THE RECORD SOCIETY OF
LANCASHIRE AND CHESHIRE

FOUNDED TO TRANSCRIBE AND PUBLISH
ORIGINAL DOCUMENTS RELATING TO THE TWO COUNTIES

VOLUME CXXXIX

The Society wishes to acknowledge with gratitude the support given towards
publication by

Lancashire County Council
The Marc Fitch Fund

ISBN 0 902593 58 7

Printed in Great Britain by J. W. Arrowsmith Ltd.

THE MEMORANDA BOOKS OF BASIL THOMAS ECCLESTON, 1757–1789

Edited and transcribed by
A.J. Gritt and J.M. Virgoe
with C.P. Brownrigg

PRINTED FOR THE SOCIETY
2004

CONTENTS

CHARTS, MAPS AND ILLUSTRATIONS   page

ACKNOWLEDGEMENTS

Thanks are due to the following:

Scarisbrick Estate Trusts, Buxton, Derbyshire for permission to publish the Memoranda Books, the University of Liverpool for a grant towards photocopying the documents and Bruce Jackson, Lancashire County Archivist for permission to copy them. To Dr Stephen Caunce for encouragement and willingness to talk about the project; Dr Henry French for his encouragement and constructive comments on the introduction; Professor Richard Hoyle for his helpful advice and enthusiasm at the start of the research; Dr Peter McNiven, the current editor of the Record Society for his patience and efficiency; Mrs Margaret Panikkar for bringing the portrait of Thomas Eccleston to our attention, and to Ann Pinder for arranging for us to copy it; Dr Michael Power for overall encouragement with this project; Mrs Skidmore of Valencia Farm House for permission to enter the garden and photograph the house; The Rev. Thomas Steel, Vicar of Prescot; Professor John Walton for checking our Spanish.

INTRODUCTION

The English lesser gentry of the eighteenth century have largely failed to capture the imagination or attention of economic and agricultural historians. There is a good deal of literature on the social milieu, local government activities and political involvement of the lesser gentry, but their economic fortunes have not been subject to extended study. Consequently, their economic significance has been systematically disregarded while historians have favoured other groups in rural society, namely, the great estates, the yeomen and the smallholders.[1] Basil Thomas Eccleston's estate stretched to around 1000 statute acres, mainly in the township of Eccleston, near St Helens in south-west Lancashire, although it extended into nearby Sutton. This placed him well above the ranks of Lancashire tenant farmers and yeomen, but well below the ranks of the greater gentry. His landed status gave him a degree of gentility which augmented his lineage. Nevertheless, he could not contend with the economic, social and political weight of his neighbours the Earl of Derby and the Earl of Sefton, but he was a member of a social group whose economic activities were, perhaps, more

---

1 See for example, R.C. Allen, *Enclosure and the Yeoman: the Agricultural Development of the South Midlands, 1450–1850* (Oxford U.P., 1992); J.V. Beckett, *The Aristocracy in England 1660–1914* (Basil Blackwell, 1988); J.V. Beckett, 'The Decline of the Small Landowner in Eighteenth and Nineteenth-century England: Some Regional Considerations', *Ag. Hist. Review*, 30 (1982), pp. 116–32; J.V. Beckett, 'The Decline of the Small Landowner in England and Wales, 1660–1900' in F.M.L. Thompson, ed., *Landowners, Capitalists and Entrepreneurs* (Oxford U.P., 1994), pp. 89–112; M. Campbell, *The English Yeoman under Elizabeth and the Early Stuarts* (Yale U.P., 1945, reprint of 1942 edition); D. Cannadine, *The Decline and Fall of the British Aristocracy* (Yale U.P., 1990); J. Cannon, *Aristocratic Century: the Peerage of Eighteenth Century England* (Cambridge U.P., 1984); W.G. Hoskins, *The Midland Peasant: the Economic and Social History of a Leicestershire Village* (Macmillan & Co, 1957); A.H. Johnson, *The Disappearance of the Small Landowner* (Clarendon Press, 1909); R.A.C. Parker, *Coke of Norfolk: a Financial and Agricultural Study 1707–1842* (Oxford U.P., 1975); M. Reed, 'Nineteenth-century Rural England: a Case for "Peasant Studies"?', *J. of Peasant Studies*, xiv (1986–87), pp. 78–99; M. Reed, 'The Peasantry of Nineteenth-century England: a Neglected Class?', *History Workshop J.*, xviii (1984), pp. 53–76; J.M. Rosenheim, *The Emergence of a Ruling Order: English Landed Society, 1650–1750* (Longman, 1998); J.A. Sheppard, 'Small Farms in a Sussex Weald Parish, 1800–60', *Ag. Hist. Review*, 40 (1992), pp. 127–42; S. Wade Martins, *A Great Estate at Work* (Cambridge U.P., 1980); M. Winstanley, 'Industrialization and the Small Farm: Family and Household Economy in Nineteenth-century Lancashire', *Past and Present*, 152 (1996), pp. 157–95; and J.R. Wordie, *Estate Management in Eighteenth-century England: the Building of the Leveson-Gower Fortunes* (Royal Historical Society, 1982).

In contrast, our understanding of the lesser gentry as a social class, their interaction with other social groups, and their economic function is much less well developed. However, the best surveys include C.F. Foster, *Seven Households. Life in Cheshire and Lancashire 1582–1774* (Arley Archives Series, 3, 2002); D. Howell, *Patriarchs and Parasites: the Gentry of South West Wales in the Eighteenth Century* (Univ. of Wales Press, 1986); P. Jenkins, *The Making of a Ruling Class: the Glamorgan Gentry, 1640–1790* (Cambridge U.P., 1983); G.E. Mingay, *English Landed Society in the Eighteenth Century* (Routledge & Kegan Paul, 1963); and B. Tyson, ed., 'The Estate and Household Accounts of Sir Daniel Fleming of Rydal Hall, Westmorland 1688–1701', *Cumberland & Westmorland Antiquarian & Archaeological Society*, XIII (2001).

significant and typical. The majority of landed estates in south-west Lancashire were under 2000 acres, and Eccleston is immediately comparable with a number of local families, most famously the Blundells of Little Crosby.[2] Interestingly, when Holt needed retrospective material in order to illustrate the agricultural development of Lancashire in the second half of the eighteenth century, it was precisely these individuals, the Lancashire squirearchy, to whom he referred.[3] Indeed, the small estates were ahead of the large estates in matters of agricultural improvement, and it took until the second quarter of the nineteenth century for the large estates to catch up.[4]

Our understanding of the social, economic and political dynamics of eighteenth-century Lancashire has deepened in recent years due to a number of ground-breaking studies. Naturally, much of this research has focused on the urban structure and industrial and commercial developments,[5] but a number of ongoing research projects have moved Lancashire historiography into previously virgin territory, exploring the nature, pace and extent of change in Lancashire's agricultural districts.[6] The work of French and Hoyle in particular has stressed the vitality and significance of the small estate owners and small farmers in the Pennine belt, work that reflects a growing interest in these highly persistent social groups in neighbouring counties and in the nineteenth century.[7]

2 M. Blundell, *A Lancashire Squire: the Life of Nicholas Blundell of Crosby, 1669–1737* (Day Books, 2002); A.J. Gritt, 'Aspects of Agrarian Change in South-west Lancashire, *c.*1650–1850 (unpublished Ph.D. thesis, Univ. of Central Lancashire, 2000); F. Tyrer and J.J. Bagley, eds, *The Great Diurnal of Nicholas Blundell of Little Crosby, Lancashire, 1702–1728*, 3 vols (Record Society of Lancashire and Cheshire, cx, cxii, cxiv, 1968–1972).

3 J. Holt, *General View of the Agriculture of the County of Lancaster* (David and Charles, 1969, first published 1795), *passim*.

4 W. Rothwell, *The Report of the Agriculture of the County of Lancaster with Observations on the Means of its Improvement* (Groombridge & Sons, 1850), pp. 106–25.

5 M.J. Power, 'Politics and Progress in Liverpool, 1660–1740', *Northern History*, xxxv (1999), pp. 119–38; M.J. Power, 'The Growth of Liverpool' in J. Belchem, ed., *Popular Politics, Riot and Labour. Essays in Liverpool History 1790–1940* (Liverpool U.P., 1992), pp. 21–37; M.J. Power, 'Creating a Port: Liverpool, 1695–1715', *Trans. Historic Society of Lancashire and Cheshire*, 149 (2000), pp. 50–71; J. Stobart, 'An Eighteenth-century Revolution? Urban Growth in North-west England, 1664–1801', *Urban History*, 23 (1996), pp. 26–47; J. Stobart, 'Geography and Industrialization: the Space Economy of Northwest England, 1701–1760', *Trans. of the Inst. of British Geographers*, 21 (1996), pp. 681–96; J. Stobart, 'Regional Structure and the Urban System: North-west England, 1700–1760', *Trans. Historic Society of Lancashire and Cheshire*, 145 (1996), pp. 45–73; G. Timmins, *Made in Lancashire* (Manchester U.P., 1998).

6 H.R. French, 'Accumulation and Aspirations among the 'Parish Gentry': Economic Strategies and Social Identity in a Pennine Family, 1650–1780', *Trans. Historic Society of Lancashire and Cheshire*, 149 (2000), pp. 19–49; H.R. French and R.W. Hoyle, 'The Land Market of a Pennine Manor: Slaidburn, 1650–1780', *Continuity and Change*, 44 (1999), pp. 349–83; A.J. Gritt, 'The "Survival" of Service in the English Agricultural Labour Force: Lessons from Lancashire, c. 1650–1851', *Ag. Hist. Review,* 50 (2002), pp. 25–50; A.J. Gritt, '"For Want of Reparations": Tenants and the Built Environment on the Estates of South-West Lancashire, 1750–1850', *Trans. Historic Society of Lancashire and Cheshire,* 150 (2001), pp. 33–55; Gritt, *thesis;* J.M. Virgoe, 'Rural South West Lancashire in the Eighteenth Century: the Land and the People' (Univ. of Liverpool, unpub. Ph.D. thesis, 2003).

7 *Accumulation and Inheritance: Browne of Townend and the Cumbrian Statesman*, symposium held at the British Agricultural History Society spring conference, St Martin's College, Ambleside,

The nature of the Memoranda Books

The *Memoranda Books of Basil Thomas Eccleston, 1757–1789,* held at Lancashire County Record Office in Preston as DDSc 127/2 and DDSc 127/3, provide an opportunity to develop further the study of this important social group. The Books of Memoranda cover a 32-year period from 1757 to 1789. They comprise two volumes of unnumbered pages, the first volume containing 91 leaves and running from 27 January 1757 to 9 April 1765. The second volume contains 171 leaves covering the period 12 April 1765 to 15 May 1789. Both volumes are approximately 32cm by 20cm (12½ by 8 inches), and are bound in redundant parchment indentures. The entries are in diary form and, with very few exceptions, were made in chronological order. Frequently the day of the week was recorded as well as the date, which suggests that the entries were working memoranda and not retrospective commentary. In all, entries were made on 1,030 days, or, on average, between 31 and 32 days each year. Basil Thomas made the highest number of entries in 1766, when he noted something on 89 days; the least number of entries in a complete year was 14 in 1781 (see figure 1). From the peak of 1766 however, there was a general downward trend in the number of entries made each year. There are a number of gaps, when Basil Thomas made no entries, the longest being from mid-May to the end of November 1768, a gap of six and a half months. Gaps of a month or two are more common. Basil Thomas offers no explanation for not entering anything during these longer gaps, but it is clear that these books were the working records of a country gentleman rather than a diary made primarily for the self-satisfaction of the diarist. Nonetheless, he occasionally recorded more personal items, especially those relating to his family.

The books are written in a large, firm hand (see figure 2), which remained reasonably consistent until near his death. The last entry was made on 15 May 1789, only eight days before his death. By contemporary standards, Basil Thomas's orthography was reasonably good and moderately consistent, although he frequently made mistakes contrary to modern accepted practice such as 'feild' for 'field'. He also made extensive use of abbreviations. He was liberal in his use of capital letters and his punctuation was erratic. He made frequent use of 'ditto' or 'do', not only in dates, but also in the text, but what he gained in brevity he occasionally lost in clarity.

The Memoranda Books mainly contain detailed information relevant to the management of the Eccleston estate, especially leases and rents, agricultural practices and mining affairs. There is no mention at any time of an estate steward, and it would seem that Basil Thomas managed the estate himself acting as his own steward, a situation not uncommon on smaller estates at the time.[8] In this respect the

2001; M.E. Shepherd, 'The Small Owner in Cumbria *c.* 1840–1910: a Case Study from the Upper Eden Valley', *Northern History,* xxxv (1999), pp. 161–84; C.E. Searle, 'Customary Tenants and the Enclosure of the Cumbrian Commons', *Northern History,* xxix (1993), pp. 126–53; M. Winstanley, 'Agricultural and Industrial Revolutions: Reassessing the Role of the Small Farm' in C. Bjorn, ed., *The Agricultural Revolution Reconsidered* (Landbohistorisk Selskab, 1998), pp. 89–110; M. Winstanley, 'Industrialization and the Small Farm'.
8 G.E. Mingay, 'The Eighteenth-Century Land Steward' in E. L. Jones and G. E. Mingay, eds, *Land, Labour and Population in the Industrial Revolution* (Edward Arnold, 1967), p. 5.

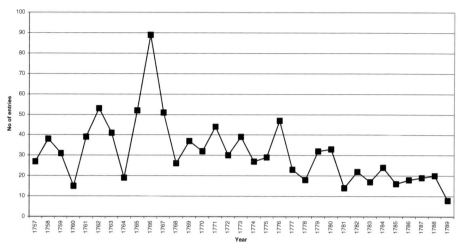

Figure 1 Number of entries in Memoranda Books, 1757–1789.

Memoranda Books formed an important part of Eccleston's estate management. That they were working books is evident from the occasional notes Basil Thomas wrote to himself (e.g. '7 June 1766 N.B. Remember the account of the nails for the Navigation') and a few gaps where he forgot to put in quantities. In addition to his Memoranda Books, Basil Thomas was also a diarist, although his diaries are not known to be extant. In the late nineteenth century, Eccleston's diaries for the years 1765, 1771 and 1772 were in the hands of the Rev. T. E. Gibson, a local historian and antiquary. They were reputedly found at Lydiate in the hands of some cottagers, having come into their possession through servants who had worked at Scarisbrick Hall.[9] Extracts from the diaries are quoted in a paper by Abram, sometimes confirming entries in the Memoranda Books, with less or occasionally a little more detail.[10]

Basil Thomas Eccleston's Memoranda Books are important for a number of reasons, but especially because of the amount of quantitative data that they contain on agricultural affairs. He provides numerous accounts of his cheese production, the weight of slaughtered cattle and pigs, and the produce of his arable crops. Some of this produce was destined for the market, and Basil Thomas provides the value of much of his output, and, in the case of his dairy produce especially, the names of the people who bought it. This preoccupation with quantitative data is evident not only in his agricultural activities, but pervades much of the Memoranda Books.

9 Attempts to trace any of Rev. T.E. Gibson's papers or Basil Thomas Eccleston's diaries through the National Register of Archives, Lancashire Record Office and Southport Public Library Local History Collection have proved unsuccessful.
10 W.A. Abram, 'Ancient Lancashire Families – The Scarisbricks of Scarisbrick', *Lancashire and Cheshire Antiquarian Notes,* ii (1886), pp. 211–54.

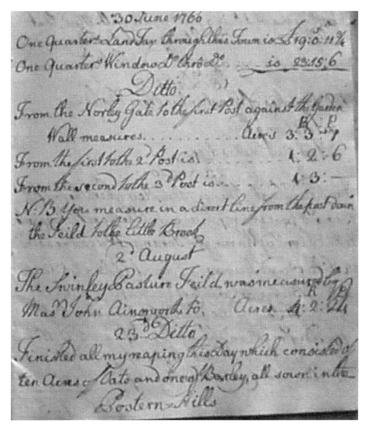

Figure 2 Entries for 30 June to 2 August 1760, Memoranda Books.

The Family

Basil Thomas Eccleston was born Basil Thomas Scarisbrick in about 1712, one of nine sons of Robert Scarisbrick and his wife Ann, who was the second daughter of William Messenger of Fountains Abbey, Yorkshire. In addition to eight brothers, Basil Thomas also had four sisters. He was educated initially at the Catholic school at St. Omer, and subsequently for three years, 1727–1730, at the Catholic seminary at Douai.[11] The family were, in general, long-lived: three of his siblings lived to over the age of eighty, and Basil Thomas himself was seventy-seven when he died on 23 May 1789. Basil Thomas was born into a strong Catholic family who were prominent supporters of the Stuarts in the seventeenth century, and his father, Robert, was suspected of being implicated in the 1715 uprising.

---

11 G. Holt, *St. Omer and Bruges Colleges 1593–1773, A Biographical Dictionary* (Catholic Record Society, 1979).

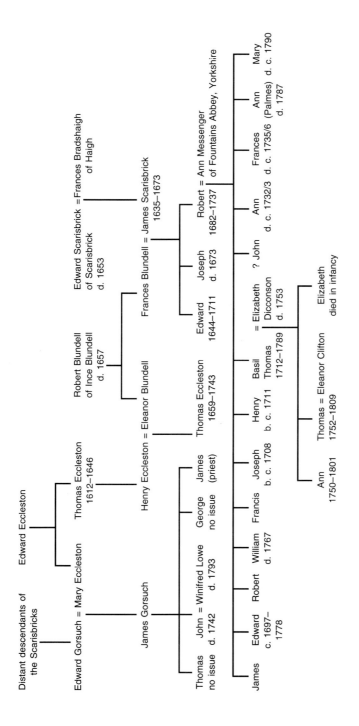

Figure 3 The Eccleston / Gorsuch and Scarisbrick families

After his arrest in 1717 he was imprisoned in Newgate prison. However, at his trial at Lancaster he was acquitted and his estates were restored to him.[12] There was no religious compromise by the family, and Basil Thomas remained Catholic until his death. Two of Basil Thomas's brothers became Catholic priests, and three of his sisters Franciscan nuns.[13] His sister Ann Palmes had her house destroyed during anti-Catholic riots in Liverpool in 1746.[14] However, Basil Thomas's siblings do not appear to have formed a close-knit family. He was reasonably close to his sister, Ann, with whom he corresponded on a regular basis, but his brothers were more aloof. Indeed, on 11 June 1770 he records that this was the first day that his brothers Edward and Joseph Scarisbrick and himself had sat and met together in a private house, though they were aged 72, 62 and 57 respectively. He records the death of two of his brothers, Will on 22 July 1767 and Edward on 7 July 1778.

The Scarisbricks' connection with the Ecclestons was tenuous: Basil Thomas's grandfather's sister-in-law, Eleanor Blundell, had married Henry Eccleston.[15] They had an only son, Thomas Eccleston, who died without issue in 1743. This Thomas Eccleston was a colourful character. He was educated at the Catholic school in St Omer and the English College in Rome, and during the wars in Ireland and after the Glorious Revolution of 1688 held a commission in the army of King James. Following a duel, in which his opponent was killed, he entered the religious life, and held various posts within the Jesuit order.[16] His portrait, with his sword thrown symbolically upon the ground, was formerly hung in Eccleston Hall and was probably later moved to Scarisbrick Hall, but does not appear amongst the portraits from the hall when it was put up for sale in 1923, unless it was one of two portraits of unnamed gentlemen in armour.[17] This Thomas Eccleston was also known as Thomas Holland, and in a letter written under this name dated 16 May 1722 to Robert Scarisbrick, the father of Basil Thomas, he outlined his intentions with respect to the disposal of his estates.[18] By a deed dated 18 August 1725, he settled the Eccleston estates upon his second cousin, John Gorsuch of Gorsuch Hall in Scarisbrick.[19] In the event of John Gorsuch dying or having no male children, reversion was in the first instance to his brother George, and secondly to a distant relation, Basil Thomas Scarisbrick.[20] John Gorsuch died without male descendants in 1742, and with George

12 W. Farrer ;and J. Brownbill, eds, *The Victoria History of the County of Lancaster*, vol. 3 (Institute of Historical Research, 1966, first published 1907), p. 269.
13 Lancs. R. O. DDSc 23/5; DDSc 19/45.
14 Lancs. R. O. DDSc 78/3. There is a considerable amount of Jacobite literature in the Scarisbrick papers, Lancs. R. O. DDSc 78/1.
15 An account of the family can be found in J.F. Giblin, 'The Eccleston Family of Eccleston', *North West Catholic History*, xvi (1989), pp. 1–6.
16 Sir L. Stephen and Sir S. Lee, *The Dictionary of National Biography*, vi (Oxford U.P., 1921/22), p. 350.
17 Lancs. R. O. DDWw 4/4/10.
18 Lancs. R. O. DDSc 9/4.
19 John Gorsuch subsequently changed his name to Eccleston.
20 Lancs. R. O. DDSc 23/1. A further document (DDSc 147/2) states that Basil Thomas Eccleston was the godson of Thomas Eccleston, which was the only reason for the estates being settled upon him.

Gorsuch also dying without male issue, Basil Thomas Scarisbrick subsequently inherited the Eccleston estate, and took the surname Eccleston.

In the early part of his adult life, Basil Thomas Scarisbrick is said to have lived in Cadiz, possibly as a merchant. This would account for his knowledge of Spanish, which he used to a limited extent in the Memoranda Books, and the possession of a number of Spanish books. It may also explain why he named the house he built in Eccleston late in life 'Valencia'. However, by 1742 he was residing in Liverpool and on 7 June 1749 Basil Thomas, by now surnamed Eccleston, married Elizabeth, third daughter of Edward Dicconson of Wrightington.[21] They had a son and two daughters, one of whom died in infancy, and in 1753 Elizabeth, at the age of 22, died in childbirth.[22] She was buried at Prescot. Basil Thomas records certain details of his children's lives, especially when they were young. On 8 May 1758, for instance, he noted in his Memoranda Book that 'my little Tom' began to write and in May 1762 he was obviously proud to record that his son shot a crow with a steel bow at the age of eight. He later records Thomas's smallpox inoculation and the birth of his son and daughter. Basil Thomas's daughter assumes less importance in the Memoranda Books, but he records the day of her marriage at Prescot to Edward Standish Townley.

During the latter part of his life Basil Thomas Eccleston was known simply as Thomas Eccleston, to add confusion with the numerous others of that name. He died on 23 May 1789, and was buried at Prescot. Although there is no memorial to him within Prescot parish church, high on the nave wall are the arms of Edward Eccleston dating from 1610, and it is believed that the burial place of the Eccleston family was under their pew at that position in the church.[23] Basil Thomas Eccleston made a will on or about 6 September 1787, and appointed his only son Thomas Eccleston as sole executor, but by the time of his death in 1809 he had still not proved his father's will.[24] A previous will is mentioned in the Memoranda Books in October 1765, when it was delivered to Mr Robert Moss of Preston with instructions to draw up a new will.

The life of Basil Thomas Eccleston has faded into obscurity, yet within the context of the much-neglected eighteenth-century agricultural revolution in Lancashire he was a remarkable character. He was to found a highly successful dynasty with a long association with innovation and economic success. His son, Thomas Eccleston, was to become better known than his father as an agricultural improver.[25] Nevertheless, the considerable influence which Basil Thomas must have had upon him is evident from the Memoranda Books.

Thomas Eccleston (see figure 4) not only succeeded to the Eccleston estates on the death of his father in 1789, but he also inherited Scarisbrick from his uncle Joseph Scarisbrick in 1786, having been in effective control since 1778, and Wrightington from his uncle Edward Dicconson in 1807. In the meantime, he had

21 *Victoria County History*, p. 269.
22 Abram, 'Ancient Lancashire Families', p. 243.
23 This information is from the Revd Thomas Steel, current vicar of Prescot.
24 Lancs. R. O. WCW 1810, Basil Thomas Eccleston of Eccleston, ltd administration.
25 Angela M. Turton, *Thomas Eccleston, 1754–1809. An Eighteenth Century Agricultural Improver* (unpub. M.A. dissertation, Univ. of Liverpool, 1995).

Figure 4 Thomas Eccleston, 1752–1809. Reproduced with kind permission of AXA Insurance UK Ltd.

added the manors of Halsall and Downholland to his holdings, so that he and his descendants, now once again under the family name of Scarisbrick, became amongst the most important landowners in south-west Lancashire. However, following the death of Basil Thomas in 1789, the Eccleston estate became nothing more than a distant satellite for Thomas and was put up for sale in 1795. Part of the estate was bought by Mr F. Peek and Mr W. R. Winch in 1805, with the remainder being sold to Colonel Samuel Taylor of Moston in about 1812.[26]

Thomas Eccleston enjoyed a widespread reputation for agricultural innovation, gaining the approbation of a number of eminent contemporaries and agricultural commentators at home and abroad. In 1789, he was awarded a gold medal by the Society for the Encouragement of Arts, Manufactures and Commerce for the drainage of Martin Mere. Throughout the 1790s his reputation as an innovator secured for him the approbation of his peers, both in Britain and Europe. He corresponded with Sir John Sinclair, the first president of the Board of Agriculture, and received numerous visitors to his model farm at Scarisbrick from British and European agriculturists.[27]

---

26 Giblin, 'The Eccleston Family of Eccleston', p. 5. The offer for sale was announced in the *Blackburn Mail*, 2 June 1795.
27 Lancs. R. O. DDSc 78/3: The Drainage of Martin Mere, 1788; M. Duggan, *A History of Scarisbrick* (Carnegie Publishing, 1996), pp. 29–33; T. Eccleston, 'The Improvement of Martin Mear', *The Transactions of the Society for the Encouragement of Arts, Manufactures and Commerce*, vii (1789), pp. 50–74; Gritt, *thesis*, ch. 6; Lancs R. O. DDSc 9, estate correspondence, *passim*.

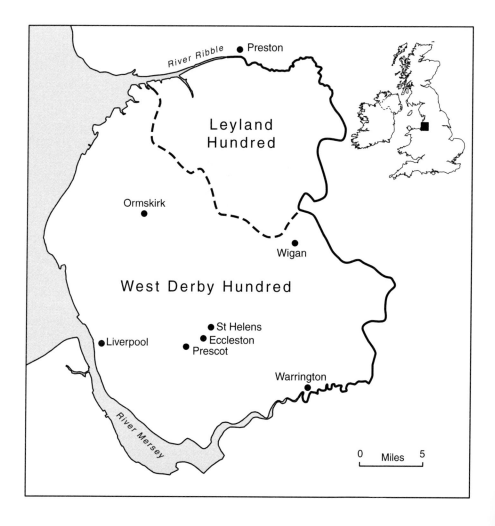

Figure 5 South-west Lancashire.

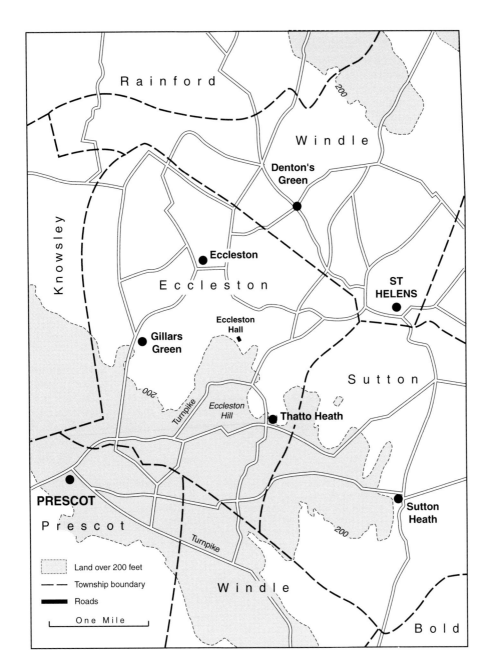

Figure 6 Eccleston and surrounding districts.

Location

Eccleston was a township within the ancient parish of Prescot, although nowadays it is part of St Helens. It was an extensive township of about 3,500 acres with scattered housing and few centres. Most of the township stood at between 100 and 200 feet above sea level, but with distinctly higher land rising above 200 feet in the southern part. At the surface much of the land is underlain by boulder clay or glacial till, which contributed to a heavy clay soil, but underneath were upper coal measures, and coal getting was first mentioned in Eccleston in 1660.[28] Some of the higher land is underlain by Permo-Triassic red sandstone which outcropped at the surface.

The township of Eccleston was strategically placed, being only a few miles from Liverpool, which at this time was growing rapidly. Basil Thomas Eccleston frequently records going to Liverpool to bring goods back and also to sell produce. In the mid-eighteenth century Eccleston was beginning to show signs of industrialisation. The Sankey Navigation, which had been opened in 1757, was extended with a branch into the eastern side of Eccleston which was first used in 1772 to come up to Mackay's colliery.[29] In 1766, Basil Thomas had carted numerous loads of stone, sand and timber for the Navigation, presumably materials used in the construction of the new branch.[30] Eccleston was also served by the Liverpool–Warrington turnpike which passed through neighbouring Prescot, with a later branch through Eccleston to St. Helens.[31]

The estate: size and rental income

At 458 customary acres (969 statute acres) the Eccleston estate was not large, and was dwarfed by the neighbouring Derby and Molyneux estates.[32] Basil Thomas clearly had to maintain a close personal interest in the commercial viability of his estate, although in the absence of detailed account books it is impossible to quantify his annual income and expenditure. Nevertheless, the Memoranda Books do

---

28 T.C. Barker and J.R. Harris, *A Merseyside Town in the Industrial Revolution* (Frank Cass, 1993), p. 3.

29 1755, 28 Geo II, c.8 An Act for making navigable the river or brook called Sankey Brook...; 1762, 2 Geo. III c.56 An Act to amend and render more effectual an Act, for making navigable Sankey Brook, and for the extending and improving the said navigation; Charles Hadfield and Gordon Biddle, *The Canals of North West England, i* (David and Charles, 1970), ch.2, pp. 39–59; Barker and Harris suggest that the branch was opened in about 1770: *A Merseyside Town*, p. 20. However, they did not refer to the Memoranda Books which clearly state that the first flat came up the Navigation on 1 June 1772.

30 See various entries for June and July 1766.

31 C.B. Phillips and J.H. Smith, *Lancashire and Cheshire from AD 1540* (Longman, 1994), p. 85; John Whiteley, 'The Turnpike Era', in A.G. Crosby, ed., *Leading the Way: A History of Lancashire Roads* (Lancashire County Books, 1998), pp. 119–82. The significant Acts of Parliament affecting turnpikes in the St Helens area in this period are: 1725, 12 Geo I, c. 21; 1745, 19 Geo II, c.19; 1753, 26 Geo II, c.65; 1771, 11 Geo III, c.91.

32 An acre in the county of Lancashire was measured as a customary acre which equated to approximately double the size of a statute acre; see E.H. Smith, 'Lancashire Long Measure', *Trans. Historic Society of Lancashire and Cheshire*, 110 (1959), pp. 1–14. All references to acres in this paragraph are customary acres.

provide frequent references to income and expenditure pertaining to all aspects of estate management. In 1760, the annual value of the Eccleston estate was just under £787, comprising £672 of rents for tenements and the 63 acres that Basil Thomas farmed himself, valued at £114.[33] By 1763, the annual rental was worth £630 with the land farmed by Basil Thomas valued at an additional £214.[34] Eccleston's most comprehensive summary is dated 1766.[35] He let to tenants 161 acres of demesne land which were worth £272, and retained 119 acres of demesne land valued at £242. Basil Thomas held a further 6 acres of land which was either out of lease or was land that he had purchased, valued at £18 per annum. He also let 172 acres of land to tenants, with a rental value of £318. In all, the 458 acres had an annual value of almost £945 in 1766. In the same year, the expenses needed to manage his estate amounted to £524, including £243 14s 3d to the dowager, about £107 in taxes, £142 in wages, and other minor rents, leaving Basil Thomas with a net income from his agricultural estate of around £420. However, land values continued to increase and in 1789 his agricultural estate had an annual value of over £1,385.[36]

Coal mining

The Memoranda Books contain much information on coal mining and show that Basil Thomas took considerable interest in, and had wide knowledge of, mining practices. He does not routinely record in his Memoranda Books his income from mining, but the scant evidence available suggests that his income from mining leases and coal royalties probably matched his income from his agricultural estate. In 1769, Basil Thomas was taking an interest in coal under land in neighbouring Sutton, which was being investigated by Adam Tyrer. Considerable quantities were indicated, one area amounting to 26,322 works of coal with a projected sales value of £16,251 based on an assumed price of coal.[37]

---

33 See entry for 27 October 1760.
34 See entry for 19 January 1763.
35 See entry for 1 February 1766.
36 Lancs. R. O. DDSc 25/27 Eccleston rental, 1789.
37 Basil Thomas uses the contemporary convention of 'works' as a measure of the quantity of coal. For lump coal, one work is 60 baskets, which according to Barker and Harris is about 3 tons, *Merseyside Town*, p. 10. However, it is clear from Eccleston's calculations that he also applies the term work to coal in the ground, one work being taken as either 5 or 6 cubic yards. Coal before extraction has no voids and one can therefore use the density to convert from volume to weight. The density of coal varies from 1.14 to 1.4 tonnes per cubic metre according to quality. To convert tonnes per cubic metre to tons to per cubic yard the multiplier is 0.7523. Therefore the density of coal varies from 0.861 to 1.053 tons per cubic yard. Thus a 5-yard work varies from 4.3 tons to 5.3 tons and a 6-yard work from 5.2 to 6.3 tons. This assumes that all the coal in the ground can be extracted with no waste. In practice, of course, this is impossible. Fines or slack will be produced, which can only be sold at a lower price. Eighteenth-century mining technology was also based on pillar and stall mining which meant that probably up to 50% of the coal had to be left in the ground as pillars to support the mine roof, so that in practice one work was likely to equate to an amount closer to 3 tons of saleable coal. However, Eccleston does not make this clear in his calculations. On this basis, the 26,322 works of coal amount to something between 80,000 and 160,000 tons. See entries for 19 April and 9 August 1769. J.G. Speight, *The Chemistry and Technology of Coal* (New York, Dekker, 1994).

Basil Thomas produced detailed cost estimates of getting this coal over an eight-year period totalling £6,658, thus showing a potential net income of £9,593 or nearly £1,200 per annum.

He does not appear to have taken part to any great extent in mining on his own behalf. Indeed, there was probably little incentive for him to do so, since he could obtain a royalty of 20 per cent of the selling price of coal without participating in the commercial risks associated with mining. In 1762, Eccleston issued a mining lease to Messrs Thomas Leigh & Co for a term of 100 years. He was to receive 20 per cent of the sales value of the coal, and even considering the long lease term was confident that this was a 'good price' and hoped that his successors would 'reap benefit thereby'.[38] Nevertheless, there is no clear statement of the actual income that Basil Thomas derived from coal mining at any point in the Memoranda Books.

These royalties occasionally led to disagreements. One such was with Charles Dagnall, and there are several references to this dispute in the Memoranda Books between October 1759 and November 1762. Basil Thomas frequently recorded the date at which papers concerning Dagnall were sent to Mr Starkie, a Preston lawyer, and to William Bankes of Winstanley, who was appointed to arbitrate in the dispute.[39] A better understanding of this affair is obtained from some separate mining papers. Dagnall had taken a lease in 1746 for a coal mine for seven years, but continued in operation without signing a new lease. In 1754, Dagnall raised the cost of his coal by ½d per basket, claiming that this was to meet his increased mining costs. However, Basil Thomas considered it 'just that I should have one half of what he got by the rise'. This demonstrates that any mine operator faced with increasing costs was unable to increase his prices without immediately losing a proportion of any benefit gained through having to pay increased royalties, whilst the landowner's income increased without any cost to him.[40]

Agricultural income
While the large estates of south-west Lancashire had abandoned farming in an earlier period, and concerned themselves with profits from agricultural rents,

38 See entry for 19 May 1762.
39 William Bankes owned a small estate in Winstanley, near Wigan. Eccleston and Bankes appear to have had a close relationship. Charles Dagnall was described as a combmaker in a lease granted him by Eccleston in 1755: Wigan R.O. DDWr 2755. After Dagnall's death in 1776 his estate leased from Eccleston still included a 'comb shop' and Rachel Dagnall, who succeeded to her father's estate, was described in 1782 as a 'comb maker'. See entries dated 7 September 1776 and 6 September 1783. Barker and Harris, in their discussion of the Dagnall affair, characterise him as 'half literate and rather dishonest': *A Merseyside Town*, pp. 32–4; Dagnall was eventually to go bankrupt: see John Langton, *Geographical Change and Industrial Revolution, Coalmining in South West Lancashire, 1590–1799* (Cambridge U.P., 1979), p. 182.
40 Wigan R. O. DDWr 2755, coal mining papers. In this collection referring mainly to the dispute with Charles Dagnall, a draft agreement for Dagnall drawn up in January 1755 indicated that he should pay 3s per work as the Lord's part. This was at a time when coal was selling at between 12s and 14s 6d per work, indicating a royalty between 20 and 25 %. Another document indicates a royalty varying with the price of coal, but which was 8.3% of the sale price.

Eccleston was typical of a group of small landowners who retained a farming interest that was not geared solely for domestic consumption.[41] With a keen eye for profit, he engaged in agricultural experiments and was himself an innovator. Moreover, he assiduously recorded much of this activity, some of which is reproduced in this publication of his Memoranda Books. But, typical amongst successful small estate owners, farming and agricultural rents were not Eccleston's only source of income, and despite rapidly rising land values and the insatiable demand of the expanding urban markets for agricultural produce, agricultural rents yielded insufficient profits to engage in expensive and unprofitable innovation and experimentation for all but the largest landowners.[42]

Despite Basil Thomas's income from rentals and coal royalties the Memoranda Books clearly indicate that his farming operations were market-orientated and driven by profit. Indeed, the commercial success of his agricultural productivity was the main motivational factor for his farming innovations. The Memoranda Books are littered with brief statements of income derived from a wide range of farm goods, although there are few comprehensive summaries. Basil Thomas documented the weight and apparent sale price of dozens of slaughtered animals. He also recorded the commercial value of a variety of arable crops including wheat, barley and oats. He provided frequent accounts of the value of his dairy produce. For example, in 1763 he provided a detailed account of his dairy produce which generated an income of £62.[43] In 1766, he summarised his income from agricultural produce in the 54 weeks from 30 April 1765 to 13 May 1766. His main income came from the sale of 468½ bushels of wheat, which was £149, and with other income derived from the sale of calves, sheep, lambs, wool, dairy produce and bacon his total income from agricultural produce amounted to £257.[44]

The management of the agricultural estate

The close bonds between the lesser gentry and their tenants assisted in the dissemination of innovative farming techniques, and the frequent contact between Basil Thomas and his tenants certainly gave him greater opportunity to influence his tenant's farming methods. This social contact was not on any formal level, and agricultural development was not simply experimental, but was based on

41 Gritt, *thesis*; Holt, *General View*.
42 There has been a protracted debate regarding who was responsible for instigating agricultural change in the eighteenth century. The traditional view makes a case for the owners of large estates whereas more recent literature has often revised this view. See for example, R.C. Allen, *Enclosure and the Yeoman: the Agricultural Development of the South Midlands, 1450–1850* (Oxford U.P., 1992); D. Brown, 'Reassessing the Influence of the Aristocratic Improver: the Example of the Fifth Duke of Bedford (1765–1802)', *Ag. Hist. Review*, 47 (1999), pp. 182–95; J. V. Beckett, *The Aristocracy in England, 1660–1914*; Lord Ernle, *English Farming Past and Present* (Heinemann, 1961 edn); M. Overton, *Agricultural Revolution in England: the Transformation of the Agrarian Economy, 1500–1850* (Cambridge U.P., 1996); S. Wade Martins and T. Williamson, *The Roots of Change: Farming and the Landscape in East Anglia, c. 1700–1870* (*Ag. Hist. Review*, supplement series 2, BAHS, 1999); Winstanley, 'Industrialisation and the Small Farm'.
43 See entry for 19 January 1763.
44 See entry for 10 May 1766.

practical commercial experience. However, this was not a one-way process, and innovations did not simply filter down the social scale from Basil Thomas to his tenants. Indeed, he was quick to recognise the improved techniques of his tenants and adopt them on his own farm. Eliza Rigby was one tenant with whom Basil Thomas had a close relationship, and he even expressed affection for her. Elizabeth Rigby appears in the Return of Papists for Eccleston in 1767, aged 78, and died aged 84 on 4 May 1773.[45] Basil Thomas recorded 'My good old neighbour and tenant Eliza Rigby died this day suddenly about 5 o'clock in the evening'. She was clearly important to him, and when he built his new barn in 1757, four foundation stones were laid. The first was laid by Lord William Molyneux, marked simply 'M'. The second was laid by a Mr Palmes.[46] The third was laid by his four-year-old son, Thomas and was marked 'TE', while the fourth was laid by Eliza Rigby and marked 'ER'. Why she alone was selected from Basil Thomas's tenants to join this company is not clear. She farmed part of the demesne with her lands extending to around 40 acres which were worth around £60 per year. Nevertheless, he treated her with generosity and affection and they regularly traded agricultural produce. In 1761, for instance, he bought 57 measures of seed oats from Rigby, which he sowed on his own land. In April 1762, he had five loads of old hay from her, a debt which he repaid two years later in clover hay. In 1765, he stored part of his wheat crop in her barn. Later in the same year he bought 20 bushels of foreign seed oats from her. Basil Thomas also did some ploughing for Rigby in October 1765, for which she paid him the following June.

This level of involvement was untypical, but Basil Thomas appears to have been paternalistic and generous towards his tenants. He had a close involvement with their agricultural practices and there was an active trade in seeds and agricultural produce between Basil Thomas and several of his tenants. A number of his tenants were Catholic, and some can be traced between the list of tenants he provided for 1766, and the Returns of Papists of the following year.[47]

Basil Thomas was not afraid to learn from his tenants. Peter Rostron, for instance, held just 11 acres of land from him in 1766, and it was said to be worth £29 per year. In April 1773, however, Basil Thomas sowed six bushels of Rostron's oats on his demesne farm, noting that 'Rostron does not know the name of his oats but says it is an early sort and produces much meal'. Peter Caddle was another tenant with whom Basil Thomas had regular dealings. In 1762, he bought all of Caddle's wheat straw, obviously thinking that Caddle's wheat was worth experimenting with as in October the same year he sowed a pint of Caddle's wheat seed.

---

45 See E.S. Worrall, *Returns of Papists, 1767* (Catholic Record Society, 1989). There were at least two other people named Eliza Rigby with whom Basil Thomas Eccleston was acquainted. He recorded the death of an Eliza Rigby on 6 December 1777 in his Memoranda Book. A third person named as Eliz Rigby wrote a will on 28 September 1779, bequeathing £8 to Basil Thomas Eccleston. £2 10s was to be distributed amongst four priests, £3 to the poor of Pemberton, Sutton, Prescot and Eccleston, and £2 10s 'for him to distribute for prayers for the repose of my poor soul'. LRO DDSc 42/12.

46 Probably the husband of his sister, Ann.

47 Worrall, *Returns of Papists.*

It was Basil Thomas, however, who took the lead in the preservation of soil fertility. Marl was to be found in abundance in south-west Lancashire, and was an important part of the system of land management.[48] Tenants were familiar with using marl as a means of conditioning the soil, and Basil Thomas would often make a rent allowance for tenants who marled their land. In some cases, marling was included as a lease covenant.[49] Basil Thomas used marl frequently and systematically on his land, and recorded in detail the cost of marling. However, he did not restrict himself to fertilisers widely available on his own estate, and at an early stage he was taking advantage of the proximity to commercially available products, primarily from Liverpool, a trade that was to grow in significance in the later eighteenth and nineteenth centuries.[50] Indeed, Mutch argues that it was the proximity to the organic waste products of towns and industries that allowed the farmers of south-west Lancashire to achieve astounding agricultural success in the nineteenth century.[51] In the mid-eighteenth century, Basil Thomas was purchasing limestone and soaper's waste in considerable quantities. Both of these materials were originally bought in Liverpool until the opening of the Eccleston branch of the canal in 1772, when it became more expedient to have limestone delivered locally. Basil Thomas records details of the cost and procedure of the lime-burning process. Lime was used in combination with other organic waste material, as Basil Thomas recorded in May 1762 when he applied manure 'which was composed of red soil as came out of the deep ditch and had lain numbers of years and which I mixt with 440 bushells of lime, horse, cow, hog dung and ashes and all kinds of rubbish'.

This general culture of improvement allowed Basil Thomas and others to achieve grain yields that were equal to or exceeded those achieved by East Anglian farmers in the third quarter of the eighteenth century. Indeed, Basil Thomas was achieving wheat yields of 27 bushels an acre by 1780, and the Blundell demesne farm was typically yielding around 20 bushels an acre in the 1760s.[52] This compares with a national average of 22 bushels an acre in 1801.[53] Moreover, the Blundell and Eccleston demesne farms were not model home farms, the playthings of socially-distant landlords who lived well from the profits of rents, but working, market-orientated farms. Their owners did not have large reserves of capital which they could invest in expensive improvement programmes, but had managerial skills complemented by an acute sense of the practicalities of farming and the workings of the market which undoubtedly helped them maintain their social position. The Earls of Derby and Sefton did not have the same degree of practical farming experience nor the bond of friendship and loyalty between landlord

---

48 Holt, *General View*, pp. 111–17. See also W.M. Matthew, 'Marling in British Agriculture: a Case of Partial Identity', *Ag. Hist. Review*, 41 (1993), pp. 97–110; Gritt, *thesis*, pp. 198–200.
49 See entries for 10 May 1757, 28 April 1760, 2 August 1766, 6 January 1768, 31 December 1771.
50 Gritt, *Thesis*, pp. 198–203; Holt, *General View*, pp. 126–39.
51 A. Mutch, *Rural Life in South-west Lancashire 1840–1914* (Centre for North West Regional Studies, Univ. of Lancaster, 1988), p. 13.
52 Gritt, *Thesis*, pp. 224–7.
53 Overton, *Agricultural Revolution in England*, p. 77.

and tenant enjoyed by the smaller estate owners. The lack of social and economic distance, and often the Roman Catholic religion, engendered strong bonds
between small estate owners and long-term tenants in south-west Lancashire.

Basil Thomas's economically rational and paternalistic style of estate management, whilst fostering good landlord-tenant relations, is also apparent in the phys-
ical infrastructure of the estate. There is strong evidence to suggest that the
buildings on Basil Thomas's estate were superior to those on many other estates
in south-west Lancashire. For instance, tenants of the Molyneux and Hesketh families were likely to find themselves occupying small timber-framed wattle and daub
thatched cottages, which had no capital value and were consequently inadequately
maintained. It was not until the nineteenth century that these estates began major
rebuilding programmes, investing in brick houses with slate roofs. Basil Thomas,
on the other hand, was building and rebuilding in brick and slate from the middle
of the eighteenth century, affording superior accommodation to people, animals
and agricultural produce.[54] He also pursued a programme of improving his own
building stock. Some of this was unavoidable such as when his 'large old barn'
was destroyed by a hurricane in March 1757, to be replaced later that year. In
October 1762, he started to build a new windmill, and recorded the construction
of its foundations in detail. Several changes were made to Eccleston Hall: in June
1767 he pulled down the hall front, and in 1779 he pulled down the chapel end
of the hall and uncovered a picture of the Blessed Virgin Mary and the infant
Jesus, which he conjectured had been there since the house was built (see figure
7). However, his most important project was the building of a new house, Valencia,
in 1785, at a cost of £435, the expenditure of which he recorded in considerable
detail. The house survives today with a datestone over the door, but it is a sur-
prisingly humble Georgian farmhouse, and it would seem doubtful whether
Eccleston built it for his own use. (See figures 8 and 9).

In terms of the legal contract between Basil Thomas and his tenants, he pursued a distinct policy. Ancient tenements or newly-purchased tenements were
generally leased for three lives whereas demesne land was leased for terms of
years.[55] The term varied, and although Basil Thomas favoured terms of fourteen
and then seven years, he also let land for terms of three, five, nine, eleven, twelve
and twenty-one years. However, he retained a preference for three life leases which
were being phased out on larger estates by the 1760s. Indeed, by the early nineteenth century a system of rack renting came to dominate south-west Lancashire.[56]

54 Gritt, 'For Want of Reparations'.
55 In eighteenth-century south-west Lancashire most holdings were leased on three-life leases, which
   involved the payment of a large entry fine and a small annual rent. The rents of three-life
   leases were only a fraction of the true rentable value and were fixed for the term of the lease.
   Gritt, *thesis, chs* 3 and 4; C. Clay, 'Lifeleasehold in the Western Counties of England 1650–1750',
   Ag. Hist. Review, 29 (1981), p.89; William Marshall, *A Review of the Reports to the Board of
   Agriculture for the Northern Department of England* (Longman, 1808), p.275; Edward Laurence,
   *A Dissertation on Estates Upon Lives and Years Whether in Lay or Church Hands With an Exact
   Calculation of Their Real Worth* (1730).
56 Gritt, *thesis*, ch. 4.

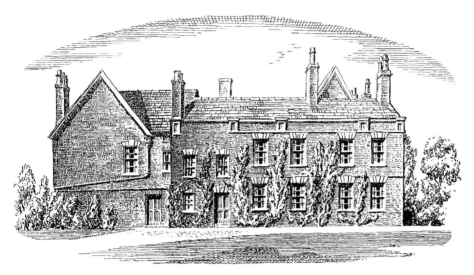

OLD ECCLESTON HALL   From a pencil drawing made in 1824.

Figure 7 A view of Eccleston Hall from 1824. Reproduced courtesy of St Helens Local History and Archives Library.

Figure 8 'Valencia', built in 1785.

Figure 9 'Valencia' datestone, 1785.

For the small Catholic estates of south-west Lancashire, three-life leases were a way of ensuring social and economic stability, and a permanent core of long-standing Catholic tenants and their families. The three-life lease provided economic stability for the family group, and, demographic failure and high entry fines notwithstanding, this system was economically beneficial to tenants in the long term.

On the small estates of south-west Lancashire, three-life leases were an extension or expression of landlord paternalism.[57] The ratio of rent to fine varied considerably, but was often lower on the Eccleston estate than it was on other estates in south-west Lancashire, although Basil Thomas rarely records the full details of a tenement. In December 1765, Basil Thomas added two lives to an existing lease for a fine of £134 3s 11d, the equivalent of 73 years' rent. In February 1771, he granted a three-life lease for £231, the equivalent of 154 years' rent. However, in March 1771, he changed all the lives in a three-life lease for the extremely generous fine of £12. Unfortunately, we do not know the acreage of the tenement, but a six-acre farm on the nearby Molyneux estate commanded a fine of £60 just five years later.[58] By January 1785, however, Basil Thomas's rents had increased, causing the rent to fine ratio to reduce substantially. For instance, the fine paid for a three-life lease for a tenement of 44 acres was £560, the equivalent of nine years' rent. A second three-life lease granted at the same time for a fine of £220 was also equivalent to nine years' rent.

Basil Thomas also recorded notes on his three-life lease covenants, and it was normal practice to make concessions to tenants for improvements. In February 1771, for instance, he agreed a new three-life lease with Ann Arrowsmith, with the condition that 'if she builds a new barn or outhouses I promised to allow her 2s in the £ for the money she lays out thereon, provided it is set in lime and

57 Gritt, *thesis*, ch. 3.
58 Gritt, *thesis*, p. 128.

covered with slate'. In February 1778, another tenant agreed to 'build a new barn of brick and set in lime and slated to be 10 yards long 7 yards backwards and at least 5 yards to the square . . . with an outheel to hold 4 cows and 2 horses' on condition that a new life was added to an existing lease without payment of a fine.

The Memoranda Books tell us considerably more about the cultivation and value of the demesne lands. The size and layout of the demesne in Basil Thomas's hands was not static. Indeed, he appears to have been pursuing a distinct policy of expanding the area under his direct cultivation in the period 1760–66. In the six years to 1766 Eccleston doubled the size of the demesne in his own hands, increasing its value by 112 per cent (see table 1). During the same period the value of the demesne leased to tenants fell by 20 per cent (see table 2). Frustratingly, he stopped recording the area of land he cultivated after 1766 although there is evidence to suggest that this year may represent a peak in the size of the demesne which he farmed himself, as thereafter he increasingly leased parts of the demesne to tenants for terms of years, including over 42 acres to Richard Greenall from May 1773 at the annual rent of £94.[59] However, the estate rental of 1789 indicates that even in the year of his death he retained 116 acres of the demesne.

The history of one demesne tenement will suffice to show how Basil Thomas varied the area of land he retained in his hands, although others could be traced in the Memoranda Books through the index. Holmes's tenement, which was a little over 14 acres, is first encountered in May 1757, when it is in the hands of

	Acreage			Annual value		
Year	*a*	*r*	*p*	£	*s*	*d*
1760	59	2	19	114	10	3
1761				137	0	0
1762				180	10	0
1763				214	5	0
1766	119	0	25	242	15	0
1789	116	3	16	288	18	3

Table 1. Demesne lands in hands of Basil Thomas Eccleston, 1760–89.

	Acreage			Annual value		
Year	*a*	*r*	*p*	£	*s*	*d*
1760				341	11	1
1761				307	7	6
1762				260	16	3
1763				232	12	6
1766	161	3	20	272	13	3

Table 2. Demesne lands leased to tenants, 1760–66.

59 See entry for 3 September 1772.

Peter Caddle for the annual rent of £40. In 1758, Basil Thomas paid the poor rate, constable's ley, land tax and highways ley for Holmes's tenement which was described in the Memoranda Books as 'in my own hands'. The tenement does not appear in the survey of demesne lands in Basil Thomas's hands for 1760, and in 1762 it appears to have been in the hands of Peter Caddle when Basil Thomas bought the wheat straw that came from it. Later in the same year it was leased to Caddle for £34 per annum, but by August it was in the hands of John Smith. The tenement was still in the hands of John Smith in 1766 but a new seven-year lease was granted to Thomas and Richard Greenall in August of that year for £42 per annum.

Even when the demesne land was in the hands of tenants, Basil Thomas monitored its use and productivity more closely than he monitored his other tenanted land. Moreover, there was a central core of tenants to whom demesne land was entrusted for terms of years, thereby allowing favoured tenants the opportunity to expand and contract their landholding. But leases for terms of years were subject to more restrictive, or certainly more prescribed methods of cultivation. As there was nothing 'customary' about these leases, they gave Basil Thomas, and other south-west Lancashire landlords, the opportunity to introduce new, progressive methods and to restrict 'damaging' practices. For instance, James Alcock's lease in August 1782 contained the covenant that Basil Thomas was 'to allow him for the first 3 years 20 tons of soaper's waste annually and Alcock to find 30 tons more annually for the said first 3 years'. Alcock was 'not to plow more then three acres in any one year without leave in writing, nor to stuble, or burn any part'.[60] In the same year, Adam Crompton's lease said that he was 'to plow no stuble nor push nor burn, but may plow 10 acres annually'.[61] He was allowed £5 annually for manure with Crompton covenanted to match this.

Labour
Yet, if Basil Thomas enjoyed good relations with his tenants, the same cannot be said of his relationship with many of his servants. He did not have a large body of permanent estate staff and typically employed a ploughman, cowman, groom, gardener, butler, chambermaid, dairy maid and horseboy. However, farm servants were not a significant body in Lancashire until the later eighteenth century, and this small workforce is further evidence of the dual personality of the gentleman farmer. Farm service was not an established system in south-west Lancashire in the middle of the eighteenth century, and with no infrastructure to support the system, hiring was scattered throughout the year, as the Memoranda Books show. The lack of an established hiring year, and competition for labour from industry, caused many servants to leave their employment before the end of their contract, and it was only in the 1770s, when the wages Basil Thomas paid to his servants were subject to significant increases, that he was able to retain a stable body of servants and an annual hiring pattern began to emerge.[62] Agricultural wages in the

60 See entry for 26 August 1782.
61 See entry for 23 October 1782.

north west were substantially higher than southern agricultural wages, and while the increases reflect the proximity of abundant alternative employment, they are also likely to represent an improvement in the standard of living that was not shared by southern labourers.[63]

As well as his regular farm servants, Basil Thomas employed casual labour for tasks such as clearing gorse, carting and marling. Some of these arrangements were contracted for on a fairly long-term basis, indicating that the labourers were local residents and not part of a casual, itinerant labour force. For instance, on 13 September 1757, Basil Thomas entered into an agreement with John Lucas

> to rid the Rushy Park of all the gorse, ollers and briars for £4 10s 0d and in case it should prove a hard bargain, I must allow him 5s more, he allso aggrees to keep it clear of all rubish for 10s p.a. for the four succeeding years.

In October 1773, Basil Thomas admitted John Lucas as a tenant, granting him a three-life lease for a 17-acre tenement. Basil Thomas also extracted boon labour from his tenants, which he would use to complement the labour of his servants and day labourers.[64] Boon labour was potentially very valuable to estates, and the monetary equivalent to boon labour in 1755 added almost eight per cent to the value of the Eccleston rental.[65]

Medicine

Basil Thomas used his Memoranda Books to record medicinal recipes for various common complaints. Some of the recipes were collected from doctors and apothecaries, but most were collected from individuals from diverse places who were not apparently medical professionals. Some recipes were communicated within Basil Thomas's family. Many of these recipes were based on herbs and plants and could be manufactured at home. On 22 May 1759, for instance, he recorded 'A receipt for an anointment of the late Mr William Lancaster'.

> Take Rue, Peter's staff, Smollage, Scettergras & Redknees or Asesmart, chopt small, fry these in May butter overnight let them stand till next morning. Fry them up again, strean them through a cloth, this will keep a whole year and good to take down any swelling.

The utility of these recipes is not always clear, but some appear to be of dubious value. On 21 November 1778 he recorded 'Mrs Townley's of Chiswick's receipt for a cough'.

> Take a piece of Burgundy pitch, the size of a nutmeg, mixed with a little peice of bee's wax and spread cold on a peice of leather the size of your

62 Gritt, 'Survival and Change'.
63 A. Armstrong, *Farmworkers: a Social and Economic History, 1770–1980* (Batsford, 1988), p. 66; A. Armstrong, 'Labour' in G. E. Mingay, ed., *The Agrarian History of England and Wales, vi, 1750–1850* (Cambridge U.P., 1989), p. 702; E.A. Wrigley and R.S. Schofield, *Population History of England, 1541–1871: a Reconstruction* (Edward Arnold, 1981), pp. 432, 451.
64 See entry for 12 April 1758.
65 Lancs R.O. DDSc 25/21.

hand, and place it between your shoulders and when the plaister is taken off, wash the place with warm milk & water.

As Basil Thomas aged he collected more medicinal recipes for complaints such as rheumatism (1779) deafness (1779), jaundice (1783), cold (1787) rheumatism (1787) and dropsy (1788). In two instances (pp. 140 and 154) where some aspects of the transcription and translation of the remedies presented difficulties, the relevant entries are reproduced photographically.

Medicine was not the only way of combating disease, however, and in late May 1771, Basil Thomas went to London where he met his son Thomas, then aged 18, who had travelled from Bruges for a course of smallpox inoculation. This was twenty-five years before Jenner developed his smallpox vaccination.[66] The process of inoculation took several weeks, and was a dangerous procedure. On 8 June 1771, Thomas took his first dose of 'Sutton's powder and salts preparative for inoculation'. Three days later he took a second dose and on 13 June, he was inoculated. On 22 June, Basil Thomas noted that 'My son was at the height of the small pox in the innoculation'. It was not until 30 July that Basil Thomas began his journey back home to Lancashire.

Basil Thomas was no less concerned about animal health than he was about human health, although the veterinary recipes he collected were even less appetising and, perhaps, of more dubious value. It is not always clear what diseases individual recipes were supposed to combat. One recipe from 16 April 1767, for instance, was designed to 'prevent calves from dying'. Calves did die, however, and in 1767 he only managed to rear one calf from his herd of 15 cows. No comment was made about the usefulness of a further recipe 'for sucking calves' collected from Mr T. Chadwick in May 1777:

Give it as soon as calv'd a glass of gin for 3 mornings succesivly & kept it low for 8 or 10 days. Near Michelmass take a handful of hen's dung, a pint of old lant & 2 or 3 spoonfuls of salt. Mix them all well togather & strain it thro' a cloth & give it the calf fasting, and bleed the night before.

It is not clear how the gin was to be administered to the calves, or what the purpose of this recipe was.

Most of the veterinary recipes Basil Thomas recorded were for cattle, although equine health was also a concern. In May 1772, he recorded a recipe for horses that had lost their hair which he had collected from his friends the Bankes family of Winstanley.

66 Inoculation involves the injection of the smallpox virus taken from a pustule of a smallpox sufferer, and produces a mild form of smallpox in the person inoculated. This procedure was first used in England in 1721 and was relatively dangerous compared with vaccination developed by Jenner. Vaccination involves injecting with cowpox taken from a suffering cow, produces resistance against smallpox but gives only a mild reaction in the person vaccinated. See P. Razzell, *The Conquest of Smallpox: The Impact of Inoculation on Smallpox Mortality in Eighteenth Century Britain* (Caliban Books, 1977).

Boil in one gallon of old urin a large handful of fox glove leaves, & make a strong lather with ½lb of sweet soap, & rub him stoutly all over with it against the grain, & when it is dry & the weather warm, turn him out and the hair will come surpriseingly fast again.

Using the Memoranda Books
The Memoranda Books contain a wealth of information on a wide range of topics, not all of which have been covered in this introduction. Using them can sometimes be frustrating because Basil Thomas was neither systematic nor consistent in his recording of details. They can occasionally test the patience of the keenest of researchers. To the unwary there are numerous potential pitfalls. For instance, the accounts of deadstock require tenacity to collate for the purposes of analysis, and yet the effort does not pay dividends because of the essential details that Basil Thomas omitted. Crucially, the breed and age of the slaughtered cattle were rarely recorded, rendering these particular accounts of little use for the analysis of eighteenth-century gains in livestock productivity. On the other hand, Basil Thomas's accounts of his arable productivity, whilst requiring considerable effort to come to terms with the variety of customary local measures, clearly demonstrate the high achievement of agricultural innovators in a rapidly industrialising setting.

The Memoranda Books await a full systematic analysis and there remain numerous, unploughed furrows to be explored and rich veins to harvest. The Memoranda Books are unique and invaluable documents that yield considerable insight into the economy and society of south-west Lancashire in the second half of the eighteenth century. It is hoped that this publication will not only bring this source to the attention of a wide public, but also encourage and stimulate further research into the economic activities and social interests of the lesser gentry both locally and nationally.

Editorial conventions
As our objective was to reproduce, as faithfully as possible, an edited version of Basil Thomas Eccleston's Memoranda Books that could be used and understood without reference to the original, without prior knowledge, and without reference to other sources, alterations to the original text have been kept to a minimum. The original capitalisation and punctuation has not been reproduced; rather, it has been silently modernised for ease of understanding. The exception to this is where the original meaning of an entry is ambiguous: in these instances the convention adopted was to transcribe verbatim and reference this in the footnotes. Much of Eccleston's original text is presented in tables, or lists going down the page. These have been largely reproduced apart from slight modifications of the original layout to improve presentation and clarity without compromising on meaning. Eccleston made extensive use of the word 'ditto'. For ease of understanding, 'ditto' is not reproduced here, but rather the word or words that Eccleston omitted have been substituted, unless the meaning is not clear in which case 'ditto' is transcribed as per the original. Eccleston also made extensive usage of abbreviations and contractions, such as 'recd.' for 'received', 'sow'd' for 'sowed', 'wt' for 'weight', most of which have been retained unless the meaning is not clear.

Eccleston did not have a convention for writing the date for each entry. For presentation purposes, and for ease of using the edited transcript, a standardised approach has been adopted. Similarly, when dates are referred to in the text they have been standardised as a modern spelling, thus 8ber and Xber become October and December respectively.

Eccleston appears to draw attention to several entries with various symbols and notations (e.g. ⊕). These have been reproduced as closely as possible in the text.

Units have been presented as £ s d, a r p, or cwt qr lbs regardless of how Eccleston presented them. Thus 'four acres, 2 roods and ten perches' is presented simply as 4a 2r 10p. Additionally, 'per annum' has been standardised to 'p.a.' throughout the text.

The transcript faithfully conveys the content and meaning of Eccleston's original manuscript which will satisfy the needs of most users of this volume. For those who are particularly interested in the exact form, style and layout of the manuscript it is readily available in the Lancashire Record Office for consultation.

June 2003

A. J. Gritt, University of Central Lancashire.
J. M. Virgoe, University of Liverpool.

Bibliography of works cited

Abram, W.A., 'Ancient Lancashire Families – The Scarisbricks of Scarisbrick', *Lancashire and Cheshire Antiquarian Notes,* ii *(*1886), pp. 211–54.

Accumulation and Inheritance: Browne of Townend and The Cumbrian Statesman, symposium held at the British Agricultural History Society Spring conference, St Martin's College, Ambleside, 2001.

Allen, R.C., *Enclosure and the Yeoman: the Agricultural Development of the South Midlands, 1450–1850* (Oxford U.P., 1992).

Armstrong, A., *Farmworkers: a Social and Economic History, 1770–1980* (Batsford, 1988).

Armstrong, A., 'Labour' in G.E. Mingay, ed., *The Agrarian History of England and Wales, vi, 1750–1850* (Cambridge U.P., 1989).

Barker, T.C. and Harris, J.R., *A Merseyside Town in the Industrial Revolution* (Frank Cass, 1993).

Beckett, J.V., *The Aristocracy in England, 1660–1914 (*Basil Blackwell, 1988*)*.

Beckett, J.V., 'The Decline of the Small Landowner in Eighteenth and Nineteenth-century England: Some Regional Considerations', *Agricultural History Review*, 30 (1982), pp. 116–32.

Beckett, J.V., 'The Decline of the Small Landowner in England and Wales, 1660–1900', in F.M.L. Thompson, ed., *Landowners, Capitalists and Entrepreneurs* (Oxford U.P., 1994), pp. 89–112.

Blundell, M., *A Lancashire Squire: the Life of Nicholas Blundell of Crosby, 1669–1737* (Day Books, 2002).

Brown, D., 'Reassessing the Influence of the Aristocratic Improver: the Example of the Fifth Duke of Bedford (1765–1802)', *Agricultural History Review*, 47 (1999), pp. 182–95.

Campbell, M., *The English Yeoman under Elizabeth and the Early Stuarts* (Yale U.P., 1945, reprint of 1942 edition).

Cannadine, D., *The Decline and Fall of the British Aristocracy* (Yale U.P., 1990).

Cannon, J., *Aristocratic Century: the Peerage of Eighteenth Century England* (Cambridge U.P., 1984).

Clay, C., 'Lifeleasehold in the Western Counties of England 1650–1750', *Agricultural History Review,* 29 (1981), pp. 83–96.

Crosby, A.G., ed., *Leading the Way: A History of Lancashire Roads* (Lancashire County Books, 1998).

Duggan, M., *A History of Scarisbrick* (Carnegie Publishing, 1996).

Eccleston, T., 'The Improvement of Martin Mear', *The Transactions of the Society for the Encouragement of Arts, Manufactures and Commerce*, vii (1789), pp. 50–74.

Ellis, W., *Ellis's Husbandry: Abridged and Methodized: Comprehending the Most Useful Articles of Practical Agriculture* (London, 1772).

Ernle, Lord, *English Farming Past and Present* (Heinemann, 1961 edn).

Farrer, W. and Brownbill, J., *The Victoria History of the County of Lancaster*, vol. 3 (Institute of Historical Research, 1966, first published 1907).

Foster, C.F., *Seven Households. Life in Cheshire and Lancashire 1582–1774* (Arley Archives Series, 3, 2002).

French, H.R., 'Accumulation and Aspirations Among the 'Parish Gentry': Economic Strategies and Social Identity in a Pennine Family, 1650–1780', *Trans. Historic Society of Lancashire and Cheshire*, 149 (2000), pp. 19–49.

French, H.R. and Hoyle, R.W., 'The Land Market of a Pennine Manor: Slaidburn, 1650–1780', *Continuity and Change*, 44 (1999), pp. 349–83.

Giblin, J.F., 'The Eccleston Family of Eccleston', *North West Catholic History*, xvi (1989), pp. 1–6.

Gritt, A.J., 'Aspects of Agrarian Change in South-west Lancashire, c.1650–1850 (unpublished Ph.D. thesis, Univ. of Central Lancashire, 2000).

Gritt. A.J., '"For Want of Reparations": Tenants and the Built Environment on the Estates of South-West Lancashire, 1750–1850', *Trans. Historic Society of Lancashire and Cheshire*, 150 (2001), pp. 33–55.

Gritt, A.J., 'The "Survival" of Service in the English Agricultural Labour Force: Lessons from Lancashire, c. 1650–1851', *Agricultural History Review,* 50 (2002), pp. 25–50.

Hadfield, C. and Biddle, G., *The Canals of North West England*, i (David and Charles, 1970).

Harris, J.R., *The Copper King: a Biography of Thomas Williams of Llanidan* (Liverpool U.P., 1964).

Holt, G., *St. Omer and Bruges Colleges 1593–1773, A Biographical Dictionary* (Catholic Record Society, 1979).

Holt, J., *General View of the Agriculture of the County of Lancaster* (David and Charles, 1969, first published 1795).

Hoskins, W.G., *The Midland Peasant: the Economic and Social History of a Leicestershire Village* (Macmillan, 1957).

Howell, D., *Patriarchs and Parasites: the Gentry of South West Wales in the Eighteenth Century* (Univ. of Wales Press, 1986).

Jenkins, P., *The Making of a Ruling Class: the Glamorgan Gentry, 1640–1790* (Cambridge U.P., 1983).

Johnson, A.H., *The Disappearance of the Small Landowner* (Clarendon Press, 1909).

Langton, J., *Geographical Change and Industrial Revolution, Coalmining in South West Lancashire, 1590–1799* (Cambridge U.P., 1979).

Laurence, E., *A Dissertation on Estates Upon Lives and Years Whether in Lay or Church Hands with an Exact Calculation of Their Real Worth* (London: printed for James and John Knapton, 1730).

Leigh, C., *The Natural History of Lancashire, Cheshire and the Peak in Derbyshire* (Oxford, 1700).

Marshall, W., *A Review of the Reports to the Board of Agriculture for the Northern Department of England* (Longman, 1808).

Matthew, W.M., 'Marling in British Agriculture: a Case of Partial Identity', *Agricultural History Review,* 41 (1993), pp. 97–110.

Mingay, G.E., 'The Eighteenth-Century Land Steward' in E. L. Jones and G. E. Mingay, eds, *Land, Labour and Population in the Industrial Revolution* (Edward Arnold, 1967).

Mingay, G.E., *English Landed Society in the Eighteenth Century* (Routledge & Kegan Paul, 1963).

Mutch, A., *Rural Life in South-west Lancashire 1840–1914* (Centre for North West Regional Studies, Univ. of Lancaster, 1988).

Newbury, K.M., 'Sidlesham Mill', *West Sussex History* no. 20, pp. 5–10.

Overton, M., *Agricultural Revolution in England: the Transformation of the Agrarian Economy, 1500–1850* (Cambridge U.P., 1996).

Parker, R.A.C., *Coke of Norfolk: A Financial and Agricultural Study 1707–1842* (Oxford U.P., 1975).

Phillips, C.B. and Smith, J.H., *Lancashire and Cheshire from AD 1540* (Longman, 1994).

Power, M.J., 'Creating a Port: Liverpool, 1695–1715', *Trans. Historic Society of Lancashire and* Cheshire, 149 (2000), pp. 50–71.

Power, M.J., 'The Growth of Liverpool' in J. Belchem, ed., *Popular Politics, Riot and Labour. Essays in Liverpool History 1790–1940* (Liverpool U.P., 1992), pp. 21–37.

Power, M.J., 'Politics and Progress in Liverpool, 1660–1740', *Northern History,* xxxv (1999), pp. 119–38.

Razzell, P., *The Conquest of Smallpox: The Impact of Inoculation on Smallpox Mortality in Eighteenth Century Britain* (Caliban Books, 1977).

Reed, M., 'Nineteenth-century Rural England: a Case for "Peasant Studies"?', *J. of Peasant Studies,* xiv (1986–87), pp. 78–99.

Reed, M., 'The Peasantry of Nineteenth-century England: a Neglected Class?', *History Workshop Journal,* xviii (1984), pp. 53–76.

Rosenheim, J.M., *The Emergence of a Ruling Order: English Landed Society, 1650–1750* (Longman, 1998).

Rothwell, W., *The Report of the Agriculture of the County of Lancaster with Observations on the Means of its Improvement* (Groombridge & Sons, 1850).

Rowlands, J., *Copper Mountain* (Llangefni: Anglesey Antiquarian Society, 1981).

Searle, C.E., 'Customary Tenants and the Enclosure of the Cumbrian Commons', *Northern History*, xxix (1993), pp. 126–53.

Shepherd, M.E., 'The Small Owner in Cumbria *c.* 1840–1910: a Case Study from the Upper Eden Valley', *Northern History*, xxxv (1999), pp. 161–84.

Sheppard, J.A., 'Small Farms in a Sussex Weald Parish, 1800–60', *Agricultural History Review*, 40 (1992), pp. 127–42.

Smith, E.H., 'Lancashire Long Measure', *Trans. Historic Society of Lancashire and Cheshire*, 110 (1959).

Speight, J.G., *The Chemistry and Technology of Coal* (New York, Dekker, 1994).

Stephen, Sir L. and Lee, Sir S., *The Dictionary of National Biography*, vi (Oxford U.P., 1921/22).

Stobart, J., 'An Eighteenth-century Revolution? Urban Growth in North-west England, 1664–1801', *Urban History*, 23 (1996), pp. 26–47.

Stobart, J., 'Geography and Industrialization: the Space Economy of Northwest England, 1701–1760', *Trans. of the Inst. of British Geographers*, 21 (1996), pp. 681–96.

Stobart, J., 'Regional Structure and the Urban System: North-west England, 1700–1760', *Trans. Historic Society of Lancashire and Cheshire*, 145 (1996), pp. 45–73.

Stratton, J.M., *Agricultural Records A.D. 220–1968* (J. Baker, 1969).

Timmins, J.G., *Made in Lancashire* (Manchester U.P., 1998).

Turton, A.M., *Thomas Eccleston, 1754–1809. An Eighteenth Century Agricultural Improver* (unpub. M.A. dissertation, Univ. of Liverpool, 1995).

Tyrer, F. and Bagley, J.J., eds, *The Great Diurnal of Nicholas Blundell of Little Crosby, Lancashire, 1702–1728*, 3 vols (Record Society of Lancashire and Cheshire, cx, cxii, cxiv, 1968–72).

Tyson, B., ed., 'The Estate and Household Accounts of Sir Daniel Fleming of Rydal Hall, Westmorland 1688–1701', *Cumberland & Westmorland Antiquarian & Archaeological Society*, XIII (2001).

Virgoe, J.M., 'Rural South West Lancashire in the Eighteenth Century: the Land and the People' (Univ. of Liverpool, unpub. Ph.D. thesis, 2003).

Wade Martins, S., *A Great Estate at Work* (Cambridge U.P., 1980).

Wade Martins, S., and Williamson, T., *The Roots of Change: Farming and the Landscape in East Anglia, c. 1700–1870* (*Agricultural History Review*, supplement series 2, BAHS, 1999).

Weatherill, L., *The Account Book of Richard Latham 1724–1767* (Oxford U.P., 1990).

Winstanley, M., 'Agricultural and Industrial Revolutions: Reassessing the Role of the Small Farm' in C. Bjorn, ed., *The Agricultural Revolution Reconsidered* (Landbohistorisk Selskab, 1998), pp. 89–110.

Winstanley, M., 'Industrialization and the Small Farm: Family and Household Economy in Nineteenth-century Lancashire', *Past and Present*, 152 (1996), pp. 157–95.

Wordie, J. R., *Estate Management in Eighteenth-century England: the Building of the Leveson-Gower Fortunes* (Royal Historical Society, 1982).

Worrall, E. S., *Returns of Papists, 1767* (Catholic Record Society, 1989).

Wrigley, E.A., and Schofield, R.S., *Population History of England, 1541–1871: a Reconstruction* (Edward Arnold, 1981).

Glossary

Bast	Probably a variant of bass; a black shale associated with coal.
Boons	Rents paid in part in kind or service as defined in a lease. Thus payment could be in eggs or a number of days work of a defined type, such as ploughing or carting. Boons could also be paid as cash equivalents.
Burr	A siliceous rock capable of being used as a millstone. Burr may be used to describe any rock hard to bore.
Butt	A strip of land.
Candlemas	Church festival celebrated annually on 2nd February. A date commonly used with reference to leases.
Clough	A ravine or steep-sided valley.
Cone wheat	A bearded variety of wheat.
Cop	A heap, pile, ridge or furrow of earth; an enclosing bank or hedge bank.
Cush	A young cow.
Feigh	The overburden above a mineral deposit. Also used as a verb meaning to remove the overburden.
Fleetings	Skimmings or curds of milk.
Ha-Ha	A sunken, unseen ditch forming a fence or boundary to a park or garden.
Hattock, haddock	Standing grain protected by slanting sheaves.
Humbles	Heart, liver, kidneys and other small innards of an animal, especially hog.
Lant	Stale urine.
Ley	A tax or levy.
Life lease	A method of granting a lease based upon the lives of (usually) three named individuals. Large entry fines were payable at the start of the lease term and on the renewal of the lives. Annual rents were very low under this form of tenure.

Michaelmas, old-, new-	Feast of St Michael. Old Michaelmas was held on 29th September but when the Gregorian calendar replaced the Julian calendar in 1752, the date for Michaelmas changed to 12th October.
Mixen	Dung hill, manure heap.
Peace Eggs	Eggs distributed to the poor by BTE at Eastertide. In certain societies it was the duty of classes of a higher social standing to give gifts at Easter and the giving of coloured eggs at Easter has a history dating back to the thirteenth century.
Platt (Plat)	Platform; foot-bridge or simple form of bridge.
Pluckings	Heart, liver, lungs, windpipe of a slaughtered animal.
Porket	A young pig or hog.
Score	Land term to describe a vertical groove either in a hillside or range of hills.
Score	Unit of weight equal to 20 lb, more commonly used for pigs or oxen.
Segg	Animal castrated when fully grown.
Set (*v.*)	To rent or lease property.
Sough	A drainage tunnel or ditch, often for mining.
Store	Livestock suitable for fattening.
Weather (wether)	A male sheep or castrated ram.
Windle	Locally varying volumetric measure used in northern England and Scotland.
Work	A volumetric measure of coal. For coal in the ground Eccleston used it as being equivalent to five cubic yards; for extracted coal it was equivalent to 60 baskets or approximately three tons. (See introduction, p. xxi).

A note on measurements

Throughout the eighteenth century it was common practice to use local customary measures for volume, weight, and linear measurements. This often results in significant difficulties in analysing issues such as agricultural productivity. In common with many other records from the North West, Basil Thomas Eccleston infrequently recorded the actual size of the units he used. Although it is apparent that he understood something by terms such as bushel, threave, load and hattock, he rarely recorded the weight of these volumetric measures. Crop yields are often calculated by historians as bushels per acre, where both the bushel and the acre are statute measures. However, Basil Thomas Eccleston uses at least three different bushel sizes (market measure, large measure, 'my own measure') although he does refer occasionally to the standard Winchester bushel, which may equate to the market measure. On only one occasion does he record the weight of a bushel of his own wheat which was 64lb 5¾oz per bushel. On two other occasions he records the market price of wheat measured in bushels of 70lb.[67]

Eccleston also used a customary acre rather than the statute acre of 4,840 square yards. The customary acre in Lancashire could vary from one manor to the next, but the acre usually used by Eccleston extended to 10,240 square yards based on an 8-yard pole. For all units of measurement used by Eccleston the safest method is to look for internal evidence within the Memoranda Books. For instance, the hundredweight used by Eccleston varies by commodity (coal, cheese, soaper's waste) which can be traced using the index.

Major units used by BTE

Units of area/linear measures
Acre
Feet
Inches
Perch
Pole
Rod
Rood
Yard

Units of volume
Basket
Bushel
Hattock, haddocks (abb. Hk(s))
Load
Measure
Peck
Pint
Quart
Rider
Sheaf, sheave (abb. sh)
Thrave, threave (abb. thr)
Windle
Work

67 See entries for 31 March 1766; 22 April 1783; 6 September 1783.

Units of weight
Grains
Hundredweight (abb. cwt)
Ounce (abb. oz)
Pound (abb. lb)
Quarter
Score
Stone
Ton

THE MEMORANDA BOOKS OF BASIL THOMAS ECCLESTON 1757–1789

Eccleston
27 January   Mr Syddall, Lord Derby's steward, gave me the following particulars out of his Lordship's lease to James Barton. The words of
the lease are as follows vizt. All that part of the Nearer Lane Croft
leaving by Eccleston's Surveyor's account for them (0a 1r 0p),
four perches & forty-two feet, for the Earl of Derby one acre half
a rod, the parcels of ground called the Dowery, Three Nooks Piece
and Further Lane Croft leaveing for Mr Eccleston two rod land
two perches and eighteen feet and the rest for the Earl of Derby
containg in the whole by estimation three acre.

a	r	p	
1	1	9	
0	3	19	Amount of what Lord Derby claims in
0	1	8	James Barton's Tenement as per the Lease
1	1	34	
3	3	30	[Total]

	a	r	p
Mr Syddall likewise said that Lord Derby claims for			
his share in the Moss Forlong near Rigby's tenement	2	0	0
Mr Rigby claims	2	0	0
Mr Eccleston claims	1	0	0
[Total]	5	0	0

and that it only measures 4a 1r 17p. Quere how this mistake
happens.

Eccleston
8 February   Brought home two loads of my own meal at 35s, £3 10s 0d.

18 February   A servant of Lord Derby's called on me this day for a quit rent.
It had not been demanded for twenty eight years & came to £3
7s 8d. I told him I paid none, but that I had a demand on his
Lordship for 4s 9d per year. John Taylor told me that the 4s 9d
had formerly been demanded and that the answer they gave was,
that Eccleston paid them some such sum, and that they ballanced
the account that way.

19 February   Permitted James Cross of Windle to get the coals in the new Pack
Lane it was taken out of that estate of lands of John Traveses
some forty years ago, and he is to give me six loads of malt for
the permission. NB. Malt was then worth 36s per load, & his malt
was made of the best barley imported into Liverpool.

25 February   Brought home one load of my own meal £1 14s 0d.

1757

4 March	Brought all the Springs in the Furthest Wood and Rutty Coppy into the Spring Head.
5 March	Paid George Booth & Richard Penketh for makeing a new cop, setting it with quick wood and hedgeing it, in length 25½ rods, in the Yew Tree Farm which I did in order to preserve the rest of the feild as they had by some means obtain'd a road through it. They had cut up the feild very much, and I made the fence to keep them in due bounds for the time to come. I paid them for it £1 6s 5d.
15 March	My large old barn was intirely blown down in a great hurricane of wind about eleven o'clock in the morning. Wind west.
28 March	Brought home four loads of meal at £1 14s 0d, £6 16s 0d.
16 April	Brought home five loads of meal at £1 15s 0d, £8 15s 0d.
18 April	Aggreed with Roger Downhall for the ground he now holds calld the Wheat Hey at £4 17s 6d p.a. & for the Long Meadow & Nobby's Croft[1] for £9, in all £13 17s 6d for fourteen years to pasture. He to do all ditching and fenceing.
21 April	Brought home five loads of meal at £1 15s 0d, £8 15s 0d.
7 May	Good Lord William Molyneux sett the first stone of my new barn this day. It is markt M.
Eccleston *10 May*	Mr Palmes set the 2d markt GP. My son Tom set a 3d markt TE 1757. My old tennant Eliza Rigby set a 4th markt ER.[2] Robert Moss aggreed with Peter Cadell, my tennant at Holmes's Estate, that he, the said Cadell, was to marle certain lands in the said Estate, in consideration of which, his first half year's rent which is £20 he was to have in his hands for three years, and at the expiration thereof, he was than to pay it me.
27 May	Brought home five loads 3 windle meal [at] £2 0s 0d, £11 4s 0d.
28 May	Brought home four & a half loads meal [at] £2 0s 0d, £9 0s 0d.
28 June	Drew on John Maire Esq. this day by order of Edward Dicconson Esq.[3]

1 Nobby's Croft inserted in place of Hill Meadow which is crossed out.
2 'My son Tom' – BTE's son Thomas was only three years old at this time.
3 Edward Dicconson – BTE's father-in-law.

1757

	£	s	d
six bills of £150 each	900	0	0
one bill of £100	100	0	0
[Total]	1,000	0	0

Which was for the remaining part of my dear deceased wife's fortune.

8 July   Reared my new barn.

29 August   Aggreed with William Ashton for all my tyth for £5 16s 0d vizt.

9 acres	middle crop of oats in the Norley
3 acres	middle crop very ordinary crop of barley in the Norley
2 acres	very good oats in Pinfold Meadow
2 acres	poor oats in Old Seddon's
16 acres	[Total]

5 September   There were 282 threave of oats in the Norley, & [...][4] of barley, and of peas two cartloads, and 66 threave of oats in Pinfold Meadow, and 46 threave of oats in Old Seddon's.[5]

13 September   Aggreed with Lucas[6] to rid the Rushy Park of all the gorse, ollers and briars for £4 10s 0d and in case it should prove a hard bargain, I must allow him 5s more, he allso aggrees to keep it clear of all rubish for 10s p.a. for the four succeeding years.[7]

14 September   Stored the following ponds with full grown fish which I tooke out of the Little Damn this day

15½	brace carp	Wall Pond	
14½	brace carp	Sleck Pond	these 29½ brace
15	brace carp	2 Isle Pond	all died
13	brace carp	Hall Lane	
15½	brace carp	Paddock	
18	brace carp	Horse Pool	
3	brace carp	in the Stew's	
6	brace carp	amongst my neighbours	
1	brace carp	house use	
101½	brace carp & 9½ couple tench in the Stew's		

11 September[8]   Housed all my oats.

---

4 Quantity not entered by BTE.

5 Tabulated in original.

6 Eccleston left a space before the surname which suggests a Christian name has been left out; possibly the intention was to insert it later. The entry for 12 April 1758 shows a payment to a John Lucas for clearing gorse.

7 Ollers (Oler) – Tree/shrub usually associated with Alder. Term sometimes applied to soft wood.

8 This entry is either out of order or misdated in the original.

1757
23 September   Put into the Old Mote 5 couple of tench, 1 brace of carps.

Monday
24 October   Andrew Valentine came to live with me this day as plough man for £6 p.a.

Monday
31 October   John Tickle came to live with me this day untill Christmass for 2s per week, and from that time he is to have £6 p.a.

Sunday
20 November   The mob came with a resolution to destroy my mill, but with fair words & some ale they dispersed.[9]

26 November   Peter Barrow desired that in case one of his lives should die within five years that I would add him an nother for £20. I answer'd in case it should happen, I would not be hard with him.

1758

Saturday
25 February   Mr Conneyrs came in the evening.

20 March   A receipt for fineing of red wine. Take the whites of eight eggs and beat them into a froth and then put a pint of red wine to it and work all together in the cask with a stick, first takeing out about two or three gallons of the wine, and work it for ten minuets and then fill the cask up, and make it close, and in a weeks time will be bright. Put a peg at the end of the cask and you will see at any time when it is fine, and then bottle it in clean dry bottles. NB the above is a receipt for half a hogshead.

28 March   Mr Thomas Beetham of Liverpool bought of BT Eccleston 1,462 feet mahogany invoice measure in Jamaica.[10]

	£	s	d
In	44	17	11½
3½ years intrest of £44 17s 11½ at 5 per cent	7	17	¾
Carting it to Eccleston	0	15	0
To sawing 471½ feet und^r two foot broad	1	3	7
To sawing 302½ feet above two feet	0	18	1½
NB it measur'd when landed 1424 feet	55	11	8¾

Settled the above with Mr Thomas Beetham 23^d January 1760.

3 April   Begun harrowing in the Tuit Hill and finished it the 12 April.

---

9   Possibly this protest was a consequence of the poor harvest in 1756 which produced famine conditions the following year because of grain scarcity and price increase. J.M. Stratton, *Agricultural Records A.D.220–1968* (J. Baker, 1969), pp. 78–9.
10   Thomas Beetham – timber merchant of Cleveland's Square, Liverpool.

1758

There were 102½ Polish & 40 measures of our own country oats sow'd in it.

12 April

Rent & charges of the Tewit Hill as it now lyes sow'd with oats.

		£	s	d
For 14 acres of ground	at 27s 6d	19	5	0
For my tame of 4 horses plowing 19 days	[at] 4s 6d	4	5	6
For boon plows charged as per rent roll 30 days		3	11	0
For keeping 4 horses 1s a man & boy 8d per diem 30 days	[at] 1s 8d	2	10	0
For ridding the gorse		1	6	0
For clearing the gorse afterwards p^d John Lucas as per rec^t		0	11	4
For one man horse & cart leading it of 7 days as per rec^t	at 1s 6d	0	10	6
For makeing the fence round the feild		2	0	0
For 102½ measures of Poland oats	at 2s 2d	11	2	1
For 40 measures of our own country [oats]	at 2s	4	0	0
For sowing ditto		0	8	0
For boon harrows charged as per rent roll 24½ days		3	1	0
For keeping 2 horses's (6d & 1 man) 5d per day 24½ days	[at] 11d	1	2	5½
For my own harrows 2 days	[at] 3s 6d	0	7	0
For reaping 14 acres	at 7s	4	18	0
[Total]		58	17	10½

12 April

Botled of the 28th ulto a pipe of beer which run to 35 doz^n & 10 and half a hogshead red wine which run 7 doz^n quarts & 5 doz^n pints.

22 April

	£	s	d	£	s	d
One double book Poor's Rate Schole End comes to				14	16	0
For which I am assessed	3	12	3			
For Holmes's in my own hands	0	7	6			
For Alexander Holland's in my own hands	0	2	0			
For Laurence Holland's in my own hands	0	3	6			
For John Thelwell's in my own hands	0	0	9			
For Henry Seddon's in my own hands	0	5	3			

1758

	£	s	d	£	s	d
One double book Hall End for the Poor is				14	12	0
For which I am assessed	0	6	9			
For late Mr Leafe's	0	11	0			
For Burrow's Lane	0	7	6			
For Hall Heys	0	1	6			
For Edward Knowles's cottage	0	0	3			
[Totals for both books]	5	18	3	29	8	0

24 April Aggreed with Richard Ascroft for himself and horse for 1s 3d per day, and to allow him half a bushel of light oats per week, & in case it rains to hinder work to receive no pay.

25 April Finished my oat ground in the Norley 5 acres.

8 May My little Tom begun to learn to write.

11 May My lame bay mare foaled a colt this morning.

Finished my three acres of barley seeding in the Norley by noon this day.

Wednesday
31 May My Badger grey mare cover'd this morning by Cavallerem at Warrington.

6 June Finished rolling all my barley & oats.

William Lancaster assigned over to me his estate for £350 at 4 per cent, the intrest to commence from the 25th March last.

Memorandum, my Dutch barn with oak posts which is next to the plantation of beech, was coverd with English dale from Wrightington, which was fell in the winter, and the other with dale posts, as is next to the stables with foreign dale in 1751.

14 June My Badger grey mare was cover'd this day for the last time by Cavallerem.

20 June My two bay mares were cover'd this day by Thomas Leigh's strong black horse.

Sunday
16 July Tom Spencer left my service at night.

17 July Aggreed with Peter Rostern for six hundred bushels of lime, he to allow one at score for 7d per bush[l], and receiv'd the following

	bushels
21st July	31
25th July	66
7th August	53

1758

		bushels	
29 August		48	
2 September		37	
7th September		56	
12 September		27	
12 September		15	for Gillar's Green
2^d October		45	for Gillar's Green
2^d October		½	for R. Moss
2^d October		½	for my wheat
16 October		64	
3 November		72	

1759

7 March	72½	
*11 14 March	58	
21 March	71½	
[Sub total]	717	
Deduct for scorage	35¾	
[Total]	681¼	

At 7d per bus^h is £19 17s 4¾d

NB there is two bushels of lime which was made of my own stones that is not accounted for in the above as he burnt it gratis.

25 July   Settled this acc^t when he paid me his rent

27 July

	£	s	d	£	s	d
One single book constable's ley						
Scholes End is				7	8	0
For which I am assessed	1	16	1½			
For Holmes's in my own hands	0	3	9			
For Alexander Holland's	0	1	0			
For Laurence Holland's	0	1	9			
For John Thelwell's	0	0	4½			
For Henry Seddon's	0	2	7½			
One single book Hall End is				7	5	6
For which I am assessed	0	3	4½			
For late Leaf's	0	5	6			
For Burrow's Lane	0	3	9			
For Hall Heys	0	0	9			
For Knowles's cottage	0	0	1½			
[Totals]	2	19	1½	14	13	6

11 The asterisk was added by BTE, suggesting that he wished to qualify this entry, but no comment was made. He entered two quantities, one of 62 and one of 58, but as the total is based on 58 bushels, the value of 62 has been omitted.

1758

	a	r	p
29 July The first barley shute in the Norley that I sow'd			
with barley & clover measured west	3	3	5
The 2^d sowed with barley and clover the middle	3	1	
The remaining part of the feild east	6	2	6
[Total]	13	2	11

12 August   Memorandum. The two stacks of hay by the Dutch barns, came out of the Crow Feild, that of the left hand next the feild is very rushy, but well got, the other is good hay, and topt with some of that which came out of the New Meadow, and was fourteen days before it was housed. It was not topt by the above, but all of the Crowfeild.

19 August   Aggreed for the reaping of 19 acres oats & 3 of barley in all 22 acres at 7s per acre.

6 September   Begun to reap my barley.

13 September   Begun houseing my oats out of the Tuit Hill.

15 September   The following is an account of my corn tyth taken out

	Threaves
10 acres in Tuit Hill Polish oats	208
4 acres in Tuit Hill our own country oats	92
5 acres in the Norley Polish oats	130
[Sub total]	430
3 acres in the Norley of barley	130
1 acre in the Norley of poor peas the tyth valued at 8s	
[Total]	560

The wheat & oats in Featherby Wood paid no tyth, this being the first year that it was ever known to be plowd, and so was considerd as new got ground & not tythable for seven years.

22 September   Finished reaping the four acres of our own country oats that were sow'd in the Tuit Hill.

Housed all my barley out of the Norley.

	£	s	d
I am assessed for land tax p.a.	16	10	0
For late Holmes's			
For Alex Holland's			
For Laurence Holland's			
For John Thelwell's			
For Henry Seddon's			
For Leafes	1	10	0

1758

	£	s	d
For Burrow's Lane	1	0	0
For Hall Heys	0	5	0
For Knowles's cottage	0	0	0
[Total]	£[...][12]		

Receivd £41 11s 3d for barley, oats, meal & peas which I sold from the 2[d] March last to this day inclusive.

	£	s	d	£	s	d
In the assesment for the Supervisors of the Highways for the Schole End one double book is				14	16	0
For which I am charged	3	12	3			
For Holmes's and Mather's	0	7	6			
For Alexander Holland's	0	2				
For Laurence Holland's	0	3	6			
For John Thelwell's	0	0	9			
For Henry Seddon's	0	5	3			
And for the Hall End it comes to[13]						
For which I am assesed for Leafe's						
For Burrow's Lane						
For Hall Hey's						
For Knowles's cotage						

28 September   Housed all our own country oats out of the Tuit Hill.

2 October   Executed a lease this day to William Hatton for three lives & twenty-one years for fourteen perches of ground which joined to my Lord Derby's on condition of his building a house. I granted the long lease, the peice being so small it might by negligence, have been lost to the family as I fear by neglect formerly it has been wronged, so for the same reason, I granted him part of a pew in Prescot church for the same term, and in consideration of which he gave me the two stone chimney peices in the old parlour and in that at the end of the Hall and 3 guineas and pays 6d p.a. rent.

4 October   Finished the wheat seeding in the fourth Old John's[14] which is three rod & twenty-eight perches.

7 October   Reced from Lancaster's kiln for 35 bushels of barley, which when malted produced 37 bushels of malt.

---

12   Amount not entered by BTE.
13   BTE left rest of the table blank.
14   Probably Old Jones's.

1758
9 October   Stored the Little Damn from Winstanley with 47 brace small carp
        & 14 couple small tench.

13 October   Put into the Little Damn, 87 brace carp of a larger size from
        Garswood.

19 October   Begun plowing the six acres in the Norley, for to lye all winter
        & for barley next year.

25 October   Walked the boundary of Eccleston township.

31 October   Advanced to William Lancaster of Eccleston £30 on an additional
        assignm^t at 4 per cent.

18/19
December   Planted in the Mill Croft Beech 16, and Elm 3, and in the Miller's
        garden Beech 7.[15]

22/23
December   Planted in the inclosure at the bottom of the Peas Croft Elm 66.

1759

Monday
15 January   Begun plowing the Peas Croft this day for oats.

        Receivd from Lancaster's kiln for 83 bushels of barley which
        when malted produced 96 bushels of malt.

        NB out of the above Richard Farrar was paid 3 bushe^s which I
        had from him for small beer.

        My brass working peices & some pumps are put in the new marl
        pitt in the Paddock, the end next to the Plantation.

3 February

	Rods	£	s	d
The lower ditch in the Crowfeild measured	22			
The higher ditch in the Crowfeild	28			
Rods at 13d	50	2	14	2
Bringing the gutter from the higher ditch to drain the old pit & other work in s^d feild cost		0	6	3
[Total]		3	0	5

26 February

	a	r	p
The contents of arable land in the Crow Feild			
The South side or higher part measured	4	1	10
The middle part	1	3	36

---

15 Tabulated in original.

1759

	a	r	p
The north or lower part 1a 3r 6p, the part amongst the trees that is now rid 0a 1r 12p	2	0	18[16]
[Total]	8	1	24

3 March Finished all my oat plowing vizt. the Peas Croft & Nighest Wood & the Smal Croft adjoining in all 10a 1r 0p

Planted the last month

In the Crowfeild	elm in hedgerows	66
In the Rushy Park	elm in hedgerows	54
In the Tuit Hill	beech in hedgerows	21
In all		141

26 March Begun sowing & harowing for oats in the Pease Croft and had finished half the feild by eleven o'clock on the 28th March when it begun to rain very hard. Begun again the 30th & finisht the 31st March at night.

5 April My Nancy begun to learn to write.[17]

6 April Mary Moore came in the evening to be housekeeper.

9 April My corn last year produced when threshed

		Bushels	
		Good	Light
129½	threave of barley	181	26
	the 4 acres of our country oats in the Tuit Hill		
93½	threave of our own country oats	217	59½
208	threave Polish [oats] in ten acres in Tuit Hill	572	101
130	threave Polish [oats] in 5a in the Norley	278	98

1759[18] The following is an account of sundry lands measured by Mas[r] John Ainsworth, the breadth is as follows vizt.

		a	r	p	a	r	p
	Hackley Moss by Prescot measured in 1755 to				2	1	11
	The Yew Tree Farme to				15	0	17
Vizt.	Zachariah Leafe's measured	1	1	33			
	Peter Orrett	2	2	08			

16 In the original manuscript 2a 0r 18p has been altered to 3a 0r 18p, but the final total of 8a 1r 24p has not been altered.

17 BTE's daughter Anne.

18 No month given.

1759

	a	r	p	a	r	p
Henry Bradburne	1	0	39			
Henry Bradburne	0	1	07			
Richard Seddon	1	2	34			
Richard Seddon	1	0	03			
Richard Seddon	1	3	18			
Richard Seddon	0	0	28			
Richard Seddon	0	0	36			
Henry Crouchley	1	0	34			
Henry Crouchley	1	3	00			
Henry Jarvaise	1	2	17			
[Total]	15	0	17			
John Forshaw's Coalpit Feild measured 1753				3	1	12
The Coppy in arable land measurd	2	3	26			
The Coppy not arable	1	1	06	4	0	32
Henry Edward's tenement at Catchall Moss				1	3	12
The contents of Featherby Wood Meadow measured as by Mas^r John Ainsworth in 1757						
John Crompton the higher part	1	0	00			
Mr Jackson the lower	1	3	34	2	3	34

15 April There was as much grass (or more) in my pastures this day, than generally one sees on the 15th May.

20 April Finished my oat seeding in the Wood.

25 April

		£	s	d
Spent in wheat this year	about 15 loads [at] 4s 6d	13	10	0
In oat meal	26½ loads about 15s per load	19	17	6
[Total]		33	7	6

To the 10th May 26½ loads meal.

2 May Begun sowing barley in the six acres in the Norley.

3 May There was perceiv'd a vent through the great bank next the broad-well in my great damn this day, so I lett it of at the pump & at the further end next Rushy Park [where I have now sett a new pump[19]] None sett (in case of a future accident) and it run of without doing further damage.

---

19 In the original this phrase has been crossed out and 'none sett' inserted.

1759
Wednesday
9 May

Finished my six & half acres of barley seeding & clover in the lower part of the Norley this day.

Thursday
17 May

My grey Badger mare, that was covered by Cavallerrem foald this morning a colt with a white blaze and two white hind feet.

20 May

Mr Mansel of Lytham made me a present of my late Ld Molyneux's two black coach horses. They are fourteen years of age.

22 May

	£	s	d	£	s	d
One book at 2d in the pound for the poor Scholes End				10	14	2½
For which I am assessed	2	9	4			
For Holmes's and the kiln	0	6	8			
For Alexander Holland's	0	1	6			
For Laurence Holland's	0	2	8			
For John Thelwell's	0	0	6			
For Henry Seddon's	0	4	6			
And for the Hall End it comes to				10	13	2
[Total]				21	7	4½
For which I am assessed	0	15	0			
For late Leafe's	0	7	6			
For Burrow's Lane	0	5	4			
For Gillar's Green new house	0	1	0			
For Knowles's cottage	0	0	2			
[Total]	4	14	2			

A receipt for an anointment of the late Mr William Lancaster's. Take Rue, Peter's staff, Smollage, Scettergras & Redknees or Asesmart, chopt small, fry these in May butter overnight let them stand till next morning. Fry them up again, strean them through a cloth, this will keep a whole year and good to take down any swelling.

The following is a copy of a note, of sundries I lent to John Patrick, the 24th April 1758, the original is in my old almanack of 1758.

An inventory taken the 24th April 1758, of the utensils of John Patrick of Eccleston blacksmith belonging to Basil Thomas Eccleston as follows: one pair of bellows, one anvil, one sledge hammer, one hand hammer. The above are the goods belonging to Basil Thomas Eccleston, as witness my hand the date above.

John Patrick.

23 May

An account of my plate. 1 silv^r ring castors & spoons, 1 new silver salver, 1 old silver salver, 4 candlesticks with nossels, 1 tankard,

1759

> 2 sauce boats, 2 salt sellers & 2 spoons, 1 punch ladle, 1 soup spoon, 18 table spoons, 1 marrow spoon, 12 four graind forks, 1 cream pot & ladle, 1 pair tea tongs, 11 tea spoons, 1 child's boat or candle cup, 1 silver tumbler.

23 May
> My lame bay mare, that was cover'd with Leigh's strong black horse, foaled this day a colt with a large star.

24 May
> Peter Johnson enter'd my service this morning as butler and groom for £4 p.a. & I allow him £2 p.a. to find his own frocks.

2 June
> My grey Badger mare, & bay lame mare were both this day covered by Cavallerem.

7 June
> Aggreed with Richard Penketh & James & Michael Roby to hew and fill eighteen rods of marle in the third Old Jones's to cover the 2ᵈ & 3ᵈ Old Jones's for 8s per rod, to have no drink but what I allow. They both measure about 3a 1r 2p.
>
> Tis said that Sᵗ Paulinus, Bishop of Nola, was the inventor of mettle bells, that before his time they made use of wood instruments. He died 22ᵈ June 420.

26 June
> Begun mowing the clover in the Norley, and the grass in the Pinfold Meadow, which is of the second year's ley.

18 July
> The marle in the pit in Old Jones's is about five yards thick. I got it to three yards, and the springs begun to rise. I then got it backwards about half a yard more, in all three and a half yards I then caused it to be bored through, and the bottom is a red sand into which they bored full four yards, which caused a great spring to arise. I made three such holes, which will make it dificult ever to empty or lave the pit.

7 August
> Henry Valentine finished cuting all his oats in the Burying Hill.

8 August
> I begun cuting oats in the Pease Croft.
>
> The sough which I am makeing at the head of the great damn from the second pump, I have turned it with an arch of brick. They are set up on large stones or flags, quite through the head, and the sides of the arch are filled with broken brick and hard ram'd with clay, and the top of the arch is ram'd likewise with clay, and each end of the sough as might be exposed to the weather is made of stone. The bricks I got made on purpose archways and they are set in clay & not in lime. The end of the arch next the great dam is not of stone, as above mentiond, but carry'd on with brick and reaches within three yards of the pump, where I let remain the old trough, being as sound as any new oak. I made a

1759

second arch upon the first for the ground work of the wall, which wall is three yards under ground, and rammed on both sides with clay, and when upon a level with the foundation of the old wall it is only rammed with clay on the rampert side. When we dug thro' the rampart & down to the pump, we found all the way trees & boughs laid mostly lengthways & piles driven to support them and keep the head from washing away, & tis immagined that the whole wall is set upon piles. The second pump that now is, lets all the water intirely of. I was told that there was a third pump, but immagine that length of time had mudded it over. However where we thought it was, we have cover'd it over with rubbish and boughs intirely to choak it up, as being of no service.

	Threave	Good measures	Light measures
The 10 acres of Poland oats that grew in the Tuit Hill last year produced	208	572	101
The 4 acres in the Tuit Hill our country [oats]	92	217	59½
The 5 [acres] in the Norley Polish [oats]	130	278	98
[Total]	430	1067	258½

The 3 acres in the Norley of barley produced 130 threave and of barley for malting 181 bushels & 26 bushels light.

		a	r	p	Threaves	Riders
16 August	Housed all my wheat out of the 4th Old Jones's	0	3	28	16	
28 August	Housed all my oats out of the Peas Croft	7	0	0	181	
8 September	Finished reaping my barley in the Norley	6	2	0		
13 September	Housed all my oats out of the Wood & Croft	3	2	0	111	1
20 September	Housed all my barley out of the Norley	6	2	0	236	2

1759[20]

20 September   Stored the Great dam from Winstanley with 170 brace carp of a year old, 200 couple of tench, same age 60 couple of small perch.

11 December   160 brace of smal carp from Winstanley.

---

20 The following accounts of fish were not entered chronologically in the original. The original entry was clearly made in September 1759 and was updated in 1760 and 1761.

1760

18 June   17 couple small tench from Winstanley.

2½ brace perch of my own.

27 June   25½ couple carp two years old out of the Horse Pool.

5 July   20½ brace carp from Standish 3 years old, 1½ couple tench from Standish & 3 years old.

3 September   1047 brace carp, 2 inch long, Horse Pool.
135 brace carp, two years old, out of Horse Pool. } 1,182 brace

1761

30 July   26 couple of pearch out of the Lower Miln Damn.

[1759]

1 October   Sent to Richard Farrar's kiln 41½ measures barley clean struck off, which produced when malted 43 meas^{rs}.

Aggreed with James Holton for two rods of rough back slate to be led to Peter Rostran's of Glugsmore in all this month at 38s per rod.

17 October

	£	s	d
Three ton of limestone of 21cwt to the ton may be had this day at Gerard's Bridge in Windle for 4s 4d per ton is	0	13	0
Carting three ton of limestone home at 1s per ton	0	3	0
Computeing the said three tons to make 66 bushels of lime we allow ½ per bush for breaking and burning	0	2	9
Drawing the said kiln	0	0	6
20 baskets of coals allowed for burning at 14s per work	0	4	8
[Total]	1	3	11

66 bush of lime at 4⅜d per bush £1 4s 0¾d

23 October   Deliver'd Mr Thomas Starkie of Preston.

Mr John Chorley's letter about the lease for the Schole on Hackley Moss.

Charles Dagnall's articles for coals in 1746.

Charles Dagnall's get of coals in 1755 & copy of my receipt to him.

Charles Dagnall's get of coals in 1756.

A note of my own of Charles Dagnall's get from 1754 to 1756 and how the money was receiv'd. Sent Mr Starkie May 1760 Charles Dagnall's letter of 1st June 1754 adviseing his haveing raised the coals a half penny a basket.

1759

23 October   Received from Richard Farrar's kiln 43 measures.

7 November   Killed a black cow, which weighed when cut up 560lb.

		£	s	d
I am charged for the Schole's End of Eccleston which is rated at	£290 p.a. at 2d per £	2	8	4
& the Hall or Moss End rated at	£90 p.a. at 2d per £	0	15	
The whole being valued in	£380 at 2d is	3	3	4

9 November   Set Peter Caddle for three years the Burying Hill & Pease Croft at 40s per acre to sew wheat the first year & the last year oats, and after they are got of he is to pasture it with nothing. If it proves a good crop to have nothing for the stuble grass, but desires me to consider him if it should prove otherwise, & I have the liberty to sew them with clover. Both contains 17a 1r 30p.

10 November   The Peas Croft was measured this day by Mas^r John Ainsworth & it contains 7a 0r 30p.

17 November   Set to Richard Tootle for seven years the little house at the head of the great damn, formerly leased to John Thelwell for £3 18s p.a. & reced 1s earnest from him which must be allowed in the first half year's rent. He has liberty to strike out a large window for his workshop which he must make up at the end of his term in the manner it now is with stone.

To make red powder.
Take Cardus pempernell termentil Bitony scabius Dragon Angellico Scordium of each a handful gatherd in fair Weather not washed but dry'd in a dry cloth bruise them and steep them twenty four Hours in three pints of white Wine then take one pound of Bole armonick beaten & searched as fine as flour then strain as much of the Wine from the herbs into an earthen dish to the Bole armonick as will make it thick & smooth as it drys in strain in more wine stir it often in the day as it drys in the sun. Strain all the Herbs hard that there be no wine left in them and when it is as thick as dough take a Quarter of an Ounce of Saffron dry'd & powder'd very fine and four Ounces's of Metridate if you have it mix all togather & make it up in little Balls or Cakes and let them dry in the sun. Keep them dry & close for use, scrape as much, as will lye on a shilling for a Man, & give it in dragon Water or Cardus posset Drink, & be sure the person lies very warm to sweat after it. NB this is good in any disease, it prevents the Extremity of the smallpox, & Measles taken early, it is good against the

plague or Fever or Surfit or for Women lyeing in Child Bed & for Children that have the Worm's.[21]

1st December   Sent to Richard Farrar's kiln 44 measures of barley clean struck of which produced 50½ measures of malt.

17 December   Dung'd that part of the New Close Meadow formerly calld the Old Jones's, with barn muck, ashes & burned sueds, and the further part in the New Close Meadow, formerly the Swingly to that part in a line faceing the ditch that devided the Old Jones's from the Pinfold Meadow with horse dung, & the Pinfold Meadow with horse and cow dung.

I bush draind the lower Kenwrick's Meadow in different parts and below the drains I have dunged it with ashes and hog dung.

Sent to Richard Farrar's kiln 48 measures of barley clean struck of which produced [...][22] measures of malt.

1760

23 January   Sent to Richard Farrar's kiln 51½ measures of barley clean struck of which produced 59½ measures of malt.

6 February   Bought of William Lancaster the tenem^t he held under me call'd Lancaster's in which there are three young lives for £700 it contains about 28 acres.

Doc^r Brian Hawarden of Wiggan sent me the 1st May 1753 34 cupple of gudgeons which I stored as follows vizt.
  6   cupple in the Horse Pond
 25   cupple in the marl pit in the Paddock
  3   cupple in the Wall Pond
 34   of gudgeons

16 February   Sent to Richard Farrar's kiln 30 measures of barley which produced when malted [...][23] measures.

The three closes of ground lately called Mr John Ashton's now Peter Moss's were measur'd by Mas^r John Ainsworth

	a	r	p	dps
the large close to	0	3	33	62
the little close to	0	1	37	00
the Intack to	0	1	00	80
[Total]	1	2	31	42

21 Because of potential ambiguities no punctuation or capitalisation has been altered in this entry.
22 Quantity not entered by BTE.
23 Quantity not entered by BTE.

1760

There was about this time a general cough amongst horses that went through the Kingdome, took away their appetites and almost reduced them to skeletons - all mine were ill, and I made use of the following, which restored them all, tho some of them lingerd nigh three weeks. 1st I took a quantity of blood from them in proportion to their age, gave them no oats but mashes of barley or brand, 2^dy warm water & in it one ounce of niter to each horse, than I smoked them with myrh half an ounce to each horse, which caused them to run much matter at the nose, and than they pritty soon recoverd. I used them more or less to moderate excercise, they horses that lay out had it and I did nothing to them and they came well thro' it.

22 March   Begun sowing and harowing my oats in the Postern Hills.

29 March   Finished my sowing and harowing the above hills with oats which consisted of full ten acres, one acre of them I reserved for barley and two acres I lett to Edmund Ligo. 104½ measures sow'd.

5 April

	Measures
Receiv'd and led from Peter Rostran's the following lime at 6d per bush^l to Richard Tootle's shop	21
brought home	25
[Total]	46

26 April   Finished sowing and harowing one acre upon the Gorsy Brow next the white gates in the nearest Postern Hill with barley & clover, which was dung'd all over.

28 April   Aggreed with Mr Lion of Warrington & Thomas Chesford to allow them £5 towards marling the Engine Coal Pit Feild, & Chesford is to have the little brick house for the damage of the small inclosure in said feild & for the soughs in the next feild adjoining.

23 May   From Michelmass last to this time, this part of the country was much afflicted with agues of a very bad kind, which people found hard to get rid of and them that had them about this time they were still more violent, tho' a vomit and the bark cured them.

The barley that grew in the 6 acres of the lower part of the Norley next Robert Moses's last year produced the folowing vizt.

	Acres		Threaves	Riders	Measures Good	Light
[Norley]	[6]	[barley]	236	2	247	28½
Wood Meadow	3¼	Oats	106	0	217	63

1760

	Acres		Threaves	Riders	Measures Good	Light
Pease Croft	7	Oats	179	0	355½	116
Old Jones's	0¼	Wheat	15	0	41	5½
[Total]			536	2	860½	213
					213	
					1073½	

In all heavy & light measures

I receiv'd for oat meal, barley, oats, & peas, from the 27th April 1759 to the 30th April 1760 inclusive £26 3s 10¾d.[24]

25 June   The following is an account of the plate my bro^r Joseph Scarisbrick of Manchester sent and deposited in my hands, which is at his disposal whenever he pleases to call for it vizt.

	oz	pho	gr
One tea kettle and lamp weight	83	3	0
One coffee pot	24	11	0
Two salvers or waiters	30	16	0
One sugar pot	16	13	12
One small tea pot	8	10	0
Three casters for sugar, pepper & mustard	41	1	0

30 June   One quarter's land tax through this town is £19 0s 11¾d. One quarter's window tax thro' this town is £23 15s 6d.

	a	r	p
From the Norley gate to the first post against the garden wall measures	3	3	7
From the first to the 2^d	1	2	6
From the second to the 3^d	1	3	0

NB you measure in a direct line from the post down the feild to the little brook.

2 August   The Swinley Pasture Feild was measured by Mas^r John Ainsworth to 4a 2r 24p.

23 August   Finished all my reaping this day which consisted of ten acres of oats and one of barley, all sown in the Postern Hills.

207 threave, and produced 28 threave.

	Threave
My 10 acres of oats in the Postern Hills produced	207
& the 1 acre of barley in the Postern hills produced	28

30 August   Housed all the above oats and barley this day.

---

24 Date changed from 27 April to 30 April and £23 6s 7½d altered to £26 3s 10¾d.

1760

6 September   I mended the clough in the Horse Pool, it formerly had two cloughs, but being filled much with mud, that which now remains lets the whole pool dry, and the other I cut away as much under the mud as I could.

18 September   Mr Bankes of Winstanley's stone roler is 5 feet long and 2 feet five inches deep.

25 September   I marled part of the next Hall Heys where the Coal Pitt Brows & coals were placed out of the marl pitt opposite to Mr Lion of Warrington's tenement, & it cost me as under

		£	s	d
4 fillers and hewers	at 1s per day	1	14	0
4 days Burgess's boon cart	[at] 2s [per day]	0	8	0
7 days Jonathan Dumbill's cart	[at] 3s [per day]	1	1	0
11½ days my man filling	[at] 1s [per day]	0	11	6
2 days my man laveing water	[at] 1s [per day]	0	2	0
11½ days my two carts marling	[at] 6s [per day]	3	9	0
[Total]		7	5	6

My tennant John Plumbley at Hall Heys new house paid a man for 9½ days laveing water & an other 10½ days for spreading the aforegoing marl. NB the pitt will be very difficult to draw, as there is a hog, or a ridge of marl that runs exactly cross the pitt in a line from one hedge to an other in the meadow, which makes that part of the pitt next the lane very nigh a yard deeper. There are several springs in the pitt.

30 September   Stored the Horse Pool out of the Wall Pond which I lett of this day with 27½ brace of carp & one single tench.

3 October   Killed a cow calld Lidiat which weighd 487lb, tallow 44lb, and hide 80lb, reckoning the meat at 2¼d and the tallow and hide at 3d she was worth something better than £6.

6 October   Put my large water engine wheel & shaft into the marl pitt in the Paddock at this end next the Plantation.

16 October   Sent to Richard Farrar's kiln 52 measures of barley for malting all clean struck of.

27 October   Put 12 brace large carp into the Wall Pond.

My estate this year is as follows vizt.

	£	s	d
I have let of the demesne lands	341	11	1
The Lord's rents are	96	0	3
Tenements & lands in my own hands which I let out to farm at	234	16	6

1760

I hold in my own hands the following

	a	r	p		£	s	d
The Postern Hills	14	0	0	[at] 30s	21	0	0
The Broad Well	3	0	0		4	10	0
The Stable Feild	0	3	37		2	10	0
The Wood Meadow	3	1	0	[at] 40s	6	10	0
The Copy	2	2	0	let	0	0	0
Part of the Swingley	1	2	2	[at] 42s 6d	3	3	9
2d, 3d, 4th Old Jones's							
new marld	4	0	0	[at] 35s	7	0	0
The New Close Meadow	6	3	30	[at] 50s	16	17	6
The Norley	13	0	0	[at] 45s	29	5	0
The Paddock	4	0	32		8	0	0
Part of the Crow Feild					7	2	0
Part of the Stand Hill	10	0	0		11	12	0
[Total]					117	10	3
Deduct for 2 acres set in the Postern Hills					3	0	0
[Sub total]					114	10	3
[Total]					786	18	1

29 October Sent by Mr Atherton to Mr Thomas Starkie of Preston, Halsal Schole deed and Charles Dagnall's letter to me dated the 28th inst. with copy of an other from Mr Dicconson to the said Dagnall.

7 November Received from Richard Farrar's kiln 54 measures of malt.

11 November Sold and deliver'd this day to Mr James Moss of Liverpool 124 cheese weight 21cwt 1qtr 22lb at 23s per cwt for which he is Dr £24 12s 11½d BTE.

5 December Killd a swine which weighed 266lb.

19 December To cure a ham.
Bay salt one pound, common salt half a pound, salt peter two ounces, black pepper one ounce. Mix all together & rub the ham well with them. Let it lay four days in this state, turning it every day. Then pour upon it one pound & a half of treacle, and let it lie a month. Then put it into cold water for 24 hours, and hang it up to dry. Do not fresh it, before you boil it.

20 December Killd a swine weight 345lb at 2½[d] per lb, £3 11s 10½d.

	lbs		£	s	d
Kill'd a cow	535	at 2¼d per lb	5	11	5½
Suit	24	[at] 5d [per lb]	0	10	0
Tallow	24	[at] 3d [per lb]	0	6	0

1760

	lbs		£	s	d
Hide	76	[at] 3d [per lb]	0	19	0
[Total]			7	6	5½

NB the head, feet &c. not reckon'd.

Beef this year produced little tallow, occasioned tis thought by the continual rains for these three months past.

26 December   Aggreed with Peter Rostran to be delivered in May, for 400 bushells of lime at 6d per bushell to allow me 22 bush[s] to the score 440 bushells.

A receipt for the chil blanes per El Rever[d] Padre Carlos de Tempesdad de la comp[a] de Jesus.

Sweet marjoram, Æsop[25], rosmary, common thyme and saven. Make a decoction of them in milk and put your feet into it as warm as possible you can and keep the feet warm afterwards.

John Bridge took Mr John Traverse's estate this year at Catchal Moss & paid M[r] £10 and cleard it of all, so it may be computed with the Lord's rent at £12 p.a.

1761

10 January   Planted in the corner by the Engine Pitt in Mr Lion's tenem[t] 22 small beech.

12 January   The barometer was 1 degree higher this day than ever I saw it before. I have markt the place.

15 January

Receiv'd from Richard Farrar's kiln	42¼	bushells of malt
And I paid him out of it what I borrow[d]	6	bushells of malt being 6 measures
	36¼	measures home

Alice Wainwright came as dairy maid at night.

22 January   Jemmy Caddle came to drive my horses's.

My 6 coulterd plow cost me as follows

	£	s	d
The wood valued by Robert Moss in	0	10	0
The iron bought of Richard Moyars of Billinge	2	2	0
Peter Barton of Pemberton for makeing it	1	0	0
Peter Barton charged for two naves he brought with him	0	0	8

25 Hyssop was a garden herb known in south-west Lancashire in this period. See L. Weatherill, *The Account Book of Richard Latham 1724–1767* (Oxford U.P., 1990), p. 4.

1761

	£	s	d
Peter Barton's board with me for six days	0	3	0
My old iron for hooping the wheels & puting it on	0	1	4
[Total]	3	17	0

Killed a porket of about seven months old.

3 February

Copy of the receipt for the Lord's rent of the Schole on Hackley Moss.

Received February the 3ᵈ 1761 from the hands of the Revᵈ Mr Ascroft schole master at the schole at Hackley Moss by the order of the Trustees of the said schole the sum of 2d, being for Lord's rent yearly due on the 25ᵗʰ day of December. This said 2d being due for the year last past. I say received the same for the use of my master Basil Thomas Eccleston Esq.

By the hands of Robert Moss.

6 February

	£	s	d
Eliza Farrar informed me this day that before the new duty on beer of 3s per barril commenced that they clear'd on each brew of four hogshead	1	10	0
That the yest made in summer 12s in Winter 8s	0	7	0
That the grains she computed at 6s and 5s each brew	0	5	0
[Total]	2	2	0

When the malt was but indiferent they used 18 measures to a brew, & when good only 17. That they allow'd one pound of hopps to each measure of malt. Each hogshead contains three barrills of 18 gallons which is 216 gallons of ale to each brew which is just 5d per gallon.

I brew two hogsheads at once which contains about 144 gallons and stands me just in 7½d per gallon, reckoning the malt at 24s per load and the hopps at 1s per lb which is £4 10s 0d.

Sunday
8 February

Jemmy Caddle went from me this evening.

Little Roby came this evening in Caddle's place.

Saturday
21 February

Henry Valentine went away from my sevice this night.

Thursday
26 February

John Tickle came to my service this mornᵍ at £6 pa.

Friday
27 February

	lb
Killd a sow whose 2 flitches weighd	263
The small meat, head, feet, fat &c.	200
In all	463

1761
Monday
2 March   Jack Roby went home this morn^g out of order, and did not return till the [...]^26.

Wednesday
4 March   James Brookfeild's boy came to drive the horses.

Monday
9 March   Burgess's boy came to drive the horses.

Tuesday
10 March   The 207 threaves of oats that grew in the Posterns there was 19½ threave taken out for the cows, remains 187½ [threaves] produced 363½ good measures [and] 122½ light measures. The one acre of barley in Posterns 28 threave [produced] 52 good measures [and] 5½ light measures. 363½ measures best oats, 122½ measures light, 486 measures in all.

Saturday
14 March   Burgess's boy went home at night.

16 March

	lb		£	s	d
Kill'd a cow that weighd	594	[at] 2½[d]	6	3	9
tallow	80	[at] 3[d]	1	0	0
hide	93	[at] 2½[d]	0	19	4½
[Total]	767		8	3	1½

Kill'd a pigg that weighed 250[lb].

Wednesday
18 March   Sow'd the Stand Hill with 95 measures of Polish oats, and it was all harrow'd & finisht this evening.

Friday
20 March   Brookfeild and Roby's boys came this morn^g to drive the horses.

Monday
30 March   I promised to allow Thomas and Richard Greenall in the next year's rent £7 towards compleating the whole at the mills.
                 From the 22^d May 1760 to the 27th February 1761 I had 36½ measures of wheat ground at the mills.

Tuesday
31 March   My dairy, which consisted of ten milch cows and the fatting beasts and score which were pastured nowhere but in the Norley made me the following money, but then I begun selling calves &c. the 15 April last and continued selling butter to this day inclusive

26 Details not entered by BTE.

1761

	£	s	d
Two rearing calves valued in	1	0	0
Eight rearing calves sold to the butcher for	5	3	11
Butter and milk sold for	1	10	2
124 cheese quantity 21cwt 1qtr 22lb at 23s per [cwt]	24	13	3
Six cows sold for	34	14	6
Three cows which I killd valued in	20	0	0
Receiv'd for the score in the Norley as per book	9	14	10
[Sub total]	96	16	8
Deduct for nine cows as I bought for feeding	35	0	1
[Total]	61	16	7

NB besides my family which consisted of fifteen persons were kept with cheese, milk and butter, only we did not eat that cheese in the parlour.

9 April   I paid Mr Richard Bankes of Liverpool for 50 measures black oats 1s 3¼d per bush, and he allowed one at the score and 34½ quarts to the bush¹ and they turn'd out good market measure and four and a half bushells over.

16 April   Finished plowing the Old Jones's this day.

15 April   I could not find that any person ever remembered so fine and so forward a spring as this year's. I cut asparagus the 1ˢᵗ of this month, and before this day the white thorn was in full leaf & the plumb & pear trees in full blossom.

21 April   Finishd sowing and harrowing the Old Jones's. This year I sowed the Standhill, Coppy, Swingley and the 2ᵈ and third Old Jones's with Poland oats quantity about twenty acres.

The Standhill, Coppy & about two acres of the Swingley were sown with 156 measures of my own oats and the remainᵍ part with 57 measures which I bought of Eliza Rigby.

This year the Tewitt Hill was sown with oats by William Billinge and Peter Caddle. I likewise sowed it with 211lb old clover seed for pasture which is about 15lb per acre and finished it this day.

13 May   My son Tom, not quite nine years of age, shot a crow with a steel bow in a tree this day, and likewise at about a rod distance shot at a mark and drove the pin that fastned it.

30 May   Plaisterd & white-washed Robison's, at the bottom of the Avenue, made an new oven, and a brew-house door, pointed the windows and repair'd the hogs-stie.[27]

---

27 To avoid ambiguity original punctuation retained.

1761
6 June

Laid a sough thro' the horse dunghill at the farmer's stable door, & paved a channel by my cow house side, to carry the urine &c. both of the stable & cow houses into the ditch in the feild calld Weldon, which I fill with straw to make manure of.

Monday
15 June

Henry Valentine came to live with me for £6 p.a.

A list of the papers delivered William Bankes of Winstanley Esq. concerning Charles Dagnall's affaire.[28]

6 November 1746 articles for a coal mine for 7 years.

1 June 1754 Charles Dagnall's letter, adviseing advanceing his coals under me ½ per basket.

1754, 1755, 1756 five papers relating to coals got & in the manner that some were paid for & the last get in 1756 being 1238w[orks] 21b[askets] at 3s, £185 15s not yet accounted for.

7th January 1755 John Taylor's letter to Mr Thomas Starkie with a note to draw new articles by for Charles Dagnall to pay 3s per work.

3d June 1755 the articles in persuance of the above letter which Dagnal never sign'd.

1760 arbitration bond.

1760 subpoena & bill in Chancery.

Tuesday
30 June

This day I begun to mow.

Monday
20 July

Housed all my hay in the following manner vizt.

	New Close Hey	
Cow house	Stables	Dutch barn
6 loads	3 loads	17½ loads
	Wood Meadow	
1 load	5½ loads	7½ loads
7 loads	8½ loads	25 loads

Friday
24 July

Hung my new gothic gates in the court this day. They were made by Peter Moss of this town, all of the best of oak, every joint was painted, when put togather and the sill was tarr'd, and the ends that goes into the pillars of the head peice also, to preserve them from wett. They were valued by the said Moss as follows:

28 William Bankes was appointed to act as arbitrator in the dispute between BTE and Charles Dagnall.

1761

	£	s	d
The value of the wood	1	15	0
The workmanship of the wood	2	13	0
Screws and springs	0	2	0
The iron work by Robert Moyars of Eccleston	1	0	0
The painting by William Forber of Prescot	0	5	0
[Total]	5	15	0

And this day we had an account of Pondichery being taken by our arms.[29]

30 July   Drained & fished the Lower Mill Damn this day, & took out some small pikes, fine pearch & a quantity of eels.

	Rods	Yards	
From the white gates by Robinson's to the white gates at the top of the Avenue by the causey measures	64	6	or 518 yards
From thence to the middle stable door	14	0	or 112 [yards]
From thence to the hall door	10	7	or 87 [yards]
[Total]			717 yards

11 August   Begun cutting my oats in the Stand Hill and I finished it the 18th so it was just five months in the ground, & I housed them all & almost all the Coppy, & half the Swingley and the wheat in the Little Old Jones's the 28th August & finished all my reaping the 31st August which was as follows vizt.

		a	r	p	thr	hks	sh	Tythe hks	sh
Stand Hill	oats	9	0	0	249	00	4	74	6
Swingley	oats	4	2	24	93	00	6	27	3
Coppy	oats	2	2	0	62	00	2	18	5
2d Old Jones's	oats	1	3	09	30	01	7	09	1
3d Old Jones's	oats	1	1	33	23	00	6	06	3
4th Old Jones's	wheat	0	3	28	13	04	6	04	3
[Total]		20	1	14					

thr	hks	sh	
457	4	1	oats
13	4	6	wheat

---

29 Pondicherry, capital of French India – defeat of the French by the British in Pondicherry, India during the Seven Years' War helped end French plans for the control of India.

1761

1761[30]   The value of Eccleston estate this year vizt.

	£	s	d
Lands of inheritance & tenements as I lett out			
Edward Parr tenem[t] at rack	32	0	0
Peter Caddle tenem[t] and lands	34	0	0
Edward Rogerson's tenem[t]	15	17	6
George Halliwell lands a malt kiln	9	0	0
Jos[a] Hewitt's tenem[t]	9	5	0
Miss Wright 20 perch & 4 feet land	0	4	6
Richard Tootle's tenem[t]	4	4	0
William Shepard tenem[t]	1	7	6
Peter Rostran lands	30	0	0
John Plumbley tenem[t]	7	0	0
Henry Sixsmith tenem[t]	0	15	0
Richard Seddon tenem[t]	24	0	0
Henry Gervase tenem[t]	6	0	0
Henry Crouchley tenem[t]	6	15	0
Zachariah Leafe tenem[t]	4	4	0
Henry Bradburn tenem[t]	4	4	0
Richard Farrar tenem[t]	50	0	0
What I have added to the estate since it was in my hands	238	16	6

The whole Lord's rents are £106 14s 6d
Deduct for tenements in my hands £10 17s 1d

	£	s	d
[Sub total]	95	17	5
Carry'd forward	334	13	11

N.B. The demesne & Lord's rents when I enter'd, did not make £500 p.a.

	£	s	d
Brought over	334	13	11

The demesne is lett as follows vizt.

	£	s	d		£	s	d	£	s	d
Eliza Rigby	60	15	0	John Crompton	28	15	5	89	10	5
Edmund Ligo	24	10	0	Samuel Ball	22	10	0	47	0	0
John Taylor	10	10	0	Roger Downhall	13	17	6	24	7	6
Richard Jackson	3	9	7	Peter Caddle	51	0	0	54	9	7
Peter Rostran	6	0	0	William Billinge	10	10	0	16	10	0
Samuel Robinson	7	0	0	George Booth	2	10	0	9	10	
D[r] Bromley	2	10	0	T & R[d] Greenalls	51	10	0	54	0	0
Margaret Liptrot	9	0	0	John Yates	3	0	0	12	0	0
[Sub total]								642	1	5

30 The following estate survey is recorded as a series of conjoined tables, the layout of which has been significantly changed for the sake of clarity.

1761

	£	s	d
The following I vallue & hold in my own hands			
The Stand & Postern Hills & Broad Well 27 acres [at] 30s	40	10	0
Stable Croft £2 10s, Wood Meadow £6 10s, Coppy £5	14	0	0
Swingley £7 17s 6d, 2d, 3d & 4th Old Jones's £7	14	17	6
New Close 6¾ acres £16 17s 6d, The Norley £29 5s, Paddock £8	54	2	6
Crow Feild £12, The Avenue £1 10s	13	10	0
[Sub total]	137	0	0
	779	1	5

		£	s	d
Pago a la Viuda	*I pay to the widow[31]*	233	14	6
Al Rey y los Pobres &c.	*To the King and the poor &c.*	93	0	0
A la Escuela	*To the school*	26	13	4
A un Senor	*To a gentleman*	2	3	4
A Otro	*To another*	0	6	4
A Diversos	*To various people*	0	3	6
A siete Domesticos	*To 7 servants*	46	10	0
A cinco Mugeres	*To five women*	17	0	0
[Total]		419	11	0

		£	s	d
Let to sundries & with the Lord's rent		642	1	5
I hold in my own hands		137	0	0
		779	1	5
	[Deduct]	419	11	0
	[Total]	359	10	0

	£	s	d
The score of 1761	37	13	10
The cheese of [1761]	36	19	11¼
Oats etc [1761]	24	6	9
[Total]	[99	0	6¼]

£	s	d	
137	0	0	
99	0	6¼	Deduct for the above
37	19	5¾	Remains lands in my hands

---

31   Translation by the editors. Possibly "la Viuda" is Winifred Gorsuch Eccleston, widow of John
     Gorsuch Eccleston from whom BTE inherited the Eccleston estate (see entry 6 Feb. 1764).

1761
31 August   I was informed that some one had got stone at Hatwell Heath,[32] and I sent to forbid them getting any more, or to cart of those that were got, and I sent my cart a whole day and brought as many of them as were got as I could to the mill, and some time afterwards I receivd a letter sign'd Henry Foster, Thomas Leadbetter, both of Sutton, saying that if I did not make Sutton satisfaction, they would prosecute my men. So in about a week afterwards I sent my cart another whole day and carted of as many as I could in order to see whether they durst venture to go to law.

12 September Housed all my oats out of the Old Jones's.

1 October

	lb		£	s	d
Killed a young heifer which weigh'd	432	at 2d	3	12	0
Suit and fat	33	[at] 3[d]	0	8	3
Hide	68	[at] 2¾[d]	0	15	7
Head, humbles & tongue			0	2	6
[Total]			4	18	4

10 October   Sowed the Moat Garden after the new husbandry, the 1st bed next to the hedge in clusters begining with 3 grains of large cone wheat and so on to 8 inclusive, then begun again with 3 grains and so on to the end, which was eight grains, & each cluster was six inches asunder. The number of grains sow'd are as follows of

3 grains   36 ⎫
4 grains   48 ⎬ The next three beds are sow'd with the
5 grains   60 ⎭ same wheat in single rows & not in clusters.
6 grains   72 ⎫ I put it into brine water 24 houres, and
7 grains   84 ⎬ then sprinkled it with lime, the whole of
8 grains   96 ⎭ the cone wheat weighd 4½oz & half quarter
Grains   396

The remaining beds are all sow'd in single rows with one pint of Eliza Rigby's wheat which weighd 15¼oz & a half, it was not in brine above an hour and was also sprinkld with lime.[33]

Peter Caddell told me he had of the Tuit Hill 53 score of oats & of the Pease Croft and & Burying Hill 20 score & 13 riders of wheat.

Thursday
15 October   Tom Reynolds came this morn^g to live with me for 50s p.a.

Sunday Evening
25 October   My great damn burst into the old place by the lowest clough, supposed to have undermined the wall, as it forced, or blew up the

---

32 Now known as Thatto Heath.
33 See entry 23 Sept. 1762.

1761

brick sough, but we never could find which way it burst. I took up both the clough, trough & brick sough and began laying clay into the damn, well ramm'd some nine yards from the wall, & upon that common green sods which were laid slopeing upon clay & sand to the top of the wall which is not three yards in height and made buttress fashion next the water in order to break the waves. Where it stands there is clay rammed from the very bottom to the top almost of the wall above three yards thick. The rest next the Broad Well is only filld with common earth and sand, and now there is only one clough to the damn which is that as is drawn to go to the mills. My engeneer was Thomas Greenall the miller. When I came to fill up the break I carted the stuff quite through the damn head which was better than any ramming, & when it was higher I carted over it crossways. I made a deep ditch the further end of the damn next to Tootle's, that in case a misfortune should happen again, the greatest part of the damn may be let of at that end. The cost was as follows vizt.

	£	s	d
To 6 Scarisbrick men at 11d per day & lodgeing 1d	4	2	10
To my own workmen 10[d] per day	4	10	5
For English spirits I gave them	1	3	3½
For cart hire 2 horses to each cart at 2s 6d	5	7	6
[Total]	15	4s	0½

Thursday
19 November   Ned Justice came in the evening to live with me.

	lb		£	s	d
Killd a cow called Caddle which weighd	596	at 2½d per lb	6	4	2
Suit & fat	76	[at] 3½d	1	2	2
The hide	77	[at] 2¾d	0	17	7¾
Head, humbles & tong			0	2	6¼
[Total]			8	6	6

23 December

	lb		£	s	d
Kill'd a hog which weighed	337				
The head	28				
The grease	15				
[Total]	380	at 2¾d per lb	4	7	1

1762

2 January   Gave James Lancaster 1s earnest & hired him this day for my cow man at £6 p.a. and he came the 3[d] inst.

1762
4 January

	lb		£	s	d
Kill'd a pyed cow bought at					
Ormskirk weighd	558	at 2½[d]	5	16	3
Suit and fat	46	[at] 3½[d]	0	13	5
The hide	89	[at] 2¾[d]	1	0	4¾
Head, humbles and tong			0	2	6
[Total]			7	12	6¾

4 February   Killd a hog which weighd (not weigh'd) lb [sic].

Tuesday
9 February   Begun to plow this morn^g the Stand Hill with one plow and at noon enter'd with an other, both my own – the 10th it frose so hard no plow could enter, and in the evening the ground was coverd with snow & continued untill the 14th even^g 15th went with 2 plows Henry Hart one, 16 with two & Cadwell ditto[34] 17. 18: 19: 20 Cad^l only ½ a day 23 Hart with 2. 26 Cadle alone. 1: 2: 3 Mar Cadwell with two. 4 ditto[35] 5th – 6 – 8: 9: 13, 15, Cadle 23. 26: Ap: Cad 6: 7. 8: 9: 10:[36]

Wednesday
17 February   For some time past numbers of poor people have got coals on Thatwell Heath & disposed of them by horse & cart loads, so I order'd Mr Wright to send each getter & carter a note which he did to the following,

Getters	Carters
George Crouchley	Stephen Wilcock
Thomas Welsby	John Wilcox
John Tunstall	Thomas Leadbeater
Thomas Hurst	James Woods
James Platt	William Woods
Edmund Forster	Peter Hewitt

upon which John Wilcox and James Platt came to make their submission to me and on Friday the 19th ins^t William Parr call'd mostly Wady Willy, came to me & said he had feighed a pitt for marl on the said Heath & askd my leave & hoped I should not be against his getting marl therein, which I gave him leave to do, but notwithstanding the above atorny^s notes, George Crouchley, Thomas Welsby, John Tunstall & Thomas Hurst continued getting coals, so I sent my cart on Saturday the 20th ins^t in the morn^g

---

34 It is not clear to what this ditto refers.
35 It is not clear to what this ditto refers.
36 This list is confusing. All attempts to improve the sense by modifying the original punctuation proved unsatisfactory. The text reproduces BTE's punctuation faithfully.

1762

& carry'd away what was upon the brow which might be some 9 or 10 baskets, but that did not hinder them from continuing getting all that day, for they said they had nothing to loose and they cared for no one, & Crouchley said his large family would protect him, as being poor they must fall to the town. On Sunday the 21st Edmund Foster came to beg pardon & on Wednesday the 24th February, Peter Hewitt came to do the like. On this 24th day I deliver'd Mr Plumb's two warrants for apprehending Crouchley, Welsby, Tunstall and Hurst.

3 March   Finish'd plowing the Stand Hill for oats and likewise turning over my mixen or dung hills.

15 March   Finisht plowing the Peas Croft by noon.

Lent John Rice on his note, and on the old mortgage of my own money £30. BTE

17 March   Promised Henry Gervase, who had his goods seized & sold by one Woods, a malster in Prescot, that as long as he finds a sufficient bondsman for his rent, he may hold the lands that he has now from me.

An account of what my dairy, which consisted of 12 milch cows and the fatning cows in the Norley, made me, besides keeping my family of fifteen persons with butter, milk, and servant's cheese from March 1761 to this day

	£	s	d
2 rearing calves which I vallue in	1	0	0
4 calves I sold in March, April & May last in	2	2	10
2 calves I sold in July £1 17s & 4 calve skins 13s 4d	2	10	4
3 calves I sold in January and February this year	2	6	6
11lb butter in April [at] 6[d] & 6½[d]	0	4	8½
37 lb butter in June [at] 4½[d] & 4¾[d]	0	14	3
10 lb butter in July [at] 5½[d]	0	4	7
11lb butter in August & September [at] 6½[d]	0	6	1½
22 lb butter in December [at] 6¾[d] & 7d	0	12	7½
9 lb butter in December [at] 7¼[d]	0	5	5¼
1 lb butter in December	0	0	7
33 lb butter in December & January [17]62 [at] 7[d] & 7½[d]	1	0	7
6 lb butter in February [17]62 [at] 7¼[d]	0	3	7½
17 lb butter in March [at] 7½[d]	0	10	7½
[Sub total] 157lb butter sold for	4	3	1¾

1762

	£	s	d
Whey butter & fleetings	0	11	4½
Milk	0	19	10
120 cheeses weight 21cwt 0qtr 18lb at 21s 6[d] per cwt	22	14	6
3 cheese for my table 64lb at 21s 6d	0	11	5
[Total]	36	19	11¼
Cows scored in the Norley	12	0	0

	£	s	d			
I bought 4 cows which cost me	14	10	6	23	10	6
2 cows of my own	9	0	0			
I killd 3 cows which were valued in				20	17	4
23 July sold 1 cow for	6	3	0			
4 January 1 cow	5	12	6	19	15	6
23 February 1 cow	8	0	0			
[Sub total]				40	12	10
[Deduct]				23	10	6
[Total]				17	2	4

Thursday Evening

18 March   Richard Ellison came along with Henry Jarvais, & offerd to give his note, or to be bound for the said Jarvais's rent for the grounds he holds under me in the presence of John Gregson.

	a	r	p
That part of the Swingley that I am now joining to the Copy was measur'd by Mas^r Ainsworth 2^d August 1760 to	4	2	24
The Copy according to the survey is	2	2	12
[Total]	7	0	36

19 March   One of my own young heifers calv'd, and the calf died.

23 March   Sow'd vetches & hay seeds in the Wood Meadow.

               Begun sowing oats in the Stand Hill.

24 March   One of my sucking calves died.

26 March   Set the following sorts of potatoes in the Stand Hill, at a foot asunder from each other. They were given me by Edward Rogerson. In the 1st butt next to the hedge, this end of the butt: early whites. Next to the aforegoing, seperated with sticks & stones: Rufford whites. Next to them, seperated as above: Three Pound Twelves. In the 4th but at this end seperated with sticks from the kidnies, a sort calld Firr Bobs. I had only four potatoes for sets of those

1762

call'd Three Pounds Twelves. I finisht setting all the potatoes the 2ᵈ day of April.

27 March   Large Dumbill slipt calf.

Saturday
3 April   Finish't soweing the Stand Hill in the following manner vizt. 23 bushˢ of Scotch Greys or Cuts are sown from the Postern Hill side to some stakes that are drove down in a but in a line with an oak tree faceing the Paddock, & the remaining with 77 bushˢ of my own Poland oats. [Total] 100 bushˢ of oats.

Teusday Noon
6 April   Finisht sowing the Pease Croft with 70 bushˢ of my own Poland oats.

Friday Evenᵍ
9 April   Finisht sowing the 4ᵗʰ Old Jones's with 7 bushells of Scotch Greys or Cutts.

Finisht sowing the Pease Croft with 106lb clover seed.

Kill'd a hog which weighd 367lb.

Thursday Evenᵍ
15 April   Finisht soweing the 2ᵈ Old Jones's with almost 19 bushˢ of my own Poland oats which finishes the oat seeding. [Total] 196 bushels of oats.

Saturday Evenᵍ
17 April   Finish'd soweing & harrowing the Burying Hill with 152lb of clover seed.

29 April   Never a finer spring was rememberd than this, fine drippling warm rains, that one might almost see the grass & corn grow.

I had 5 load of old hay from Eliza Rigby for which I am to give her as many of new. I pᵈ her in clover hay this 12ᵗʰ April 1764.

Saturday
8 May   Finish'd cross cutting the barley ground in the Swingley and Copy, which I have now laid into one feild, and had both my cultivator & a common plow broke this day.

John Vose came at night as cowman for £6 pa.

18 May   Begun plowing & sowing barley in the Copy & Swingley.

19 May   Set my coal works in John Barnes's tenements in Sutton to Messʳˢ Thomas Leigh & Cᵒ for one hundred years. The Lord's part to be one fifth of the value the coals are sold for, & hope that none of my successors will think I have done wrong in setting them at so

1762

long a term, being judged a good price and hope they will reap benefit thereby.

22 May

Finished carting all the manure to the Copy & Swingley, which was composed of red soil as came out of the deep ditch & had lain numbers of years & and which I mixt with 440 bushells of lime, horse, cow, hog dung & ashes and all kinds of rubish, which very nigh cover'd both the feilds, except the lower part of the Copy, by a little elm where I have left a few stones. Down to the deep gutter is coverd with cow dung, and the half acre of moist ground on the other side of the said gutter is cover'd with horse dung.

Wednesday
26 May

Finisht my barley seeding of seven acres by noon. I sow'd it with 32 bushels, being advised to put no more in on acc^t of the strong set of compose I had lain on it, judgeing that if I allow'd more the corn would not stand. It was finisht in seven days with two plows.

Begun cros cutting my summer works in the 3^d Old Jones's.

An account of sundry weights as I have vizt.

of lead	of lead	of iron
1 of 1lb weight	1 of 6lb weight	2 of 56lb weight
1[of] 2 [lb weigh]t	1 [of] 12 [lb weight]	2 [of] 28 [lb weight]
1 [of] 3 [lb weight]	1 [of] 24 [lb weight]	2 [of] 14 [lb weight]
1 [of] 4 [lb weight]		

27 May

Finisht cross cutting my summer works & Caddle went home.

1 June

Aggreed with the Commisioners of the Turnpikes to pay 10s 6d yearly, which is to clear me of all toll at the Eccleston Gate for all my horses, carts, coaches &c. &c. &c.

9 June

Finished sowing & harrowing my clover seed in the West Norley for which I allowd 20lb per acre, my reason for not sowing it sooner was on acco^t of the great heat & dryness ever since barley seeding. Yesterday we had a fine shower which I took the advantage of.

12 June

I had five tubs of Irish soaper's waste, which was very dry, weigh'd this day at Liverpool in my old six inch wheel^d cart & altogather was

	Cwt	qtr	lb
	26	3	10
Tare for the cart	9	2	20
Neat	17	0	20

NB five tubs are reckon'd to contain one ton.

18 June

Peter Moss markt forty trees for Pitman's, Denton's, Thomas

1762

Owen's & John Barnes's where Mrs Tingle lives & sold the bark to Mr Chorley of Prescot for £4 10s 0d.

My book of house expenses from the 10th June 1761 to the 16th June 1762 inclusive amounted to £56.

My large oak harrow was valued by Peter Moss, the wood to 6s, workmanship 5s. Fifty-one pinns [...][37] binding painting.

1 July

Aggreed with Peter Caddle for all his wheat straw that grows in my estate of Holmes's at 10d per threave.

Prime cost & charges of sixty and a half tons of Irish soaper's waste bought in Liverpool & brought home in 52 carts vizt.

	£	s	d
22½ tons at 4s 10d & measureing at 2d is 5s per ton	5	12	6
Shoveling it up 10d, drink 4d, expenses procureing w. room 1s 8d	0	2	10
2 carts one day 8s, a man 1s, drink &c. 1s 9d	0	10	9
[Sub total]	6	6	1
38 tons at 5s & measureing at 2[d], 5s 2d per ton	9	16	4
My two men one day 2s, two carts 8s	0	10	0
Expences for 2 days not being measur'd the first day	0	3	6
[Sub total]	16	15	11

		£	s	d
My carts brought home	23 loads at 4s	4	12	0
John Crompton's	11 loads at 4s	2	4	0
Samuel Ball	10 loads at 4s	2	0	0
Peter Hewit	6 loads at 4s	1	4	0
Eliza Rigby	2 loads at 4s	0	8	0
[Total]	53 loads	27	3	11

Tons 60 at 9¾s per ton £27 3s 9d. [sic – should be £29 5s 0d]. Tons 60 at 5s 7d, £16 15s 0d.

Wednesday
7 July

Never was so general, early & long a drought rememberd by the oldest man liveing, haveing lasted almost 3 months. The best pastures were burnt the most, little grass in the meadows, & the crops of barley & oats very poor. The wheat in general good. One would almost have immagined the cattle could not have subsisted as all was burnd up, but we had large honey falls, which most immagin'd maintaind the cattle, and all of them looked very well. This day the weather broke, and we had very fine rains which continued more or less untill the next day at noon.[38]

---

37 Space left in the original by BTE.
38 Generally this was a year of great drought; Stratton, *Agricultural Records*, pp. 79–80.

1762
23 July

My oats & wheat of last year produced as follows vizt.
Threaves of oats

412½	produced 888 measures good & 310¾ measures light
45 & 1 sheaf	was given to fat beasts
457½ & 1 sheaf	and the 13:4 haddocks and 6 sheaves of wheat [produced] 49 measures

Out of the above oats I made into meal

626	measures
166	measures I sowd &
49½	measures I sold
46½	measures I keep for house use besides the 310¾ measures light oats
888	measures good oats

Finished drawing into buts the Old Jones's for wheat.

Thursday
29 July

Begun mowing the oats in the Stand Hill.

Monday Morn[g]
2 August

Begun houseing oats out of the Stand Hill.

3 August

Finished mowing the Stand Hill & Pease Croft oats.

10 August

Finish'd leading all the oats out of the Stand Hill & Pease Croft.

My Scotch Grey seed oats that came out of the Stand Hill are placed at the further end of the 2[d] bay on the right hand.

Peter Moss valued my large oak harrow as follows vizt.

	£	s	d
The wood 6s, workmanship 5s, painting 5½[d]	0	11	5½
1cwt 0qtr 25½lb iron & wormanship	1	19	6½
[Total]	2	11	0

My 6 inch wheels cost as follows.

	Cwt	qtr	lb		£	s	d
2 barrs Voiage iron	0	1	17	at 2¼d per lb	0	8	5
Liverpool iron	3	2	17	[at] 18s	3	5	8
More iron	0	2	8½	[at] 18s	0	10	0
[Total]	4	2	14½		4	4	1

	£	s	d
4 frets 5s 4d, 24 bolts & nuts 2s 6d	0	7	10
Riveting the wheels 1s, two hortars 6d, 8 clouts 1s 4d	0	2	10
2 warpins 4d all which weighd 0cwt 2qtr 27lb	0	0	4
To setting on the wheels 3cwt 3qtr 15½lb at 1s per score	1	2	2

1762

17 *August*   Begun sowing turnip seed in the Stand Hill.

18 *August*   Finishd five acres of the above, which was all I sow'd this season as being so far advanced. I coverd it with soaper's waste about ten tons to an acre.

I paid the following taxes in 1761 for the undermentiond estates vizt.

	£	s	d
For Lancaster's held by Richard Farrar in the sum of	50	0	0
4 books poor £3 6s 8d, land tax £1 12s 0d, highway £1 5s 0d, constable £0 8s 4d. In all	6	12	0
[Sub total]	43	8	0
Leafe's by Richard Seddon	45	3	0
4 books poor £3 0s 0d, land tax £1 10s 0d, highway 15s 0d, constable £0 7s 6d. In all	5	12	6
[Sub total]	39	10	6
Burrow's Lane Edward Parr	32	0	0
4 books poor £2 2s 8d, land tax £1 1s 4d, highway £0 8s 0d, constable 5s 4d, Farnworth bailiff 6d. In all	3	17	10
[Sub total]	28	2	2
Henry Seddon's, Glugsmore, Peter Rostran	27	0	0
4 books poor £1 16s 0d, land tax 17s, constable & highway 9s	3	2	0
[Sub total]	23	18	0
Holmes's set to Peter Caddle	34	0	0
A malt kiln to George Halliwell	9	0	0
	43	0	0
4 books poor £2 13s 4d, land tax £1 4s 0d, highway 13s 4d, constable £0 6s 8d. In all	4	17	4
	38	2	0
Laurence Holland, Edward Rogerson	15	17	6
4 books poor £1 1s 4d, land tax 9s, highway 6s 10d, constable 2s 8d, Farnworth bailiff 6d. In all	2	0	4
	13	17	2
Alexander Holland, Jos[a] Hewitt	9	5	0
4 books poor 12s, land tax 5s, highway 3s, constable 1s 6d. In all	1	1	6
	8	3	6
Hall Heys, John Plumbley	7	0	0
4 books poor 8s, land tax 5s, highways & constable 2s 6d	0	15	6
	6	4	6

1762

	£	s	d
The aforegoing estates setts for	229	5	6
Taxes & leys deduct thereunto	27	19	0
[Total]	201	6	6

£229 5s 6d at 2s 6d per £ or 12½ per cent £28 12s 6d.
at 3s per £ or 15 per cent £34 7s 0d.

28 August

                                            Threaves

The whole of Peter Caddle's
wheat in the seven acres of
Holmes's, now John Smith's,
was 453 riders, whereof there
are in my barn   87
And in Glugsmore barn   17   & for these last I am to
                                                     give for the straw 1s 6d
                                             ___   per threave
                                             104   threave in all

3 September   Sold Mr Ellison of Liverpool all my cheese for which [...][39] to
give me in the present 26s per hundred and whatever the ruleing
price may be at Michelmass, which it is thought will be higher
than at present to make it good to me, & this day I delivered 73
cheese which weighed 14cwt 0qtr 28lb for which I receiv'd

	£	s	d
	18	9	10
I paid turnpike toll & charges	0	2	2
	18	7	8

23 September   The wheat ground by the Mote measur'd 448 square yards, which
is 23 parts of an acre wanting one square rod, and it produced as
follows vizt.

	lb	oz	
150lb 2oz common wheat	32	8½	cone wheat
15¼ & ½oz deduct for seed	8	8	cone wheat produce of
			396 grains
	41	0½	
	4	0½	light wheat
	45	1	

The 396 grains of wheat produced sixty-five thousand five hundred & sixty-five large good grains 65565, which is 165 grains
for one & 225 over in the whole.[40]

39 Space left in the original by BTE.
40 See entry 10 Oct. 1761.

1762
5 October

	£	s	d
Cost of 48 tons of soaper's waste from Ireland which now lyes in a yard as I have hired at 4s 10d & measureing 2d	12	0	0
Paid a special messeng^r with advise thereof	0	1	6
One day my 3 carts removeing it at 4s	0	12	0
For nine loads carted by town carts at 8d	0	6	0
For carts of my neighbours helping ditto		[...]^{41}	
To one Liverpool filler & two of my own	0	3	4
To exp^s in meat, drink, turnpike &c.	0	7	5
To cash to Mr Richard Tate for his trouble	0	5	0
[Total]	13	15	3

7 October John Standish came at noon as plowman for £6 p.a.

8 October Sowd the Moat Garden in rows with a pint of wheat of Peter Caddle's which weighd 15¾oz. I brined it in salt & water 22 hours and than limed it.

9 October Peter Moss sett the ridding the gorse, alders &c. and clearing the Coal Pit Brows & makeing a cross ditch five & a half feet wide & three spadeing deep in late Woods's tenem^t to a parcell of muggers for £5 10s certain & if to my likeing to allow them 5s more.

12 October Finished sowing with 4 measuers of wheat the 3^d Old Jones's which is 1a 1r 33p, the wheat was springled with urine & limed.

13 October Finishd cutting my barley in the West Norley, which came at two or three comeings, on acc^t of the very dry spring, & was very full of Lambs Quarter & B Nettles, especially that part as was calld the Copy had a great quantity of them nettles and one sees plainly by experience that the barley was sow'd too late for it is impossible to ripen so late on as this.

	£	s	d
I bought 5th January last, 40 ewes & a tup for £9 11s 6d, which I sold to Richard Ellison at 13s 6d per ewe & lamb, & they produced 26½ couple vizt. 30 ewes & 23 lambs	17	17	9
Received of Richard Ellison for 2 skins & 2 skins & fleeces	0	2	4
[Sub total]	18	0	1
He had the tup gratis and 5s return'd	0	5	0
[Sub total]	17	15	1
I received for 2 skins 1s & five I have to sell 2s 6d	0	3	6

41 Quantity not entered by BTE.

1762

	£	s	d
I received for 54lb of wool	1	7	0
I kill five, they weighd 35lb or more, each 7s 6d	1	17	6
[Total]	21	3	1

15 October   Mas^r John Ainsworth's survey of Glugsmore & Holland's Nookes

	a	r	p
The close next Edward Rogerson's	3	0	0
The close adjoining the Little Damn	4	0	24
The close next Thelwell's tenement	4	0	20
[Total]	11	1	4

The old rough's & Pitts are not measured tis good 11 acres arable lands.

21 October   I sough'd the Slack in the Paddock, next the Broad Well Lane, with brick two courses high, & cover'd it with stones from Seddon's Delf, & in the lower part for some way I flag'd it at bottom with old slates; ten rods cost me as underneath, so one may judge of the whole by it

	£	s	d
Cost of 1,280 bricks for 80 yards or 10 rods at 10s	0	12	9
Covering stones 80 yards at 2d per yard	0	13	4
A mason & a labourer each 3 days at 2s 4d	0	7	0
[Total]	1	13	1

10 rods at 3s 3¾d per rod £1 13s 1½d.

80 yards at 5d per yard £1 13s 4d.

22 October   This day I begun to lay the foundation of my new wind mill, which is three yards underground, in some parts rather more. It is laid upon the growing clay, except in one place just by the clough, where there was a kind of a sand grit & gravel, on which they rammed several bricks, than it was made solid. Than begun laying it with brick one course quite round & one brick & a half thick, but without mortar. Than all above that one row was set in lime mortar & in a round manner, the same as the work above ground. And on that side next the damn as high as the water comes is well rammd with clay, the inside fill'd up with rubbage, every fourth course above the ground was fill'd with running mortar.

23 October   Late Samuel Wood's estate in Sutton was let for £17 p.a.

	£	s	d
It pays land tax 4 books 4s 8½d each	0	18	10
Poor 4 books 5s 8d	1	2	8
Constable 5s 8d, highway 5s 8d	0	11	4

1762

	£	s	d
p.a.	2	12	10
The Lord's rent & boons were	1	16	8
[Sub total]	4	9	6
	17	0	0
	4	9	6
[Total]	12	10	6

	£	s	d
Computation of the cost of marling the two Heath Heys in the above estate from the top of the Midgeley's by the Slack where there is a very good marl, four yards thick or more. I to lay 4½ rods of marl or, 1,500 loads on an acre, the breadth of the feilds being 4½ acres which will make 20 rods of marl in the whole at 24s per rod	24	0	0
Hewing (not falling) & filling 4½ acres 9s [per rod]	9	0	0
Spreading 4½ acres [at] 2s [per rod]	2	0	0
Feighing computed	2	0	0
[Sub total]	37	0	0
For the Midgeley's the carting would only be 14s per rod & marling them 4½ acres would be about	27	0	0
[Total]	64	0	0

26 October Deliver'd Mr Thomas Starkie the old & new articles of Charles Dagnall's and the rough drafte drawn by Mr Henry Wright for Mr Thomas Leigh & Cº.

27 October Housed all my barley.

Tuesday
2 November Deliver'd Mr Peers Legh the award against Charles Dagnall which he said he would give to Mr Starkie of Preston on Saturday next.

10 December Finished planting all the hedge rows by the lane sides, in the late Samuel Woods's tenement in Sutton, with 103 very fine beech of 6 yards long & upwards and 8 very fine beech much smaller next Sutton Heath. In all 111 plants. By my gardiner Robert Spencer & Henry Hart.

27 December Mr John Barnes's tenent Thomas Clayton informed me this day, that the said Barnes makes the following of Tickle's tenemᵗ Part of which said Clayton holds vizt.

1762

	£	s	d
Clayton pays him for what he holds	21	10	0
Clayton pays poor leys £2, land tax £1 13s 2d,			
highway 4s 6d, constable 5s, church leys 6s 9d	4	9	5
[Sub total]	25	19	5
Barnes sets of to Ralph Cook	5	15	0
To Nehemiah Cook	5	10	0
To John Mollyneux	7	8	0
And that Barnes holds himself 2 acres	3	6	0
[Total]	47	18	5

	£	s	d	
£29 p.a. at 15 years purchase	435	0	0	
£40 p.a. at 8 years purchase				
two lives	320	0	0	
[Sub total]	755	0	0	Barton head
Deduct £2 17s Lord's rent	22	16	0	for 8 years Barton head
[Total]	732	4	0	

28 December

	£	s	d
Deliverd Mr Ellison of Liverpool the remainder of my cheese which were 50 & weighd, 822 which at 120lb per cwt is 6cwt 3qtr 12lb, for which he paid me at 28s per cwt.	9	11	9½
He also paid the advance on 14cwt 0qr 28lb which were deliver'd to him the 3ᵈ September last at 2s per cwt.	1	8	5½
[Sub total]	11	0	3
I paid John Vose's expˢ (they went per Chesford).	0	1	1
[Total]	10	19	2

[Loose sheet dated 1762.]

	£	s	£	s	d
I have let this year the tenements in my hands for			240	16	6
I have let of the Demesne lands with the mills			260	16	3
The Lords rents to be receiv'd are			95	17	5
I hold in my own hands	180	10	180	10	0
Whereof I have for score	42	0	778	0	2
	138	10			

	£	s	d
I have now the late Samuel Woods's tenement of Sutton which I let at £24 deducting £1 16s 8d Lord's rent is	22	3	4
[Total]	800	3	6

1763

19 January   Kill'd a third cow which I bought of my little ones. It weighd 546lb which at 3d per lb is £6 16s 6d, fat 30lb 7s 6d, hide 72lb at 2d [total] £7 16s 0d.

An account of what my dairy made from the 25th March last

		£	s	d
44½lb	butter from March to June, [at] 6d & 7d per lb	1	3	10½
37lb	butter from July to the 12 January ins[t] 6½[d] & 8d [per lb]	1	3	9
81½lb				
	Of milk whey & fleetings	1	5	3½
	21cwt 0q 10lb of cheese in 123 cheeses at 28s per cwt	29	10	1½
	4 reareing calves computed at 10s each	2	0	0
	4 calves for the butcher in May & September	2	12	2
	1763, 11 calves in March, April, May & June for the butcher	6	12	0
	[Sub total]	44	7	2½
	I had in the Norley 3 cows at score [at] 40[s]	6	0	0
	I had for feeding 4 cows & 2 for my children [at] 40[s]	12	0	0
	[Total]	62	7	2½

I milk'd 15 cows which at 40s per head is £30

The value of Eccleston estate this year 1763

	£	s	d
Lands of inheritance & tenem[ts] let to sundries	264	16	6
Demesne lands let to sundries per rental	232	12	6
Lord's rents to be receiv'd	94	0	9
[Sub total]	591	9	9
Lands as I hold in my own hands as under			
Stable Croft £2 10s, Wood Meadow £6 10s, Copy £5	14	0	0
Swingley, £7 17s 6d, 1st, 2[d], & 3[d] Old Jones £7	14	17	6
New Close £16 17s 6d, Norley £29 5s 0d, Paddock £8	54	2	6
Crowfeild £12, Avenue £1 10s	13	10	0
Postern Hill £21, Tuit & Pease Croft £31 10s	52	10	0
Stand Hill £15, Burying Hill £18 15s, Broad Well £4 10s	38	5	0
Glugsmore Nook & Slutch Field in score	10	10	0
Holland's Nook to be marld	4	10	0
Kenwrick's Meadow & Norley Acre	12	0	0
[Sub total]	805	14	9

1763

	£	s	d
The New Wind Mill as per aggreement	17	14	9
Ann German's to sundries, deducting 20s 6d			
Lord's rent	20	15	3
[Total]	844	4	9

5 April   Finshd sowing and harrowing the Stand Hill, as far as the pathway, computed to be six acres with twenty-one bushells of vetches, all struck off.

14 April   Finshed sowing and harrowing the Crowfeild, with eighty bushels of our own country oats, bought at Ormskirk.

15 April   Finished sowing and harrowing the Little Old Jones's with 2½ bushels of tares or vetches, and the Head Lands with one peck of blew peas, bought of John Smith.

16 April   The measurement of the late John German's estate, taken this day by Mas^r John Ainsworth.

	a	r	p
Building, orchard, fold, & hemp yard	0	1	29
Orchard Feild	2	0	03
Owler or Alder Hey	2	1	10
Old Meadow	1	1	13
Three Nooked Hey	2	0	11
Clover Hey	2	0	04
Barn Hey	1	2	05
Damn Stid	1	0	06
[Total]	12	3	01

20 April   Finish'd rolling the vetches in the Stand Hill, & setting potatoes.

21 April   Finish'd rolling the vetches in the Little Old Jones's.

23 April   Finishd sowing the New Close Meadow with 64 bushells of Scotch Grey oats.

NB the Pinfold Meadow & part of the Old Jones's meadow, as lies next to it, & as far as the forked stick in the gutter, are of them oats that grew in the little Old Jones's, which were extraordinary good, the others were of the Stand Hill.

Mr Hollinshead's directions, (of Chorley) for setting potatoes.
The potatoe beds to be thrown up in ridges, as soon as the potatoes are got 4 feet asunder, & to lye all winter. In the spring the ridges are opned and the sets put in, ten inches asunder, and when they brewer'd or break ground dig up the allys and after some time, hoe the beds of each side, not on both & let that lye in the ally. Afterwards hoe the rest. If you throw dung upon them,

1763

when brewer'd it will make them strike more into roots than wisels.[42]

24 April Finishd sowing & harrowing the 2ᵈ Old Jones's, of 1a 3r, with 16 bushells of Scotch Grey oats. NB 13 bushells were of the best sort as above, the remainᵉ are sown with the other sorts at the right hand at the bottom of the feild, & terminates where I have stuck a stick in the gutter & the two low headlands are the same oats.

6 May From the 18ᵗʰ May to the 30ᵗʰ April last I used sixty-two measures of wheat.

14 May

	£	s	d
Bought 11 weathers & one ewe, 11 in all	6	1	0
18 ewes and lambs Shropshire	4	4	0
28 ewes & lambs Shropshire at 8[s] 6[d] per couple	5	19	0
16 ewes & lambs Welch [at] 6[s] 6[d]	2	12	0
20 ewes & lambs Welch [at] 8[s] 6[d]	4	5	0
93 in all put into the Paddock – charges	1	1	0
[Total]	24	2	0

30 May Begun marling Holland's Nook from Hatwell Heath.

7 June Sold Richard Ellison the following sheep & lambs, all to be taken away by New Michealmass vizt.

	£	s	d
41 couple ewes and lambs at 15s per couple	30	15	0
6 weathers, 3 barren ewes, 2 rams, in all 11 at 12s each	6	12	0
He is to allow me if they prove well to him	0	10	6
To pay the whole at Michealmass	37	17	6

The contents of the several commons or waste land lying in the township of Ditton, when the publick roads of 12 yards broad and the pits are deducted in the measure of 8 yards to the perch vizt.

	a	r	p
Marsh Green	9	3	38
Ditchfeild Green	16	1	11
Hough Stone & a pˢ in Old Lane	2	1	15
Hough Green	3	1	27
Little Heath	5	1	33
Broad Heath	25	1	14
[Total]	62	3	8

Measured in June 1763 per John Eyes.

---

42 Wisels (Wizle, Wyzle) – stalk or top of carrots, parsnips, potatoes, etc.

1763

28 June Fished the Little Damn & took out 229 fine carp & 9 tench, 238 in all, which I put into the Recevoir, Stews & in the pit at the bottom of the Avenue. 10 fine pike, & 4 eels.[43]

2 July Begun mowing my clover in the West Norley.

4 July Turn'd my bull amongst the milch cows.

14 July Cost of ridding and marling Holland's Nook quantity 3 acres

	£	s	d
Ridding the feild of gorse & feeighing the pitt	3	15	0
Getting and filling 18¼ rods at 8s	7	6	0
Paid them for pumping	0	5	0
Paid Ned Justice for pumping day & night 26 days	1	6	0
Paid day wage for carting with 3 horses 18¼ rods, 4[s] 6[d]	20	14	0
Paid spreading 18¼ rods 1[s] 8[d]	1	10	5
Paid & gave them to drink	0	2	6
Paid ridding & levelling the cops around the feild	0	11	1
[Total]	35	10	0

NB The marl pitt is just at this end of Hatwell Heath by Mr Edwards's.

21 July Finish'd leading all my clover out of the West Norley, which contain'd twenty-seven very large loads.

1 August Housed all the hay out of the little wood, which contain nineteen very large loads in very good order, and the best grass I ever saw, being cheifly trefoil, tarvetch & wild clover. Two years ago, I run it over with the six coulter, and laid a thin set of compost upon it. I put 5 loads in the cowhouse, 7 into the nighest Dutch barn, 6 in the stable & 1 into the paddock, in all 19 large loads.

12 August Housed all the hay in good order out of Kendrick's Meadow & the Norley Acre, which consisted of 18 large loads, 3 were put into the cowhouse, 1 over the stables, & 14 into the Dutch barnes. 18 in all.

20 August Housed all my vetches in very good order, out of the Stand Hill, which was plowed as far as the path way from the gate, which I compute to be five to six acres, & it contain 41 large loads, but there was amongst it a great quantity of bee-golds, catelock and yaw. The best were put into my own barn, the rest into Rigby's & over the coach stables.

31 August Housed my vetches out of the Little Old Jones's quantity 3 rods,

43 Tabulated in the original.

1763

consisting of 4 loads, 3 were put into my barn & 1 in the low^r stable.

Housed 3 loads of white hay out of the Crowfeild, which was put into the higher stable.

15 September   Finishd boreing for coals at the bottam of the Tuit Hill next to the great ditch faceing 2 little oak trees that grows on the cop in the marld Holland's Nook & board thro'

2½   Yards soil & blew clay
11   Yards black bast
4   Stone
4½   Yards, very fine flag & almost [...]⁴⁴ ½ an inch
0½   Yards very black bast & then thro' a little coal and gave up
22½

Housed all my wheat out of the 3^d Old Jones's containing 1a 1r 33p consisting of 33 threaves.

19 September   Finished boreing in the Green Slack the bottam of the Stand Hill next the Little Damn & went through.

1   Yard at top
5   Yard bast
½   Yard burr
6   Yard woolen & woone & broken stuff & left off
12½

26 September   Housed all my oats out of the 2^d Old Jones's 1a 3r 0p cont^g 56 threave.

28 September   Sold all my cheese to Mr David Ellison of Liverpool at 26s per cwt certain, but if the prices are higher at Lancaster Fair, to have the medium price over & above the 26s per cwt advance, & receiv'd 10s 6d earnest on acco^t. He has markt out 91 cheeses which he will have next week or the week following, and the remain^r he fancies he shal not order away then February next.

4 October   Put 40 brace of carp into the Little Damn from Winstanley. They might be about 3 to a pound.

12 October   Housed all my oats out of the New Close 6a 3r 0p cont^g 216 threave.

13 October

	£	s	d
Deliver'd to Mr David Ellison of Liverpool 91 cheeses which weighed 19cwt 1qtr 0lb, for which I receiv'd at 26s	25	0	6

44 Space left in the original by BTE.

1763

	£	s	d
I paid turnpike toll and charges	0	1	2
[Total]	24	19	4

14 October — Housed my 2ᵈ crop of clover, out of the West Norley quantity 16 loads.

17 October — Housed all my oats out of the Crowfeild quantity 213 threave.

19 October — Paid for 21 ewes & one ram North Country £5 19s 6d.

21 October — Finishd sowing the Little Old Jones's with wheat, quantity 0a 3r 0p with 2½ bushells.

22 October — Soap muck'd the lower part of the Stand Hill from the pathway to the wood side with 27 loads or tuns.

26 October — Killd a hog which weighd 314lb.

4 November — Finished sowing the Stand Hill with wheat quantity 9 acres, 22 measures were sown on the 1ˢᵗ shute, next the path road, and 11 measures on that next the damn wood, in all 33 measures.

5 November

	£	s	d
Received for 79 sheep and lambs at 7[s] 6[d]	29	12	6
11 weathers [at] 12[s]	6	12	0
[Sub total]	36	4	6
I return'd them back, as haveing a hard bargain	1	1	0
[Sub total]	35	3	6
Received 25ᵗʰ August for 94¾lb of wool	2	12	3
[Sub total]	37	15	9
They cost	24	2	0
Proffit	13	13	9

7 November — Paid for 20 North Country weathers at 7s 3d, & driving 2s 6d, £7 7s 6d. They were mark on the further side TE the ewes, & ram on the nigh side.

5 December — Killd a hog which weighd 330lb.

In October & November 1763 — Joseph Stafford, the collier and Will Wilcock of Hatwell Heath bored at the top end of the Little Hurst in Lancaster's tenement next the ditch at the corner of William Moss's Meadow, and went into black bast, at about 6 yards deep, then about five rods from the top end of the Long Feild in Holmes's tenemᵗ next the Little Hurst into black bast at about ten yards, then to the edge of the pitt in Peter Moss's Alder Hey thro' the marl into a kind of flag and then came to stone about seven yards deep, then into the east

1763

side of the Old Meadow in ditto's tenem[t] about 2 rods above the old pit 14 yards deep thro' a flag & then into bast, from thence into ditto's Lower Sheep Hey thro' marl and then into sand & could get no further. Then into Holmes's Meadow at back of the Orchard 14 yards deep thro' marl, and under that thro' a rocky red sand, and raised a large spring and then about three rods from the top end of Peter Moss's Alder Hey next to the acre about six yards from the ditch, and bored thro' marl into a flag, then into hard stone & thro' a kind of a burr & then into a soft stone incline-ing to flag to about 27 yards deep, and into ditto's Richard's feild the side next to the Meadow about three rods from the top end into a crop of coal about an inch thick and under into a warren earth about five yards deep from the top.

Teusday
13 December   The barometer was lower, in the morning, by one degree, then ever I knew it. It rain[d] at 9 o'clock and then clear'd, and a smal gale of wind South East & East and almost due East.

21 December   Kill a cow which weighed 550lb, tallow & fat 59lb, the hide 79lb, [total] 138[lb].[45]

Joseph Bolton miller & labourer, Samuel Robison joiner & Peter Arrowsmith jun[r] shoemaker, came to ask my leave to carry Samuel Robison's corps thro' the hills & down the Avenue which I grant-ed conditionally, that they should ask leave of my servants John Vose, Robert Spencer, John Standish, Jos Glover & Charles Standish at each gate they passd through.

28 December   Bob Rainford came as plow boy at 45s p.a.

1764

3 January   Edward Kirshaw came as plowman for £6 p.a.

9 January

	lb
Killed a cow which weighd	480
Tallow 55lb, the hide 64[lb]	119
[Total]	599

21 January   Kill'd a hog which weighd 335lb.

24 January   Begun plowing the Postern Hills with two plows.

25 January   Sent to Mr David Ellison's 34 cheeses weight 5cwt 3qtr 3lb at 26s per cwt for which I receivd £7 10s 2d.

45 Tabulated in the original.

1764

I received of Mr David Ellison 13 October last for 91 cheeses weight 19cwt 1qtr 0lb at 26s [per cwt] £25 0s 6d.

He is to pay more on 25cwt 0qtr 13lb at [...][46] per cwt advance.

Monday
6 February

Tender'd Mrs Eccleston of Cowley Hill £40 for one year's intrest of £1,000 due the 5th ulto from Eccleston Estate, which she refused, insisteing upon £50, but would have given a receipt for it in part.

Tuesday
7 February

	lb
Killd a cow which weighd	694
Fat 67lb, hide 86[lb]	153
[Total]	847

The head, humbles & feet not included.

Manchester Mercury. The following is recomended as a preservitive from the rot in sheep, at this very wet season.

Bruise a quantity of Rue leaves well & press out the juidce; to which add an equal weight of salt. When sheep are in danger of being rotten, give them a tablespoonful of the mixture once a week. It should always be given to new bought sheep, as it will keep them well if they are in danger. If not, it will do them no harm.

24 February

William Parr, that purchased the late Mr Hesketh's tenem[t] of Robert Gwylim of Atherton Esq., the side of Hatwell Heath, took in some small part of the Heath, & so brought the brook nigher this way, in order to enlarge his garden some small matter, & to keep the floods from riseing into his fold, askd my leave & whether I would permit it to stand, that he might plant quick wood on the cop to make fence, which I aggreed to.

5 March

Cover'd the higher parts of both the Norley Acre, & Kendrick's Meadows, as far as the footpaths, with fine old rotten compost of all kinds of dung & ashes.

14 March

Begun sowing the Postern Hills with our country oats, & 4 pair of harrows.

20 March

Finished sowing the Postern Hills with our country oats, 120 bush[s] and the Low[r] Gorsy Shute by the white gates of about 3 rods with 8 bush[s] of Scotch Grey oats. In all 128 measures.

Pears planted.
The Bureau, Summer Borgomet, Admirable Pear, Orange Borgomet, Winter Borgomet.

---

46 Amount not entered by BTE.

1764

2 April Finishd sowing and harrowing at noon, with 3 harrows the 3^d Old Jones's, with 6 measures & a half, & half peck of white makeing pease, quantity 1a 1r 33p.

5 April Finish'd sowing and harrowing the marld Holland's Nook quantity 3 acres with 25 measures of Scotch Greys.

6 April Finish'd sowing the 4th Old Jones's quantity 0a 3r 0p with seven measures of Scotch Grey oats. NB the head lands & 7 tong sharps are in wheat.

Friday
27 April My dearest children left Eccleston & went to Scarisbrick.

9 May Aggreed with Richard Ellison for 13 cupple of ewes & lambs to be taken away by the 29th September at furthest at 15s per cupple makes, £9 15s 0d. Paid.

12 May Aggreed to allow Thomas & Richard Greenalls £5 in their next years rent for them to buy dung with for German's.

21 November

		£	s	d
Killd my white cow which weighed 598lb	at 2¼[d]	5	12	1½
87lb fat	at 3d	1	1	9
hide 74lb	[at] 2½[d]	0	15	5
[Sub total]		7	9	3½
Hide weighd 10lb more		0	1	10½
[Total]		7	11	2

	£	s	d
Received of Messrs Brown & Birch of Liverpool for 124 cheeses which weighed 24[cwt] 0[qtr] 13[lb] at 29s per cwt[47]	34	19	0
Turnpike toll and expences	0	2	8
[Total]	34	16	4

27 November The four acres of ground in Edward Rogerson's estate proposed to be marled from Thatwell Heath will stand in about £1 8s 8d per rod vizt.

	£	s	d	
Compute the feighing at	0	3	0	per rod
Hewing & filling	0	9	0	
Carting	0	15	0	
Spreading	0	1	8	
[Total]	1	8	8	

Which at 6 rods of marl per acre is £8 12s 0d.

---

47 Messrs Birch and Brown – merchants of North Side, Old Dock, Liverpool.

1764

5 December

Aggreed with Rachael Dagnall for late Lawton's estate for £13 p.a. She to repair & keep the house in order & to allow Dr Leigh a cart road through it, he paying her trespass for the same.

	£	s	d
Aggreed with Mr Parker of Liverpool to add two lives to Mrs. Jane Wilkinson's tenement vizt. George Wilkinson aged 7 years and Thomas Wilkinson aged 6 years, both sons of the late Mr Samuel Wilkinson of Middle Witch, Cheshire for the sum of	147	0	0
To deduct 7 years Lord's rent of £1 16s 7d p.a. is	12	16	1
To be ready in February & the sum to be receiv'd is	134	3	11

My dairy, from the Norley made from the 28 March 1763 to 12th May 1764

	£	s	d
25cwt 0qtr 3lb cheese at 26[s] 6[d]	33	3	2
Butter, whey, & milk sold for	4	18	10½
One heifer £3 3s, two rearing calves £1	4	3	0
Two calves to the butcher £1 16s 6d, one calf to the butcher £1 1s	2	17	6
Four cows of my own £8, 3 of my children's & score £6	14	0	0
[Total]	59	2	6½

I had the following oats in 1763

	Measures	
302½ threaves & 5 sheaves of Greys which produced	655½	best & 201½ light
192 threaves of our own country which produced	331½	best & 110½ light
	987	of the best
	312	light
[Total]	1299	measures in all

I made into meal

623½ meas^{rs} which produced 52 loads 4 windles 41lb & 117lb of groats

	£	s	d
I sold 37 loads & 36lb of oatmeal & ½ peck groats in	39	2	6½
And 120¾ measures of oats in	13	11	4½
623½ made into meal [Total]	52	13	11

744¼

242¾ sown & gave to horses &c.

987 measures of the best oats

1765

5 January	Killd a cow which weighd 620lb at 2¾[d] per lb, 86lb fat at 2¾[d], hide 75lb.
6 January	Jack Hoole came at night as plowboy for 40s p.a.
7 January	Begun plowing the Tuit Hill in the afternoon with two plows for oats.
Saturday *12 January*	Sold Richard Ellison of Prescot 59 weathers at 13s each all to be taken away by Candlemass, in case it shoud prove a hard bargain to make him an allowance. He is to run all risks of them.
22 January	Promised to allow John Crompton 15s towards clearing the brows in the Alder Hey.
23 January	Sold Richard Ellison of Prescot my little black heifer for £5 15s. I am to keep her a fortnight longer.
25 January	Aggreed with Eliza Rigby that she may plow the cow pasture this year for oats, and the next year with barley on condition that she puts thereon 30 tons of soaper's waste & mucks the remaining part over with dung. She may sow clover, & mow it twice in 1767, and only mow it one in 1768.
	Planted the following against the long wall vizt. 1 Smith's Newington Peach, 1 Red Magdalen Peach, 1 Newington Nectairne, 1 Red Roman Nectairne, 1 old Black Newington Nectairne. They were bought of Thomas Caldwell of Knowsley, and cost 7s 6d.
28 January	Killd a cow which weighd 592lb at 3d, fat 43lb [at] 2¾[d], £0 9s 4d, hide 69lb.
	Killd two hogs which weigh'd 261 & 289lb both 550lb.
31 January	Made a brick sough in the Spout Hey in Edward Rogerson's farm and brough the water across the top of the feild, & fill'd up the large gutter in the middle of the feild where it used to runn to Hatwell Heath. The sough contains 1,300 brick, they are laid two in height, & cover'd with brick, & where it had a sand bottam I have set the bricks upon slate. Richard Farrar was seven days with two carts about it, and I had one half day four men filling soil from Hatwell Heath for it. The rest was filld by them, which I account as nothing, because they were feighing the pitt from the Heath out of which I intend to marl said closes, so that it was rather an advantage to the men than otherwise.

1765
9 February

Marld the middle of the Great Feild of the Spout Estate, which I bought, where a hedge stood, about 3½ yards broad, quite cross the feild, with three large carts, two with four & the other with three horses, and laid thereon fifty-two large loads. I likewise laid twenty-two large loads at the side of the bank, where the stream runs in the lower feild. I had four fillers.

Monday
11 February

Finishd plowing the Tuit Hill in 23½ days with two plows, & what is remarkable from the 7ᵗʰ ulto to the 1ˢᵗ insᵗ I was never hindred one day by rain &c. The 2ᵈ insᵗ it set in & froze for six or seven days which keept the plow out of the ground till this day.

Begun late this afternoon plowing the Pease Croft with 2 plows.

12 February

Deliver'd Mr Turner of Warrington, Mr Starkie's engrossd articles of Messʳˢ Mackay & Leigh's aggreemᵗ for coals, with his own, Mr Moss's, & my notes thereon.

13 February

Delivr'd Mr Moss of Preston, an original latin deed (in old court hand) for my holding Eccleston Court, which he promises to transcribe out fair, and send them both back to me.

Peter Moss's valuation of late Knowles's tenement vizt.

	a	r	p	£	s	d
House, barn, fold, orchard, garden & croft	0	3	10	2	10	0
Meadow	1	2	00	3	10	0
Great Heys	3	1	19	5	10	0
Hall Heys	3	0	00	4	10	0
Widdow's Heys	2	0	11	3	10	0
Warhouse Lane & Croft	2	1	18	4	10	0
[Totals]	13	0	18	24	0	0

20 February

I bought at Liverpool

		£	s	d
720	measures of soot at 3d per measure	9	0	0
36	measures were allow'd for scorage	0	0	0
756	measures, carting at 3s per 40 measures	2	16	8
[Total]		11	16	8

NB I carted the whole myself except 40 measures by William Bankes for which he charged 3s and my carts took 45, 55, 60, 63 & 65 each which was computed at 16cwt. I coverd all the Crowfeild with 630 measures which is 70 to an acre, and the remaining 126 measures I devided equally on the lower parts of the 2 meadows next the lower mill damn.

1765
Friday
1 March

Ann Rigley, daughter of Roger, came to live with me as cook lass this evening. The girl did not stay, being too young.

8 March

	£	s	d
Bought of Catherine Birkett of Liverpool, 12 tons of soaper's waste at 8s[48]	4	16	0
I brought home when I first bought it, 1 ton 7cwt in 2 carts, 4s	0	8	0
Paid three men removeing it to the sand hole	0	4	6
Expences in drinks &c. on [the men]	0	3	10
Employ'd my 3 carts with seven horses removing it 4s	0	12	0
[Total]	6	4	4

NB I have laid in the feild about 2 ton 7cwt. I carted it to the hole in the following manner.

	Tons	Cwt
8 carts with 1,500lb each is	6	0
5 carts with 1,200lb each is	3	0
3 carts with 1,100lb each is	1	13
What I first brought home	1	7
[Total]	12	0

11 March

	£	s	d
Bought of James Foden 5 tons soaper's waste at 8s[49]	2	0	0
Paid one man filling 1s 6d, & expences in ale &c. 2s 4d	0	3	10
Employ'd my 3 carts with 7 horses removeing &c.	0	12	10

NB I brought home about 1 ton 10 cwt 0lb. I carted it to the hole in the following manner.

	Tons	Cwt
6 carts with 1,500 each	4	10
1 cart with 1,000	0	10

4 April

Killd a hog which weighd 411lb.

6 April

Finish'd sowing the Spout Land with 6 meas^{rs} of vetches.

9 April

In a hurricane of wind betwixt 10 & 11 o'clock in the morning the top of my Dutch barn next the stables was blown of, and I might loose about a load of hay. Wind west.

12 April

Finish'd sowing the top end of Holland's Nook with five measures & half a peck of peas. It is not quite an acre.

Planted 648 winter cabbages in the little Old Jones's.

48 Catherine Birkett – tallow chandler and soap boiler of High Street, Liverpool.
49 James Foden – tallow chandler and soap boiler of Pluckington's Alley, Liverpool.

1765

Sowed a large bushell & a half of vetches in the Pease Croft, next to the hedge by the Postern Hill side, which sowed 6½ butts.

Begun sowing our own country oats in the Pease Croft, three harrows.

18 April

The weight of iron that was used for my two pair of six inch wheels was 824lb. The rivetts for both pair were the old ones of my other carts, and are not included in the 824lbs.

	£	s	d
Received of Richard Ellison for 59 wheathers at 13s	38	7	0
Received of Richard Ellison for a year old lamb	0	9	0
[Total]	38	16	0
Return'd him	0	5	0

	£	s	d
Paid Richard Ellison for 80 ewes [at] 5s 9d	23	0	0
And for 6 ewes [at] 7s	2	2	0
86 ewes expenses driveing &c.	0	17	0
[Total]	25	19	0

My dairy from the Norley made from the 13th May [17]64 to the 18th May 1765

	£	s	d
124 cheeses weight, 24cwt 0qtr 13lbs of 11 milch cows at 29s per cwt	34	19	0
Butter & milk £4 10s 1½d, bulling cows 16s	5	6	1½
Score of one cow 40s, three calves to the butcher 38s	3	18	0
5 feeding cows £10, two rearing calves 20s	11	0	0
[Total]	55	3	1½

24 April

Put into the Little Damn from Winstanley 69 carp of eight to 12 ounces each.

25 April

Finished by eight o'clock in the morng sowing & harrowing the Pease Croft with our own country oats.

Put into the Little Damn from Winstanley 20 carp of the size of the above.

30 April

Finish'd early in the morning, sowing & harrowing the Tuit Hill with 124 measures of our own country oats, & the Pease Croft took 57 measrs of our own country oats & 1½ measures of vetches. [Total] 181 measures.

Sow'd in the Little Old Jones's ¾ of a pound of burnett and one pound of carrot seed.

20 May

Finish'd cross plowing Holland's Nook & the 3d Old Jones's for wheat.

1765

21 May   Made a kiln of our own oats of 65 measures into meal which produced 6 loads one & a half windles & 7lbs.

22 May   Begun marling with three carts, at noon from Thatwell Heath, three closes in Edward Rogerson's farm cont^g four acres.

Marked 110 oaks & 16 cyphers, the bark of which was sold to Mr Chorley for £16. The wood is intended for the new bay of the barn & a new barn in Sutton & for Joseph Houghton's, James Greenhough's & Peter Barrow's buildings.

29 May   Sold all my ewes & lambs to Roger & Richard Downall for 15s 3d per couple to take the lambs as soon as they are ready & the ewes by old Michaelmass. They to run the risk if any of them are destroyd after new Michaelmass.

30 May

	£	s	d
Bought of Catherine Birkett of Liverpool 8 tonns soaper's waste [at] 8s	3	4	0
3 men removeing it 4s 6d, ale 3s, horse, hay & tunp^k 5d	0	7	11
4 carts & 8 horses half a day	0	8	0

I brought home 4 loads which might be 2tonns 12cwt. It was carted to the hole in eleven loads.

1 June   I used from the 30 May to the 31st October 1764 wheat 12¾ bushells, & from the 31st October to the 8th May ulto inclusive 29 bushells in all 41¾ bushells.

22 June   Cost & charges of 48,901 bricks made in the Paddock

	£	s	d
Clay for them at 3d per 1,000 12s 6d, sand 8 loads 5s 6d	0	18	0
Loads & getting 3s, drink 1s	0	4	0
5 works 40 baskets coals at 12s 6d	3	10	10
Carting coal at 4s	1	2	8
Casting, tempering & moulding the clay & burning at 5s	12	4	0
[Total]	17	19	6

48,900 bricks at 7s 3d per [1000] is £17 15s 6¼d.

24 June   Let of the Sleck Pond by the house of office, & took out 1 brace of made carps & 61 brace of very fine carps storers, larger than those from Winstanley and I put 53 brace into the Little Damn, the others into the Stews, & there was about 20 ells. It run of in about 7 hours & required about an hour's laveing. It is very full of mud.

1765

8 July   Begun mowing the West Norley with two men, & housed the whole being about twelve loads the 15th July.

15 July   Begun mowing the Middle Crowfeild with three men.

Fished the Horse Pool & took out 28 brace of fine carp which I put into the Sleck Pond in the New Orchard.

My dairy from the Norley made from the 13th May 1764 to the 10th April 1765, £55 3s 1½d vizt.

	£	s	d
Score of 5 feeding cows [at] 40s	10	0	0
4 calves to the butcher	2	10	0
2 rearing [calves]	1	0	0
Butter, whey and milk	3	18	1½
Score of one milch cow 40s, bulling sundries 16s	2	16	0
24cwt 0qtr 13lb of cheese at 29s per cwt	34	19	0
[Total]	55	3	1½

29 July   Paid Robert Billinge for casting, moulding and burning 45,400 bricks in open fires at 5s, £11 7s 0d.

Housed the following loads of hay vizt.

15th July	12 loads out of the West Norley
20th July	12 loads out of the 3 Crowfeilds
22 July	2 loads out of the Avenue & Stable Croft
25 July	11 loads out of the Wood Meadow
29 July	10 loads out of Kendrick's & Norley Acre
[Total]	47 loads

6 August   Finished sowing the Little Old Jones's with 3½lb turnip seed. The Burnet carrots & cabbage, as I had sow'd & planted before in it being almost intirely destroy'd by the dry weather.

9 August   Finished slutching the Horse Pool, the mud thereof I laid in large heaps in the Avenue & Stable Croft. It had not been cleansed before for forty years & was as full as possibly it cou'd be. There is a lower clough or sluice which is quite racked up, which will make it very difficult to be drawn, as the net will be apt to catch upon it unless care is taken. It cost cleaning as follows viz.

	£	s	d
John Tickle 4 days, John Watkinson & Henry Hart 7½ days each	0	19	0
Randle Ligo 6 days, Ned Kirshaw 7½ days	0	13	6
3 carts with 2 horses 7½ days, one cart with 2 horses 1 day at 3s each	1	5	6
[Total]	2	18	0

NB I gave them a pint of beer each per day.

1765

17 August   Begun reaping wheat with five reapers in the 2^d Old Jones's.

21 August   Housed three loads of vetches out of the Spout Lands which was all the two acres contain'd.

23 August   Finished houseing all my peas out of Glugsmore Nook, where I sow'd not quite an acre which produced seven loads, two of which I put into my own barn & five into Ned Rogerson's.

20, 23, 26, 30 August   Housed all my wheat out of the 2^d Old Jones's & the New Meadow which measured 8a 2r 22p, & of plowd land only 8a 1r 0p & all in very fine order, large bands & remarkably well headed & containd as on the other side, verte.

30 August

	[Tythe]		In the barns		
	thr	sh	thr	sh	thr	sh
In the 2^d Old Jones's	37	12	3	8	34	4
In the higher shoot of the New Meadow	64	19	5	16	59	3
In the Pinfold Meadow in the New Meadow	48	11	4	8	44	3
In the next Old Jones's in the New Meadow	44	0	4	0	40	0
[Total] threaves	194	18	17	8	177	10

I put into Eliza Rigby's barn in one bay intirely filled	67 16
In one bay of my own, with 2 loads peas & 3 of vetches	45 11
In the other end of my barn	20 23
In the new bay over the cart houses	43 8
[Total] threaves	177 10

NB one of my bays will hold about 68 threaves of wheat of large band, and that over the cart houses will hold about 49 threaves of wheat of the large band.

2 September   The names of those who have licence to sell ale.
Anne Robison, Robert Lawton, John Whitlow, James Seddon, Rachael Ball, William Halliwell, Mary Southern, Eliza Hatton, Eliza Leland, Henry Hart. In all ten.

9 September   I perceivd on my oats this year in the Tuit Hill & Pease Croft millions of little black flies settled on the corn, & when it was ripe & cut a multitude of lady cows. Quere, whether the lady cows do not come from the black flies.

Alice Wainwright, my dairy maid, run away from her service about ten o'clock at night.

1765
10 September   Begun with two plows sowing wheat in Holland's Nook. The ground was in very fine order.

Thursday
12 September   Sowed on the 3ᵈ Old Jones's 5 tonns & 9cwt of soaper's waste, & begun plowing & sowing it with wheat this afternoon with two plows. It contains 1a 2r 3p.

Saturday
14 September   Finish'd the above which was in very dry fine order by five o'clock in the evenᵍ with 3¾ bushells market measure. The 12ᵗʰ I had two plows all day, the 13ᵗʰ one all day, & another till noon, & the 14ᵗʰ two plows to five in the evenᵍ.

Threshd five threave of wheat which producd 19¾ measʳˢ all struck of, and of small 0¼ measʳˢ. In all 20 measures.

Monday
23 September   Finishd sowing Holland's Nook with wheat with 9¼ bushells all struck of, the 3¾ in the Old Jones will make 4 bushells when all is struck of, so that I have sow'd in all 13¼ bushl bare measure.

Teusday
24 September   Aggreed with Richard Farrar to take all my new malt of him at 30s per load.

Saturday
28 September

	£	s	d
Mrs Davenport's estate in Upholland set to Thomas Yates	70	0	0
The Eagle & Child in Upholland to Peter Platt	11	0	0
A house garden &c. in Upholland to James Atherton	5	10	0
An other in Upholland to Widdow Pryor	3	0	0
An estate in Eccleston with an new house	25	0	0
Mr John Davenport in Farnworth, Parish of Dane[50], James Berry	40	0	0
A coal mine let to his Grace of Bridgewater for 1,000 years	50	0	0
An estate in Little Lever let to Jacob Fletcher for 1,000 years	10	10	0
A lease of 8 houses in Bolton to John Bothwell for 7 & 14 years	11	5	0
All that Mr Davenport is possessed off	226	5	0

---

50 Parish of Deane, near Bolton.

1765
Monday
14 October   Aggreed with Elizabeth Rigby for twenty bushells of[51] her for-reign seeds oats at 2s 6d per bushl in presence of Mr Weldon.

Teusday
15 October   Plow'd this day with two plows with three horses each for Eliza Rigby, drawing her ground into butts. Paid 7 June.

Wednesday
16 October   Plow'd for Eliza Rigby with two plows with three horses each, paid 7 June.[52]

Friday
25 October   Deliverd Mr Robert Moss of Preston my will & codicill a list of the tenem[ts] & lands & a note of instructions to draw a new will by. He has also an old court book of 1736 and the amercements of 1760.

I N.N. Esq. of the Mannor of E in the County of L, do hereby nominate, authorize, and appoint N.N. of E in the said county to be my gamekeeper of and within my said mannor of E with full power, licence and authority to kill any hare, phesant, partridge or any other game whatsoever in & upon my said mannor of E for my sole use and immediate benefit. And also to take and seize all such guns, bows, greyhounds, setting dogs, lurchers, or other dogs to kill hares or conies, ferrets, travels, lowbells[53], hays, or other nets, hare pipes, snares or other engines for the taking and killing of conies, hares, phesants, partridges or other game, as within the precincts of my said mannor of E shall be used by any person or persons who by law are prohibited to keep or use the same. Given under my hand & seal this 7 day November in the year of our Lord 1765.
Sealed and deliver'd on paper duly stamp'd in the presence of [...][54].

2 December   Winnow'd the 5 loads of peas that were in Rogerson's barn and there were 34 measures all struck off & ½ a measure light.

3 December   Killed Richard Farrar's old cow.

---

51 'for' crossed out in the original and replaced with 'of'.
52 The entries for 15 and 16 October have been lightly crossed out, presumably when the account had been settled.
53 Lowbells – bells with lights, used in conjunction with other tools to help snare birds. Primarily for night use.
54 Details not entered by BTE.

1765

	£	s	d
She weighd 450lb at 2½[d]	4	13	9
The hide 68lb at 2¼d, 14s 2d, suit 12lb [at] 4d, fat 32lb [at] 3½d per lb, 9s 6d	1	7	8
[Total]	6	1	5

Killd & weighed a hog of 230lb, & his head 40lb, in all 270lb.

9 December

	a	r	p	£
Let to John Crompton for no certain term all the grounds that Samuel Ball held being	16	0	6	28
And the Crowfeild being	9	0	0	13
[Total]				41

The Middle Old Jones's of 1a 2r 0p sow'd with peas in 1764 produced

	£	s	d
5 bushells & ½ a peck which I sow'd this year at 5s	1	5	7½
24½ bushells & one quart sold at 5s	6	2	7½
2¼ [bushells] & 3 quarts used in the house at 5s	0	11	9
[Total]	8	0	0

32 bushells in all is £5 6s 8d per acre

18 December Planted the Bruges onions under the rails in the court on the left hand, a foot asunder, the first eight are old roots, the rest all young ones.

1766

4 January Killd a hogg whose head weighd 26lb, plucking & grace 30lb, and the two sides 249lb, in all 305lbs.

Thursday 16 January Cover'd the lowest & furthest part next Eliza Rigby's Wood Meadow of my Wood Meadow, in all about 1½ acres, with the mudd and sand that came out of the Horse Pool.

The labourers begun about this time to raise their wages from 10d and 12d per day to 12d and 14d per day.

Tuesday 21 January Old John Barrow died in the poor house.

Tuesday 28 January Begun plowing the Burying [Hill] with two plows.

Friday 31 January Kill'd a hog which weigh'd 295lbs.

Eccleston Estates sets as follows.

No		a	r	p	£	s	d
1	Eliza Rigby with a road thro' the hills	39	2	12	61	5	0
2	John Crompton with Balls & Crowfeild	55	1	03	66	10	0
3	Edmund Ligo Maids Hills & Sand Croft	23	0	07	24	10	0
4	Roger Downhall	9	2	11	13	17	6
5	Ann Robison the Court House	0	0	11	7	0	0
6	Mr Thomas Weldon	1	1	05	3	0	0
7	George Rice Glugsmoor Nooks	8	0	34	12	0	0
8	Pater Rostran Rushy Park	7	1	12	9	0	0
9	Thomas & Richard Greenalls Mills & Damns	14	3	07	69	4	9
10	John Smith Brook Meadow	2	2	38	6	6	0
	I have set of the Demesne Acres	161	3	20	272	13	3

The following remaining part of the Demesne I hold in my own hands, it was valued per Peter Moss and is as followeth.

	a	r	p	£	s	d
Stable Croft with stables & shippons	1	3	34	4	0	0
Wood Meadow and Croft	3	2	06	12	0	0
West Norley	7	2	37	16	10	0
2^d, 3^d, and 4th Old Jones's	4	1	22	9	19	0
New Meadows	6	3	00	14	0	0
All the Norley	14	1	08	42	0	0
The Paddock	3	3	03	13	0	0
The Avenue	1	1	10	1	1	0
Postern Hills	14	1	08	23	0	0
Tuit Hill	16	0	11	22	0	0
Pease Croft	7	0	17	11	0	0
Stand Hill	10	0	23	19	0	0
Burying Hill and Half Acre	10	2	27	16	10	0
The Broad Well and Lane	5	0	12	7	0	0
Holland's Nook	3	1	28	8	10	0
Kendrick's Meadow	2	1	10	8	10	0
Norley Acre	1	3	13	5	5	0
George Booth's Meadow	1	0	04	2	10	0
Grange Meadow	4	0	30	7	0	0
I hold of the Demesne in my hands	119	3	25	242	15	0
I lett to tenants of the demesne	161	3	20	272	13	3
The Lords' rents which I receive are				90	15	3

1766

	£	s	d
Henry Sixsmith's cottage 15s, Mr Davenport's rent 4s 6d	0	19	6
Two seats in the church 17s 6d, Schole rent 2d	0	17	8
The Demesne according to the valuation &c.	608	0	8

The following are lands, or tenem[ts] that I have purchasd or what is fallen loose to me & first of them that I hold in my own hands.[55]

	a	r	p	£	s	d
Brimilow's Land	2	0	26	8	0	0
Rogerson's Spout Hey tenem[t]	1	2	14	3	15	0
Rogerson's feild next to it tenem[t]	1	2	08	4	5	0
Rogerson's Meadow next to the Heath tenem[t]	1	0	0	2	15	0
I hold in my hands	6	1	08	18	15	0

I let the following Lands & Tenem[ts] to.

	a	r	p	£	s	d
Edward Parr Burrow's Lane tenem[t]	29	1	13	32	0	0
John Smith's Holmes's tenem[t] 14a 3r 25p John Smith's Mather's Land 7a 3r 39p	22	2	24	35	14	0
Edward Rogerson	5	3	25	10	0	0
George Halliwell Malt Kiln Land				9	0	0
Jos[a] Hewitt tenement	3	2	27	9	5	0
Richard Tootle tenement	0	2	03	4	4	0
Peter Rostran Seddon's Land	11	3	25	29	0	0
John Plumbley Hall Heys tenem[t]	4	2	04	7	0	0
Richard Seddon, Yew Tree Farm tenem[t] [56]				24	0	0
Richard Ellison in Yew Tree Farm tenem[t]				6	0	0
Doctor Zachariah Leafe in Yew Tree Farm tenem[t]	15	1	22	4	4	0
Widdow Bradburne in Yew Tree Farm tenem[t]				4	4	0
Widdow Crouchley in Yew Tree Farm tenem[t]				6	15	0
Richard Farrar Lancaster's tenem[t]	28	3	30	50	0	0

---

55 This sentence is repeated in the original.

56 The five entries for Yew Tree Farm are ambiguous. However, comparison with the estate survey and valuation for 1759 (see above, pp. 13–14) shows that tenements within Yew Tree Farm were leased to people named Seddon, Leafe, Bradburne, and Crouchley.

1766

	a	r	p	£	s	d
Thomas & Richard Greenall's German's tenem^t	12	1	14	20	15	3
Thomas & Richard Greenall's Houghton's Sand Hey tenem^t	1	2	30	5	5	0
John & Robert Sutton Woods's tenem^t	14	1	20	24	0	0
Rachael Dagnall Lawton's tenem^t	8	2	01	13	0	0
Thomas Lyon, Robert Knowles's tenem^t	13	0	18	24	0	0
Let to sundries as above	172	3	26	318	3	3

	£	s	d
The demesne is valued as on the other leaf to	608	0	8
The lands and tenem^{ts} that I have purchasd &c. as specify'd on the other side amounts to	336	18	3
The whole amount	944	18	11

	a	r	p	£	s	d
I hold of Demesne lands	119	3	25	242	15	0
Of Lands and Tenemt^s	6	1	8	18	15	0
I have in my hands	126	0	33	261	10	0
I pay in taxes for tenem^{ts} about				48	3	7
In taxes for the demesne				59	1	0
To Mrs Eccleston £193 14s 3d & £50 interest				243	14	3
Halsal Schole rent				26	14	4
Rent to the Vicar of Prescot				1	13	0
To Mr Leigh & Miss Bold about				2	8	0
In wages £62 10s Labourers &c. £80				142	10	0
[Total outgoings]				524	4	2
[Net profit]				420	14	9

3 February The papers mention'd at this time that there was consum'd in London & a little ways round 14,000 sacks of flour and 6 to 7,000 quarters of oats weekly.

I find that of earth or mudd 240 cart loads are required to set an acre with, and it is no strong set.

8 February Coverd the lower part of the Norley Acre with the mudd and sand that came out of the Horse Pool, & the headland next the brook with the marl and mudd as came out of it, and the top square part with brick kiln bottoms, and the top part of Kendrick's Meadow next to the Norley Acre with the Horse Pooll mudd and the furthest part next the damn, and the brows of the lower part with the marl and mudd as was taken out of the brook.

	£	s	d
1766			
27 February			
Killd Richard Farrar's little cow, which weighd			
472lbs at 3½[d]	6	17	8
The hide 60lb at 2¼[d] 11s 5d, fat 60lb at			
3½[d] 17s 6d	1	8	11
[Total]	8	6	7

Saturday
1 March

Begun sowing & harrowing the Burying Hill with our own country oats & with three double harrows.

Monday
3 March

Begun plowing for oats in Edward Rogerson's with two plows.

Thursday
6 March

Continued sowing the Burying Hill with three sowers and twelve pair of double harrows. vizt. 3 of my own, 2 of Richard Greenal's, 2 of Richard Farrar's, 1 of Edmund Ligo's, 1 of Thomas Chesford, 1 of John Smith, 1 of Jonathan Dumbill and 1 of Thomas Lyon.

It was a very fine, calm sunshineing day and the ground cou'd not be in finer order, and I finish'd the whole with 107½ bushells of our own country oats.

Monday
10 March

Received 14½ hundred of soaper's waste from young Travese.

Tuesday
11 March

Finishd plowing the four acres in Edward Rogerson's.

Wednesday
12 March

Begun plowing the Spout Land with two plows.

Satturday
15 March

Finishd plowing the Spout Land, at 11 o'clock, & begun sowing & harrowing in Rogerson's Further Spout Hey. 3 harrows.

Sowd some Saintfoin by the south asparagos bed.

Monday
17 March

Continued sowing in Rogerson's lands, & with my 3 harrows and 2 of Richard Greenall's.

Tuesday
18 March

Fnish'd sowing & harrowing, with my 3 harrows Rogerson's grounds. The Furthest Hey had 16 bush^s of our own country oats, the second 17, & the Meadow 8. In all 41 bushells, and five butts next to the gate in the meadow are sow'd with 11lbs 9¼oz of naked oats. All were got in very well.

1766
Wednesday
19 March   Begun with 2 plows in the Little Old Jones's for peas.

Thursday
20 March   Never a finer equinox known, not a breath of wind & a fine sunshine day, but a sharp frost, the wind northeast, & it has been for some time past east, & now & then a point to the north. It turn'd in the afternoon to west.

Finishd by noon with one plow &c. sowing ¾ of a bushell of vetches and 5lbs of clover seed in Old Booth's Meadow.

Finishd with 1 plow the Little Old Jones's & plow'd the potatoe butt in the Stable Croft.

Friday
21 March   Finishd with a single harrow, sowing the Little Old Jones's with 4½ bush⁵ and half a peck of white peas, and the potatoe butt in the Stable Croft with 1 peck of vetches & about two hatt crowns full of our own country oats.

This even⁵ past 10 o'clock it began to rain & there were fine showers in the night, there not haveing been any since the 6ᵗʰ insᵗ.

25 March   I paid only 4 books Poor Ley this year, & the demesne, Spout Lands and Sand Hey are £6 9s per book at 4d per £ which is £25 16s & £270 for tenemᵗˢ out of lease £4 10s per book at 4d is £18. [Total] £43 16s.

Wednesday
26 March   My two loads of pease produced 11 bushells, the five loads in Rogerson's barn, all struck off 34 [bushells], [Total] 45.
Allowing one at the score it is 42¾ bushells, which at 5s per bushˡ is £10 13s 9d. The ground they were sown on was not quite an acre.

Tuesday
31 March   I sent to the mill 45 bushells of wheat clean struck off, & I had return'd back 99lb as overweight, so that a bushell clean struck off weighs 64lb 5¾oz so that allowing the scorage it would weigh 67[lb] & 7oz.

Tuesday
8 April   Begun sowing the Spout Lands with Hewitt's Grey oats and 2 harrows.

Wednesday
9 April   Finish'd the above with two harrows & 18¼ bushells of oats.

Sow'd a bed with carrot seeds in the Little Old Jones's. Fine weather.

1766
Friday
11 April   Finish'd sowing 9½ bushells of Rigby's Grey oats in the Paddock. The rest I have reservd for turnips.

Monday
14 April

	£	s	d
Kill'd a spade heifer which weighd 590lb at 3½d per lb is	8	12	2
Hide 80lb [at] 2½d, 16s 8d, 32lb fat 9s 4d, 20lbs suit [at] 4½[d] 7s 6d	1	13	6
[Total]	10	5	8

Tuesday
15 April   Begun carrying dung with 3 of my carts, one of John Smith's and one of Richard Greenall's to the Old Jones's for barley & four fillers and finished. Byart workd for Richard Greenall all day.

Wednesday
16 April   Begun plowing the above with two plows.

I had at this time thirteen sucking calves.

Monday
21 April   Begun dunging the higher part of the New Close Meadow with 3 of my own carts & one of John Smith's. At noon I took one of my own of and drudged with the 2 horses.

Tuesday
22 April   Continued dunging the above with 2 of my carts only.

Begun sowing William Moss's barley in the Old Jones's with 1 double and 1 single harrow, & finish'd it with 9 bush^s struck off.

Wednesday
23 April   Began plowing the New Close Meadow with 2 plows at 9 o'clock morn^g.

Thursday
24 April   Continued plowing with two plows & in the afternoon sow'd Moss's barley with a single harrow.

Friday
25 April   Continued plowing with 2 plows and Henry Hart sowd the Old Jones's with clover. It was rainish and raind at 11 o'clock.

Saturday
26 April   It rain'd greatest part of the day.

1766
Monday
28 April   Continued sowing Moss's barley in the New Close & with 1 harrow, & sowd likewise with clover & a 1 horse drudge. It was in tolerable order but rather to moist.

xxx Never was a finer spring known, in these parts in the memory of any man, all the feilds look'd very green & a great prospect of a plentiful harvest both of corn & grass.

Wednesday
30 April   Begun dunging the Old Jones's in the New Close with 3 of my carts & one of John Smith's & betwixt 4 & 5 o'clock the rain drove us away. Wanting about 15 loads to have finishd the feild.

Friday
2 May   Begun plowing about ten o'clock the Old Jones's in the New Close with 2 plows.

Sold Eliza Arrowsmith my cheese of last year's make for 28s per cwt to be taken away in six weeks. They consisted of 105 cheeses & weighd 22cwt 2qtr 23lbs, £31 15s 4d. I kept for the kitchen 32 & for my table 5 cheeses, all which would weigh 7 cwt, which makes £9 16s besides my family has eat all along of them since May last. I may have reckond what I have kept to much, so I will say only 5cwt which is £7.

My servants consisteing of 5 men, two boys & 3 maids, in all ten, consume about ten hundred of cheese p.a.

Saturday
3 May   Continued plowing the Old Jones's with 2 plows. There were heavy showers about 11 o'clock.

Monday
5 May   Continued in the above with two plows in the afternoon.

Tuesday
6 May   Continued in the above with 2 plows & finish'd by noon all but the long headland, & begun at 10 o'clock sowing Randle Ligo's barley in it and with 4 single harrows.

Joseph Edwards's new close on Catchall Moss is 1a 1r 16p and Helen Eccles's is just one acre. Both measured this day by Mas^r John Ainsworth.

Saturday
10 May   Mutton & beef were at this time at 5d per lb.

1766

Reced from the 30th April 1765 to the 13th May 1766.[57]

	£	s	d
For 13 calves	9	16	6
127lb wool	3	3	7
Butter, milk & whey	3	11	10
Bacon	2	2	6
Cow fat	1	9	5
Pease	8	0	0
105 cheeses 22cwt 2qtr 23lb [at] 28s [per cwt]	31	15	0
Hills score £10 7s, Norley 40s	12	7	0
3 rearing calves	1	10	0
468½ Bushell's by weight of wheat	148	19	6
	222	15	4
Proffit on sheep & lambs	34	13	0

Receivd from the 10th June 1766 to the 17 March 1767

	£	s	d
For 1 calves	0	11	0
Butter, milk & whey	4	10	9½
Bacon & pork	3	10	6
Cow fat	1	19	11
Hides & one skin	5	1	8
Honey 4½lb	0	2	7½
One load of meal	1	6	0
186 cheeses 30cwt 1qtr 23½lbs [at] 26s [per cwt]	39	17	4
Hills score	25	17	0
Norley 40s one calf & eathidge	2	6	6
Booth's after grass	0	10	0
	85	13	4
Sold an in calf heifer	6	12	0
Proffit on 2 fat cows	6	13	0
6 rearing calves	3	0	0

Friday
16 May   Begun in the afternoon with 3 carts dunging the Pinfold Meadow.

Saturday
17 May   Continued dunging with 4 carts & 4 fillers, & finishd the compost at noon & cover'd the rest next the gate, which is about half an acre, with ashes.

Monday
19 May   Begun plowing with two plows in the afternoon Pinfold Meadow.

Tuesday
20 May   Continued with two plows in Pinfold Meadow in the afternoon, and sow'd out the Old Jones's with barley.

57 This is inserted on a loose sheet of paper.

1766
Wednesday
21 May   Continued till noon with two plows in the Pinfold, in the after-
                noon only one, & with 3 harrows, sowing barley in the Pinfold
                & finishd sowing the Old Jones's with clover.

Thursday at noon
22 May   Finishd sowing all my barley & clover. I had one bushell from
                the mill, so I sow'd 41 bushells & 190lb clover seed on the before
                mention'd ground which is eight acres. It was only winter fallowd
                and now in the spring I harrow'd it both with the large & small
                harrows & then led the dung & plowd it in.

Saturday
24 May   Went to Liverpool with two carts for corn for Richard Greenall.

Monday
2 June   Carted ten loads of stone with 2 carts & 3 horses each for the
                navigation.[58] A whole day.

Tuesday
3 June   Carted quarry stone with 2 carts & 3 horses for the navigation till
                noon and than brought 2 loads of flaggs from Moss Bank. A whole
                day.

Wednesday
4 June   Carted for the navigation with 2 carts & 3 horses stubbs and rails
                from Rainhill one half day.
                NB To charge the planks carted twice down & up again.

Thursday
5 June   Carted from Rainhill with 2 carts & 3 horses stubbs &c. 1 whole day.

Friday
6 June   One cart a day laiding stones for the platts for the navigation.

Saturday
7 June   2 carts from 9 till 3 o'clock carting wood to the navigation from
                Rainhill.
                Remember the account of the nails for the navigation.

Friday
13 June   Carted half a day stones for the navigation platts with one cart 3
                horses.

Monday
16 June   Carted stones with 4 horses for the navigation one cart a whole
                day.

---

58 The Navigation – extension of the Sankey Navigation into Eccleston, then under construction.

1766
Wednesday
18 June

Aggreed to add James Barton, son of Mr Thomas Barton callender man of Wigan, to Thomas Houlding's lease for £30, & aggreed that he should not pay the writeing of the lease.

Capt Mathias Holmes receipt to kill rats or mice.

2 quarts of oatmeal, 2 dropps of rhodium, 2 grains of musk, 4 red beans alias nux vomica, made into powder, mix them well all togeather and lay it where they frequent. Enlarge the receipt or diminish according to the number you have to destroy.

Thursday
19 June

Carted 2 loads of sand & 1 of brush wood for the navigation with 4 horses half a day.

Friday
20 June

Carted 1 load of sand & two loads of stone for the navigation with four horses half a day.

Monday
23 June

Carted 4 loads of cropwood from Rainhill for the navigation with 2 carts 3 horses each one day vizt. from 4 to one o'clock.

Saturday
28 June

Went with 2 carts 2 horses each for Richard Greenall to Liverpool.

Aggreed with Thomas Houghton to keep the road from the furthest gates on the Postern Hills to the Mill Gate in repair for 30s p.a. The millers to pay 10s & myself 20s for doing it.

30 June

Carted 200 piles from Rainhill for the Navigation with four horses half a day.

Wednesday
2 July

Begun moweing the Stable Croft.

Saturday
5 July

Sow'd 3lb Dutch turnip seed in the Paddock.

Friday
18 July

Mr John Robison, schole mas^r in Prescot, informed me that John Maddocks, tallow chandler late of Leeds, died about three years ago in Vicar Lane, Yorkshire.

Carted the 15th ins^t with 2 carts & 3 horses planks to the Navigation about three hours.

Saturday
2 August

Aggreed with Thomas & Richard Greenall for Holmes's for seven years for £42 p.a. They to do all the ditching & make stone platts in the ground where they are wanted at their own expences & if

1766

the stock they keep upon the ground does not make 30 good loads of dung, they in each year are to set that quantity on some part of the lands, to plow six acres p.a. & have liberty once to push the bottam part of one feild, & may have liberty in some years to sell a load or two of hay & to leave all their dung on the premises at the end of the term, & if they marl I have promised not to raise 'em for that improvement if they continue on the farm.

Tuesday
5 August   Rear'd my barn in Sutton.

Finish'd all my mowing.

Friday
8 August   Sow'd some few seeds of turnip cabbage in the little garden for a trial.

Tuesday
12 August   Sold all my cheese of this year's makeing to Eliza Arowsmith at the governing price other cheese will be sold for, & she is to take them as fast as she disposes of them & each lot to be weigh'd out to her, as she takes them away.

Saturday
16 August   Slutched part of my lower mill damn next to the Norley. I was exactly six days in it. I had four carts with two horses each and six fillers and a setter which was John Watkinson, and he unloaded it on the Norley. The bottam is very good being gravelly & hard as farr as a ridge of sand as runs almost cross the damn, the other side of which has a bad botom. I slutched it as far as the ridge of sand just twenty years ago & put it on the Mill Meadows. The part next to the mill Richard Greenall slutchd five days with 4 carts and 6 fillers & Richard Ascroft was the setter. The botom was very bad & cut much being marl.

NB I cut the damn head to drain it, just by the two little oaks that grows on it. It cost as follows vizt.

	£	s	d
Paid the fillers and setter	2	14	8
Four carts two horses each at 4s	4	16	0
[Total]	7	10	8

Tuesday
19 August   Lead marl for Richard Greenall with three carts & two horses each, a whole day out of Arrowsmith's Lane into the late Richard Brotherton's feild adjoining it.

Wednesday
20 August   Lead marl for Richard Greenall 3 carts & six horses, half a day.

1766

NB there is very good marl in the deep ditch, at bottom of the Norley next to the Avenue, but it is only seven feet thick. I bored thro' it. It crops towards the Mill Meadow, it has 4 feet of feigh.

30 August

The breadth of the ground delved in my gardens as follows

	Perches
Bee garden contains	32½
The Court in front	5½
Onion garden	16
New orchard border	1¼
Long walk border	3¾
Mistres's garden	5½
Wall pond border B. front	2¼
Moat garden	7
[Total]	73¾

The whole contains 0a 1r 33¾p.

Finish'd threshing out all my wheat of last year 1765

	Threave		Best Measures	Small Measures
September 14	5	which produced	19¾	¼
1766				
January 4	6½	[which produced]	20	1½
February 8	7	[which produced]	22	3
March 15	38	wanting 5 sheaves		
		[which produced]	115	15
April 19	18½	[which produced]	58	5
June 14	26	[which produced]	74	5
June 21	23½	[which produced]	72	3
June 27	17½	[which produced]	53	5
August 29	38	[which produced]	112½	12
[Total]	179	& 19 sheaves	546½[59]	49¾
		what it produced in all	596 measures	

			£	s	d
I sold	13	bushells	at 6s	3	18	0
	39	bushells for house use	at 6s	11	14	0
	49¾	bushells small	at 3s	7	7	9
	260	bushells sold by weight	at 6s 2d	80	3	4
	120	bushells sold by weight	at 6s 4d	37	16	8
	88½	bushells sold by weight	at 7s	30	19	6
	570¼			171	19	3

59 Figures actually add up to 546¼.

1766
Saturday
6 September   Paid Peter Smith for 3 days new laying two of the Navigation platts, 5s.

Sunday
7 September   Old John Vose my cowman and brewer run away from his service about five o'clock in the afternoon after haveing much abused & crushed Mary Talbot the dairy maid, leaving me in the midst of my harvest & just about brewing, he haveing ready 18 bushells of malt ground & was to have gone the 8th to Ormskirk Fair.

Thursday
11 September   James Smith came to live with me as cowman till Christmas at the rate of £6 p.a.

I bought 64 tonns of limestone in Liverpool at five tubs for a tonn which at sundry prices cost £13 13s 2d. Expences in drink & labourers in moveing them to Sir Thomas Gerard's coal yard £1 1s 4d. [Total] £14 14s 6d.

64 tonns at 4s 7¼d per ton is £14 14s 8d.

NB I reckon nothing for cart hire, because my carts brought each of them part of a load home.

	£	s	d
I had 4 tubs weighd in Liverpool which weighd exactly 26cwt so that at 2 tons or 10 tubs should weigh 65cwt which I only call 3 tons of 21cwt each which cost in Liverpool	0	9	2½
Carting 3 tons home	0	12	0
15 basketts charcoal 3s 7½d drawing the kilns 6d	0	4	1½
Breaking & burning 66 bushells at ½[d]	0	2	9
[Total]	1	8	1

NB the kiln when well fired will only require 12 basketts.
66 bushells at 5d is £1 7s 6d.

If I was to deduct my carting out of the £1 8s 1d for the limestone there would only remain 15s 5½d the bare cost of the stones, & according to that 66 bush[s] of lime at 2¾[d] would be 15s 1½d & at 3d per bush[l] 16s 6d.

Wednesday
17 September   Botled of a quarter cask of Cap[t] Holmes red port which ran to 10 doz[n] & 5 bottles. Part are ale bottles.

The following is an account of my hay & corn this year vizt.
                                                    Loads of hay
I had out of the Stable Croft   6
Out of the Stand Hill   22

1766

	Loads of hay
Wood Meadow	28
West Norley	40
Mill Meadows	24
Crompton's Grange Meadow	13
George Booth's Meadow	4
Norley a pasture	6
In all	143

large loads

			Tyth		Home	
	Th	Sh	Th	Sh	Th	Sh
Spout Land Grey oats	72	00	6	16	65	08
Part of the Paddock oats	49	09	4	08	45	01
Burying Hill our country oats	212	20	19	00	193	20
Ned Rogerson's feilds our country oats	107	14	9	00	98	14
Holland's Nook with wheat	79	13	7	08	72	05
3ᵈ Old Jones's with wheat	27	19	2	08	25	11
New Close with barley	332	00	30	00	302	00

1 October   I finish'd houseing all my corn. Gracias Dios.

4 October   Sent 38 measures, all struck of, of Old Jones's clover barley to Richard Farrar's malt kiln.

Friday
10 October   Finish'd sowing the Little Old Jones's with Ormskirk wheat. There was sown on it 2¾ measures, market measure. NB there was no manure laid on the feild.

Tuesday
14 October   Aggreed with Thomas Greenall for all my barley that I don't use for 4s per measure, but if it rises to 4s 2d or more per measure he is to give me 4s 2d & no more.

Wednesday
15 October   Sent Ned with a plow & 2 horses to help Richard Farrar in his wheat seeding. I sent no driver.

Thursday
16 October   Ned went with a plow & 2 horses to Richard Farrer but no driver.

Monday
3 November   Aggreed with John Sutton that he might set the Yew Tree Farm in Sutton for the remainder of the term to the best advantage for the benefit of the widdow, to act according to the articles and whatever he setts it for more than he has it for from me to be for

1766

the benefit of the widdow, he paying a proportionable part of the taxes according to the rise.

Spanish books belonging to B. Thomas Eccleston Esq. and Cornelius Morphy and the survivor of them.

Folio Ribadeneira, Flores Sanctorum, Sveyro Annales de Flandes 2 vol., Carnero Guerras Civiles de Flandes, Mariana, Historia General de Espana 2 vol., Stephens's Spanish and English Dictionary, Quarto Obras de S Teresa 4 vol, Obras de Quevedo 2 vol, Octava Diana de Montemayos Imperf 12 mo Dialogos de Oudin.

Friday
14 November

	lb
Kill'd a segg which weigh'd 834lb, fat 50[lb] in all	884
The hide at 2½[d] weighd	114
[Total]	998

Tuesday
3 December

72cwt of limestone of 120lb to the 100 & 16 baskets of charcoal made 63½ bushels of lime, of my measure.

Wednesday
17 December

Went with a cart and three horses to Liverpool for barley for Richard Greenhall.

Monday
22 December

Sent to Richard Farrer's kiln 45 bush^s barley struck off.

1767

Friday
2 January

Thomas Sankey came to live with me as plowman &c. for £6 10s p.a.

Thursday
15 January

	£	s	d
My iron plow cost me in Scotland	3	8	6¼
Freight to London 10s 2d, freight to Liverpool 8s 6d, carriage 9¼d	0	19	5¼
[Total]	4	8	0

Friday
16 January

Kill'd a hog which weigh'd 14 score 10lb which at 3½d per lb is £4 4s 9d.

Wednesday
21 January

Last Friday's & Sunday's posts did not come before this day at

1767

> 12 o'clock (and the Tuesday's post did not arrive) occasion'd by the heavy snows, and I receiv'd a letter this day from London marked by the office the 13th January. The Tuesday's came on Friday, and the Friday's on Sunday, & Sunday's on Monday, & Tuesday's on Wednesday morn[g].

Tuesday
27 January

Sold to Mr Wilmore all my cheese's at 26s per cwt.

Sent to Richard Farrar's 15 bushells of barley.

30 January

Killed a cow (Brookfeild) which weighd 592lb, fat 52lb, hide 76lb. 128[lb].

Tuesday
10 February

Gave Richard Greenall leave to take my 2 large stone troughs from Holmes's to German Hall.

Kill'd 2 swine which weigh'd 30 score & 7lb.

Wednesday
11 February

My slutch in the Norley cost as per acc[t] 16th August last £7 10s 8d. I have mixt with it 675 measures of lime of my large measure which is 7½ quarts above the sale bushell, which I only call 20 per cent, the difference is 135 bush[s] which in all 810 at mixing 11 kilns at 3s 6d per kiln, £1 18s 6d. Cost of the slutch and lime. £[...][60].

Aggreed with Helen Ascroft for £36 to add her son, Robert's life (aged six years) to hers and Dorothy Turner's daughter of Thomas Turner of Upholland aged 17 years, the money to be paid 24th June next. She ask'd for something to make gates & for posts.

Tuesday
17 February

Kill'd a cow (dun) which weigh'd 603lb, fatt 67lb, and the hide 75lb, 142lb.

Mix'd in the Long Cop in the Norley, at the side of the Sand Hey, 134 of my large measures of lime, allowing 20 per cent difference for the size are 160 sale measures. Mixing 134 bush[s] at 3s 6d per kiln, £0 7s 7d.

Thursday
19 February

Planted 98 willows & poplars on the Navigation Mill Cop.

Saturday
21 February

The valuation of the late Richard Bushell's estate taken this day per Peter Moss. It was leased in 1695 & fell loose this month; it

---

60 Amount not entered by BTE.

1767

belong'd many years to William Leadbetter and in 1742 was let at £12 p.a. but said Leadbetter, alias Hacko, run it out almost to the last degree.

	a	r	p	£	s	d
House garden & croft	0	0	35	1	0	0
Backhouse Hey	0	3	31	1	10	0
Round Meadow	0	1	35	1	0	0
Clover Hey	1	1	0	1	17	6
Pingot	0	1	18	0	12	0
Barn & Barn Meadow	1	0	26	2	4	0
Acre	1	0	9	1	11	0
Two acres in 2 pt[s] A	0	3	19	1	1	0
Two acres in 2 pt[s] B	0	3	8	0	16	6
[Total]				11	12	0	p.a.

Mix'd in the cop in the Norley by P Moss's, 50 bushels of large measure of lime which at 20 per cent are 60 of sale at [...][61]. Mixing the above at 3s 6d per kiln, £0 3s.

Thursday
26 February   Mixed in the cop in the Norley, by the Mill Gate 103½ bushels large measure of lime which at 20 per cent are 124 of sale at [...][62] mixing lime £0 6s.

Monday
2 March   The 7 cheeses that were weighd the 29th January last were 103lb & only weighd again this day 101lb, notwithstanding the weather had been mostly moist and rainny.

Saturday
7 March   Begun plowing in the West Norley for oats with 2 plows.

Monday
9 March   Mixed in the cop in the Broad Well Lane 165 large measures of lime which at 20 per cent are 198 bushells. Mixing the above at 3s 6d per kiln, £0 9s 0d.

Received of Mr Thomas Wilmott for 159 cheeses weight 25cwt 2qtr 20lb at 26s [per cwt], £33 7s 4d.

Took out of the Avenue Pond 8 large carp.

12 March   Sow'd my turnip cabbage seed.

Friday
13 March   I advised Mr Johnson that I paid 34s 6d p.a. for the newspapers.

61 Detail not entered by BTE.
62 Detail not entered by BTE.

1767
Saturday
14 March   Begun plowing the Grange Meadow wth 2 plows for our own oats.

Sold 186 cheeses weight 30cwt 1qtr 23½lb at 26s per cwt, £39 17s 4d.

30 March   Mr Scarisbrick of Holt's receipt for makeing of ink vizt.
Take one quart of rain or river water, put 3oz of Gall well bruised, a full ounce of Gum Arabic, of Coperas and Roach Allum each one quarter of an ounce, half an ounce of common salt and a full spoonful of brandy. Shake all up together in the bottle 2 or 3 times a day & in a fortnight fit for use or sooner. NB if made by the fireside or in the hot sun t'will bring it on faster with shakeing it well 2 or 3 times a day, & when made & not to your liking black enough, place it in the hot sun, or near the fire so as to steam gently & exhale the watery fluid & by so doing with the cork out you may bring it to what consistency of black you please.

Thursday
16 April   Finish'd soweing the West Norley the 14th inst with 56 measures of Scotch Greys & this day finisht soweing the Grange Meadow with 39½ measures of our own country oats.

Mr Joseph Cowling's, apothecary, of Wigan's receipt to prevent calves from dying vizt.

Take Gentian Root, the root of birthwort, or what is called aristolochill, bay berries, myrrh, cummin seed of each 1 ounce, take care these are all good in kind, let them be powder'd fine and well mixt together. Take half an ounce of this powder, which is to be given to a young calf in a little table beer with a little treacle milk warm.

Good Friday
17 April   I had this day 209 poor people a begging & for peace eggs.

Saturday
25 April   Begun sowing barley in Holland's Nook, without manure on wheat stubble.

Tuesday
28 April   Finishd sowing the above with 15⅛ bushs of barley.

Friday
1 May   Begun sowing the 3d Old Jones's with barley. It was cover'd with 170 of my measrs of lime of 204 sale measures, the part next the Little Old Jones's was set the thickest.

1767
Saturday
2 May   Finish'd sowing the 3ᵈ Old Jones's with 7½ measʳˢ barley less one quart.

Monday
11 May   Thomas Peters came to live with me as cowman at £6 p.a.

Tuesday
19 May   Sow'd the 3ᵈ Old Jones's with clover.

Thursday
21 May   Sent 2 carts with 3 horses each to Liverpool for barley for Richard Greenall.

Friday
22 May   Finishd sewing the lower part of the Paddock with 10 bushells of Greys.

	£	s	d
Bought 31 tons of limestone at 4s & measuring 2d per ton	6	9	2
2 men 3s, drink 4s 4d, yard room 2d per ton 5s 2d	0	12	6
3 carts & 7 horses, which on accᵗ of bringing home about one tonn I only charge	0	8	4
[Total]	7	10	0

31 tons at 4s 10¼d is £7 10s 5¾.

Sunday
31 May   I had 3 cows this year slipt calf, and out of 12 more that calved, I could only rear 1, the rest all dieing, but of what distemper no one could tell.

NB I had fed them in the winter with turnips. Quere whether that was not the cause.

This month was the coldest, I believe, ever remember'd but within these 3 days we have had fine showers, & the weather somewhat warmer, & now a great shew for grass, & hope the corn will do well.

Wednesday
3 June   Sow'd Burnett in the Paddock & 379 wild vetches.

3/4 June

	£	s	d
Paid for 39 tons 1 tub limestone at 4s and measuring at 2d	8	3	4
Expˢ 5s 3d, two men 3s, three carts with 7 horses 8s 4d	0	16	7
[Total]	8	19	11

1767
Monday
15 June

The Ciborium in the chapple was given to me this day by Mrs Eccleston of Cowley Hill.[63]

Promis'd Richard Greenall to give him forty tonns of limestone. He is to cart it & to buy forty tunns more. The price it bore this day was 4s per ton.

Tuesday
16 June

Paid Thomas West & his companion Chesford, one guinea for pulling down the brickwork of my windmill which stood on the bank of the Lower Mill Damn, by the clough. NB they pulld it down in 2 days.

Wednesday
17 June

Paid for 24 tons 4 tubs of limestone at 4s, £4 19s 2d. Measure^g & exp^s 4s 8d, [Total] £5 3s 10d.

Monday
St Albans Day
22 June

Begun pulling down the hall front. The foundation was only 1 row of large flat stones, or ashlers, & the two heightes of large ashlers that stood above the ground was only placed one upon an other loose, being neither set in lime mortar, nor daub, or mudd.

Monday
29 June

Begun mowing my clover in the New Close.

Saturday
4 July

Planted in the Paddock in rows of 5 feet asunder in length and six feet crossways asunder 1805 turnep cabbage plants.

Saturday
11 July

	£	s	d
The land tax for Eccleston township when 4s per £1 comes to	76	0	0
My part for the demesne & penny rents is	14	3	0
When 3s per £ is	57	0	0
My part than is	9	12	3
Mrs Eccleston's year's tax is	3	16	11
	0	8	6¼
[Total]	4	5	5¼

Wednesday
22 July

+ Poor broth^r Will Scarisbrick died this morning betwixt five & six o'clock.

63 Ciborium – a vessel for the Host used in the Eucharist, sometimes suspended from the roof or wall of a chapel.

1767
Saturday
25 July

Aggreed with Thomas Lion to lead me 21,500 bricks from Pikes to late Leadbetter's tenem᷑ at 5s for every 1,800 bricks, or to go six times a day & take each time 300 brick, which makes 1,800, which makes £2 19s 9d. I am to allow a man to fill, which will be 12 days.

Friday
21 August

Cost of the stone & work for the door case & windows in the hall paid to William Sephton of Billinge as per bill

	£	s	d
For 112 feet solid stone for the door & windows at 6d	2	16	0
For 312 feet dressing [at] 6d	7	16	0
For 12 yards of copeing stone for the turretts 1s 10d	1	2	0
For his trouble in fixing the stones & casements	0	10	0
The cost of the stone & work for the hall	12	4	0
The window rods and casements cost	2	12	0½

Teusday
25 August

	£	s	d
Finish'd fixeing the windows in the hall which cost with the lead that covered the 2 turrets weighd [...][64] & cost and the lead of the 2 spouts & gutter cost as per bill	20	15	7
Paid the masons that run it up	6	7	7
Paid the carpinter per Peter Moss's bill	6	5	9½
Bricks and lime	11	0	0
A new door, locks, bolts, hinges, knocker, painting &c.	6	15	0
[Total]	66	0	0

Monday
31 August

Begun reaping oats in the West Norley.

The weight of the new lead that is to be returnd to Prescot is 221lb at 20s per 120lb, & of the old lead 428lb at 15s per 120lb.

Monday
7 September

Sign'd for all that had ale licences last, & likewise for Peter Cadwell, but he got none.

Wednesday
23 September

The warmest day we have had all summer, being the equinox, the sun very bright & little or no wind, but what there was was in the East.

2 November

Gave soul loaves to 138 persons and 1s 5d to 34 more, in all 172 persons.

64 Weight not entered by BTE.

1767
Thursday
12 November   Kill'd a hogg which weighd nineteen score.

Friday
27 November

		lb
Kill'd Cadwell a black cow, white face which weighed		838
Tallow 54lb, suit 40lb, the hide 95lb in all		189
[Total]		1,027

Friday
18 December   Finish'd my large mixen, or dung hill, which was put togather as follows vizt. The bottom stratum was fine soil got out of the calf house foundation, & levelling, than a set of lime, than the barn muck, and than a set of lime, and than promiscuously, horse, cow, & hogg dung, but betwixt every layer of each sort of dung, was a set of lime. In the whole there was eight large kilns full of lime, each of which might contain 80 bushells of sale measures, which makes 640 bushells of sale measure. NB there were some 100 bush[s] of spent turnips in this mixen.

Monday
21 December   Killd a hogg which weigh'd nineteen score less 2lb.

1768

Monday
4 January

	£	s	d
Half a year's land tax at 3s per £ comes to	5	6	1½
Mrs Eccleston's share computed at two fifths is	2	2	5½
[Total]	3	3	8

Housed my hay & corn of last year in the following manner

In the stack	Nearer Dutch barn	Further Dutch barn
16 loads clover 2d crop	22 loads clover 1st crop	18 loads clover 1st crop
18 w. hay Mill Meads	1 loads clover 2d crop	1 load clover 2d crop
—	2 loads w. hay Mill Mead	1 load Mill Mead w. hay
34	25	20

Stables	Cart House	Cow House
1 w. hay Avenue	2 loads clover 1st crop	7 loads clover 1st crop
7 w. hay Wood Meadow	10 w. hay Wood Mead	15 Carthouse
—	3 w. hay Mill Meadows	8 Stables
8	15	20 Further Dutch barn
		25 Next Dutch barn
		34 In the stack
		In all 109 loads hay

1768

I had the following corn

	Thr	Sh		Tyth		Remains	
				Thr	Sh	Thr	Sh
In the West Norley	197	11	Grey oats	16		181	11
Grange Mead	130	22	Common oats	11		119	22
Paddock	45		Grey oats	4		41	
Threaves of oats						342	9
3ᵈ Old Jones's	44	14	Barley	4		40	14
Holland's Nook	125	16	Barley	10	8	115	8
Threaves of barley						155	22
4ᵗʰ Old Jones's	16	23	Wheat	1	12	15	11

Wednesday
6 January

Let to James Clayton the Burying Hill for seven years to pasture at £17 p.a. He is never to plow it unless he marles it. I am to find him a gate & two stubbs & he is to fix them and at the end of the term he is to make up the wall where he now fixes the gate, in the condition it is in now and he is to allow me a coach or cart way through the bottom part of the said Burying Hill to the turn-pike road.

Thursday
21 January

Killd a hog which weighd 17 score & 12lb.

Friday
29 January

Begun stirring the Grange Meadow with 2 plows for wheat.

Monday
8 February

	lb
Killd a segg which weighed	788
Tallow 48lb, suit 33lb, the hide 106lb	187
[Total] 975	

Friday
9 February

John Whitlow the wheel wright's shop at the Four Lane Ends was broke open early this morning. They forced two locks to get in & took out a very large iron crow & an old hatchet and came from thence to Ann Robison's, the Eccleston Arms, at the bottom of the Avenue & got into the house thro' a window and forced open the town's chest, but not meeting with any money they contented themselves with eating bread & cheese & black pud-dings & went away about 3 o'clock in the morning. They light-ed themselves with burnt paper & rolls of cotton which they greased with fat.

1768
Thursday
25 February   Edward Whitlow of Prescot died either the 20th or 21st instant.

Tuesday
8 March   This day was fallen by The Right Honble Edward Earl of Derby's orders, an ash, by George Howard & James Prescot, in James Barton's feild adjoining to my meadow at the bottom of the Avenue, in that part of the feild next to the stile going into my meadow, which I say belongs to His Lordship, tho his steward Mr Culceth says that part is mine. But by falling the tree it showes otherwise, & that this part next the Avenue is mine which was always told me. It was given to John Crompton of New House, Eccleston.

Monday
21 March   Begun sowing our own country oats in the Stand Hill & with 3 harrows.

Teusday
22 March   Continued sowing our own country oats with 3 of my pair of harrows & with 2 of Richard Greenall's and in the afternoon with annothr pair of Richard Greenall's harrows.

Wednesday
23 March   Continued sowing with 3 pair of mine & 3 of Richard Greenall's harrows.

Thursday
24 March   Continued sowing with my own 3 pair of harrows & finishd the whole with 96 bushells of seed.

Monday
11 April   Sunk in the Damn Wood at the side of the Stand Hill two holes for coals, but the water overpower'd me & I gave up. There has been coals got there & some part under the hill, but I was only upon the crop where I found them at about 6 yards deep. NB there is good clay there for bricks.

Monday
18 April   Bored in sundry places in Lancaster's barn Hey (now held by Richard Farrar) that runs down to Ned Patrick's garden for coals, but found they were all gotten throughout the feild, & I bored quite through several hollows.

Friday
29 April   Hung my new, large, hall door, the cheecks it is hung to are of oak & it is made of the best Riga dale.[65] The pannells

65 Riga dale – Baltic timber from Riga, Latvia which is either pine or fir, possibly in planks.

1768

are double & painted on the inside to preserve them, & all the joints of the whole door were painted before they were put togather.

Wednesday
4 May   Went with three carts & six horses to Liverpool for Richard Greenall.

Thursday
5 May   Went with three carts & six horses to Liverpool for Richard Greenall. Both times they came back with oats for him.

Friday 6
& Saturday
7 May   Cover'd the Little Old Jones's with compost of 2 large kilns of lime mixed with coal ashes.

Tuesday 10
& Wednesday
11 May   Sow'd the above with 4⅛ bushells of barley.

Sunday
22 May   Subscribd to Mr John Collier of Milnrows near Rochdale book of heads, which is to contain 120 & be compris'd in 15 numbers at 1s per Nº containing eight heads.

               The Scarisbrick method of brewing 18 measures of malt to make good & strong, which produces 100 gallons ale, 50 gallons table beer & 60 gallons small beer. 16lb the best hops to the brew. Let it lye on the malt 4 hours before you run it off, work it very cool, & when done working, close it well up. To tap the ale not in less than 3 months. Put into the casks spent hops.

               Lord's rent & boons £158 9s 8d, Bescar Meadow hay £78 10s, the lower part of Bescar Meadow set for £30 10s.

30 May   The owner of Sutton lime is Mr Frogat in Ashley near the chappel.

               Begun stirring with 2 plows the Grange Meadows.

               Mr John Cook lives on Peel Green near Barton Upon Irwell.

Thursday
10 November Came home with my daughter to dinner from Manchester.

15 November Mr John Chorley of Prescot dʳ for the bark of 58 trees and 28 cyphers. Paid £7 18s.[66]

               The value of the land taken by the town out of German's estate is 7 rod & 53 yards at £90 per acre, £4 8s 1½d.

---

66 BTE has crossed out the £7 18s presumably having been paid.

1768
6 December

		score	lb
Killd 2 hogs, the one for my own use whose flitches weighd 14 score 2lb, chines[67] & head 2 score & 13lb, grace &c. 37lbs, in all		18	12
The whole of the other 18 score 6lb, and pluckings 15lb, in all		19	01

	£	s	d
I sold half of this to Leland being 181lb. at. 3½d per lb paid	2	12	9½
The other half to Thomas Fazackerly 185lb at 3½d per lb paid	2	13	11½
15lb of pluckings			

Saturday
31 December Set to Thomas Lion, late of Mr William Lancaster's tenement for fourteen years. He to clear it of all Leys, taxes & Parliamentry impositions whatsoever, & to do all ditching & hedgeing & keep & leave the windows in good repair as also all gates & stiles, to reap seven acres annually, & neither to push, burn or sow stubble wheat nor let the estate to any other, and to pay annually at two equal paym[ts] for it £60. I have promis'd to allow him £5 worth of limestone the first year in consideration of the small quantity of dung that is upon the premises. He is not to sell either hay or straw of the premises & only to leave at the end of the term two & a half acres of wheat on the ground.

1769

Monday
2 January John Owen came this evening to live with me as plowman for £7 p.a.

Thursday
12 January Mixed all my coal ashes with 100 large measures of lime.

Friday
13 January Kill'd a hog which weigh'd 18 score & 4lb.

Tuesday
24 January Kill'd a hog which weighd 18 score & 14lb.

Thursday
2 February Thomas Owen of Fenny Bank acquainted my man Peter Johnson

67 Chines – Spine or backbone of an animal.

1769

this day, at Thomas Greeenall's sale at Holmes, that John Barrow of London, a life in his lease, had broke his neck of a scafold.

Sunday
26 February
Robert Orrell came to live with me this even^g as cowman for £5 10s p.a.

Thursday
9 March
Eliza Growcock came at noon as chambermaid at £4 p.a.

Thursday
16 March
Bored in the Pitt Hey in late Samuel Woods's tenement in Sutton, in an old coal pitt at the top of the Hey next to the Four Lane Ends, & it was 20¾ yards deep.

Wednesday
22 March
Begun this morn^g sowing our own country oats in the Postern Hills, and went with three pair of harrows.

Thursday
23 March
Continued sowing our own country oats with 3 of my own & 2 of the Miller's, 5 pairs.

Friday
24 March
Continued sowing our own country oats with 3 pair of my own.

Saturday
25 March
Continued sowing our own country oats with 3 pair of my own.

Wednesday
29 March
Continued sowing our own country oats with 3 pair of my own.

Thursday
30 March
Continued sowing our own country oats with 3 pair of my own.

Friday
31 March
Continued sowing our own country oats with 3 pair of my own.

Saturday
1 April
Continued sowing our own country oats with 3 pair of my own, & finishd the whole. It took 132 measures of seed.

Thursday
6 April
Killd a Welch cow, bought by Richard Ellison, which cost £11 12s 6d

	£	s	d
She weighd 524lb at 4½[d] per lb is	9	16	6
The fat or suit 47lb, 4[d] per lb	0	15	8
The hide weighd 71lb, 3½[d] per lb	1	1	0
[Total]	11	13	2

1769

The butcher is paid 1s 6d for killing it; & I have the head, tongue, feet, tripes, heart &c. not valued. It is the dearest purchase of the kind I think as was ever made. Beef sold at this time at 4½d per lb.

19 April

Adam Tyrer's estimation of what coals may be laid dry in the estate George Makeing now lives at in Sutton, by the levell of that rank of coal pitts, which was brought up by Peter Berry from Mr Barnes's tenement at Alder Lane, into Mrs Tingle's Meadow.

	yards	feet	inches	
NB the fall betwixt an old coal pitt in George Makeing's Pitt Hey to Alder Lane Brook is	42	2	3	the fall on the surfice.
The depth of the pitt in Pitt Hey	20	2	3	
	22	0	0	the fall at the coals

Suppose the dib be seven yards in breadth, for two in depth what will be the breadth at 22 yards deep, answer 77 yards.[68]

The length of the run is	768 yards
The breadth	77
	5376 yards of coal
	53760
	59136
	59136 The coals being 2 yards thick must be doubled
Suppose five yards to a work	⌐118272⌐ [equals] 23654 works of coal

Now we are informed that there is 14 yards in breadth, lost by the being fallen in, so we must take 14 yards from 77 [leaves] 63.

The length of the run as before	768
	63
	5⌐96768 [equals] 19353 works

In the two Heath Heys for 230 yards in length, we find an additional breadth of coals, on the crop of 28 yards, example

The length	230 yards
The breadth	28
	6440
	6440 the coal being 2 yards thick is doubled
	5⌐12880 [equals] 2576 works of coals

68 Dib – the hole at the bottom of a mine shaft which collects water for pumping for drainage. Eccleston also seems to use it for a dip or inclination of strata.

1769

Allow 6 square yards to a work 6 $\overline{118272}$ [equals] 19712 works

Allow 6 square yards to a work 6 $\lceil\overline{96768}$ [equals] 16120 works

Allow 6 square yards to a work 6 $\lceil\overline{12880}$ [equals] 2146

NB. I bored down in the furthest old coal pitt in the highest Heath Hey & it was 19¾ yards deep. The borers were Henry Hart & Michael Bibby.

Saturday
27 May

I promised my millers, Thomas and Richard Greenall, to allow them at the end of their term for the expence they would be at in bringing a new cut by James Greenhough's to convey more water to the Lower Mill damn, an estimate of which they deliver'd to me the 18th February 1765 before they begun the cut, which is as follows vizt.

	£	s	d
Laying a damn head in Chesford's Meadow	2	0	0
Cutting a sluice from the damn head thro' Chesford's Meadow	0	16	0
Two plats in Chesford's Meadow 16 rods	1	10	0
28 rods from Chesford's to Greenhough's House [at] 2[s] 4[d]	3	7	4
2 plats for Greenhough's	1	0	0
Turning the pavement	1	5	0
Scoureing from Greenhough's to Hall Lane Pitt	1	11	6
50 rods scoureing from the Lane to the damn at 5d	1	1	10
[Sub total]	12	11	8
Hall Lane plats	0	15	0
[Total]	13	6	8

NB the pavement was not turn'd & but little, if any, alteration to the plat in the Hall Lane.

Sent to late William Lancaster's tenemᵗ five new oak gates.

Sent to late William Holmes's tenemᵗ four new oak gates.

Friday
16 June

Brought 1 rod of slate to Lancaster's from Ball's Delf, and 0¼ of a rod from Ball's home.

Saturday
17 June

Brought ¾ of a rod of slate home from Ball's.

Friday
23 June

Brought 1 rod home of slate from Ball's.

1769
Wednesday
9 August

Weighd a flat load of limestone at Gerard's bridge which weigh'd 22 ton 18cwt.

Adam Tyrer's estimation of the vallue of 26,322 works of coals which are supposed to be got dry in the estate commonly call'd Woods's in Sutton where George Making now lives, Saturday 27th May 1769. Supposeing the coals to sell at 12s 6d per work, the whole is £16,251 5s.

The charge of getting computed as follows:

1769

	£	s	d	£	s	d	£ (cost)	s	d	£ (Makes)	s	d
I suppose there will be six pitts in the run on the deep level 40 yards deep each which makes 240 yards the whole at 11s per yard	132	0	0									
Also 6 pitts on the crop, 30 yards deep, makes 180 at 9s 6d	85	10	0	241	10	0	0	0	2¼	246	15	4½
Also 6 old pitts to be scoured up, 20 yards each 120 at 4s	24	0	0									
Brick, timber & powder for 12 pitts at £6 per pitt				72	0	0	0	0	0¾	82	5	1½
For getting 26,322 at 2s 6d per work				3290	5	0	0	2	6	3290	5	0
For winding & banking 26,322 at 1s				1316	2	0	0	1	0	1316	2	0
By 768 yards the deep levell at 1s 6d	51	12	0									
By 768 yards the dry levell at 1s	38	8	0	107	11	0	0	0	1	109	13	6
By 462 yards upbrows at 6d	11	11	0									
By props & waydrawing at 2d				219	7	0	0	0	2	219	7	0
By utensills as whimseys[69], ropes, baskets &c.				273	17	1	0	0	2½	273	17	1
I suppose there will be 3,000 works of coal got each year, so they will be 8 years in getting												
The clarke's salery for 8 years at £30 p.a.	240	0	0	400	0	0	0	0	3¾	411	4	7½
The underlooker's for 8 years at £20	160	0	0									
By discount loss & expences				658	1	0	0	0	6	658	1	0
By eight years trespass at £6 p.a.	48	0	0	79	10	0	0	0	0¾	82	5	1½
By clearing the pitt brows at £1 15s per brow	31	10	0									
Cost of getting 26,322 works of coal as per the above				6658	3	1	0	5	1	6689	15	10

69 Whimsey – A winding engine.

1769
Friday
11 August

Computation of what a kiln of lime stands me in.

	£	s	d
7 tons 12cwt of stone at Gerard's Bridge at 5[s] per ton	1	17	10
Carting 7 ton 12cwt of stone 1s per ton, I can go 4 times per day with 3 horses	0	11	4
40 bask^s of charcoal from the ashes 3 times per day with 2 horses [at] 14s per work	0	9	4
Carting charcoal as above estimated at 4s per work	0	2	8
Breaking, burning & drawing	0	6	0
[Total]	3	7	2
A kiln should contain 150 bush^s which at 5½[d] per is	3	8	9

Monday
28 August

Begun reaping wheat in the West Norley.

Thursday
14 September

Cover'd in my new vault. It is arched over twice, & the bricks set edgeways, so that it is 9 inches thick, and both layers are run with run mortar. Then I cover'd it about six inches thick with clay daub, and that I sanded well over, & then I cover'd that with soil.

Wednesday
20 September

Sold John Ashworth of Prescot my whole dairy of cheese of thirteen cows which milked remarkably ill this year, only makeing beside my own consumption 16cwt 2qtr 12lb at 30s per cwt, £24 18s 0d.

Monday
25 September

Kill'd a cow comeing four years old which weighd 368lb, fat 16lb, hide 61[lb]. Beef now sold at 3¾d & 4d per lb.

Tuesday
3 October

Begun sowing wheat in the Stand Hill.

Thursday
2 November

There were only this day 178 persons for loaves.

Tuesday
7 November

Killd a cow which weighed 31 score 16lb or 636lb, the hide 85lb suit 47[lb], 132[lb].[70]

Wednesday
22 November

Aggreed with Henry Lyon to grant him a full lease of Henry Holland's for £130. Boons 5 days sheering or 5s. Rent 16s. The lease to be ready for Candlemass.

---

70 This was tabulated in the original.

1769
Friday
24 November   Aggreed with Mr Mathew Illum[71] to let his mas^r Jonathan Case Esq. Wood's tenement in Sutton cont^g 14a 1r 20p for £24 p.a., clear of all leys, taxes & repairs.

Saturday
25 November   Set to Thomas Mather, wheelwright, of St. Helens, Sprey's tenem^t in Eccleston cont^g 8a 2r 1p for £14 p.a. clear of all leys, taxes & repairs, to hold the same for seven years with a promise of granting him a further term of seven years, if I live to see this present term expired. I am to allow him £5 in the first year's rent towards repairs, some two or three trees, only to plow two acres yearly & neither push nor burn. The payments to be on the 25 December & 25 March annually.

Tuesday
5 December   The following are the lives that are to be put into Henry Lyon's tenem^t vizt. William aged 25, John 23, Henry 12 years. They are his 3 sons.

Thursday
7 December   Set to James Clayton the Grange & Grindley Meadows, the latter to mow this next year, the other to pasture containing 10a 0r 30p for £18 10s p.a. but in case he manures them to my satisfaction the next year, I have promis'd to abate him the 10s. He gave me 1s in earnest.

Saturday
23 December   Killd a cow which weighd 643lb, hide 86lb, fat or suit 36lb, 123[lb].

1770

Saturday
13 January   Kill'd a pig which weighd 80lb, the head 10lb in all 90lb.

Memorandum. I put upon the Stand Hill that is now in wheat 19 kilns of lime & coal ashes, the quantity as my ash house holds twice filld.

Friday
26 January   Kill'd a hog which weighd 17 score & 15lb or 355lb.

Wednesday
7 February   Kill'd a hog which weighd 17 score & 8lb or 348lb.

---

71 'Illum' is probably a corruption of Ellam. Matthew Ellam was agent to Jonathan Case.

1770

Carted for Richard Greenall from Hatwell Heath to the higher mill 1,500 brick & 15 measures of lime with 2 carts & 3 horses each.

Thursday
8 February

Set upon the lower part of the Little Old Jones's a kiln of lime mixt with ashes & 2 loads of barn dung mixt with the lime.

The 2^d Old Jones's from the bottom part upwards I have set with barn dung mixt with lime. It is about ⅔ of the feild cover'd.

Monday
12 February

Killd a segg which weighd 650lb, the hide 110lb. He had two winters keep & yet prov'd very ordinary, having little or no fat.

Friday
23 February

Finish'd covering about ten acres of the Norley with slutch & lime (for the quantity of lime examine this book) & 2 large kilns full of lime mixt with soil & about 15 bush^s more of lime mixt with soil & barn door muck.

Sent a four barr'd gate on Tuesday the 20th ins^t to Bradburne's and brought home from Hackley Moss a large bow that was blown from of the trees on said moss.

Wednesday
11 April

Begun sowing our own country oats in the New Close Meadow with two harrows.

Saturday
14 April

Finsh'd sowing the above with 63 bushells of our own country oats.

Killd 2 hogs which weighd 29 score, they eat two loads of meal less five pecks.

Tuesday
17 April

Aggreed with Richard Pye to grant him a full lease of his late fath^r James' tenem^t for sixty guineas & to give two guineas to my daugh^r. The Lord's rent to be 10s p.a. The lease to be paid for 24th June.

Friday
27 April

Begun sowing Holland's Nooks with Dutch oats.

Saturday
28 April

Finishd Holland's Nook with 23½ meas^{rs} Dutch oats.

Thursday
10 May

John Eccleston, apprentice to Thomas Mawdsley, came to live with me this day at noon as gardener for £10 10s p.a.

The cost of six new gates which I have hung in the Postern Hills & in the entrance to the court valued by Peter Moss.

1770

	£	s	d
Wood for 2 gates and makeing	1	5	0
Three stubbs & two sills for them	0	18	0
Dressing stubs, stubs setting & hanging the gates	0	13	6
Four gates, 7 stubs, 4 sills dressing, setting, & hanging	5	18	0
Paid for 132½lb iron for gates at 5d per lb	2	15	2½
Paid John Hatton painting them all as per bill	1	19	6
[Total]	13	9	2½

Friday
18 May

Begun sowing the West Norley on Monday 14th ins[t] & finished it this day with thirty-five bushells of barley which I had all stept in spring water before sowing.

Thursday
24 May

Finish'd sowing in the above feild by Thomas Sankie 164lb of clover seed.

Thursday
7 June

Finish'd setting one & a half bushells of potatoes in the Little Croft in the nearest or Mistress's Wood Meadow.

My grey mare was cover'd the 8th & 15th ulto by a black horse called Smiling John, the property of John Horn of Silsden near Skipton.

Monday
11 June

This was the first day that ever my broth[rs] Edward & Joseph Scarisbrick & self met togather in a private house, tho' the first was 72, the second 62 & the third 57 years of age.

Copy of the note I gave to Sarah Jump vizt.
Eccleston 27th June 1770. I aggree that Sarah Jump buys the old house & garden at the Four Lane Ends in Eccleston for the term of the lease that Samuel Ball holds from me. BTE
NB She gave sixty guineas for it.

Friday
29 June

Paid Thomas Cliffe and John Tickle for sletching the Little House pond and that next to it, which they did with wheelbarrows, and laid it in the stif quarter, or New Orchard, and performed it with three hands all but two days when the had four.

	£	s	d
They lump'd the little house pond at	2	0	0
The other was 2 rods & 49 yards at 16s per rod	2	4	3
[Total]	4	4	3

1770
Monday
9 July

My daughter begun to ride out betwixt 5 & 6 o'clock in the morning.

Moll calved on Thursday the 5th ins[t] the bull which I rear.⊕

Wednesday
11 July

Begun mowing the 2[d] year's crop of clover in the Little Old Jones's with two mowers.

Sunday[72]
11 July

I did not put on summer cloaths before this day the weather haveing been very cold.

Sunday
29 July

John, the son of Peter & Cecily Talbot, about 17[73] years of age was drownded about noon this day in the Great Damn, by the old clough or sluice. He is the first that ever I heard of as was drownded in the Damn.

Wednesday
1 August

Told George Haliwell I would pay for sixteen bushells of lime to lay a new floor at the Malt Kiln if he would cart it.

Tuesday
4 September

Brought home my chesnut colt from Scarisbrick for which I paid £18 18s. They say is four years & two months old.

7 September

Cephalic Tobacco.[74]

Get the tops of marjoram, rosemary, betany, sage, lavender, eye bright, colts foot, but of this last double the quantity of any of the others & dry them, but not in the sun, & mix equal quantites of them togather, except the colts foot of which you must have double the quantity to any other, & you may smoak them as tobacco, or powder them & take it as snuff. Add a small quantity of cascarilla, shaved or grossly scraped.

14 September

James Pye's lives are to be Richard Pye 48, Richard 16 & William 8.

Wednesday
19 September

	Th	Sh	Th	Sh
The wheat in the Higher Shute of the Stand Hill was	78	0		
In the Lower Shute	51	8		
[Sub total]	129	8		
Tyth	11	8	118	0

72 BTE obviously made an error here since both Wednesday and Sunday are dated 11 July.
73 Originally '15' but crossed out and inserted '17'.
74 This is on a loose sheet dated 7 September 1770 but is also written in greater detail in the Memoranda Book; the editors have transcribed the entry from the Memoranda Book.

1770
Thursday
27 September

	Th	Sh	Th	Sh
Wheat in the 2^d Old Jones's	25	13		
Tyth	2	4	23	9
Wheat in the Wood Meadow & croft	47	5		
Tyth	4	0	43	5
Oats in Holland's Nooks, Dutch	84	11		
Tyth	6	19	77	16
Oats in the New Meadow, our own country	189	8		
Tyth	17	8	172	0
Barley in the West Norley	256	16		
Tyth	23	16	233	0

Saturday
29 September

I had only of hay this
  year 83 loads vizt.
Out of the Little Old
Jones's   4
Middle Old Jones's 3   I begun mowing the 11th July & finished
Avenue   3   it all the 13 August safe in the houseing.
                                 I begun reaping the 3^d September &
Mill Meadows   16   finish'd it the 29 & all was in the house
all the Norley   57   the 6th October.

Thursday
11 October

Bottled of a quarter cask of old red port bought of Capt Mathias Holme which run to 11 doz^n & one bottle.

Begun sowing the six acres of Rogerson's & Spout Land on Monday the 17 September & finishd it on Monday 8th October. I sow'd it with 19 bushells. The wheat was limed, I laid 50 tonns of soaper's waste upon the lands. ⊕

Friday
2 November

I put into the Great damn twenty-eight couple of carp from Winstanley of about a ¼lb each.

Saturday
10 November

Sold Richard Greenall all my wheat at 6s 6d per bushell of 70lb per.

Saturday
17 November

Killd a little young cow which weighed 420lb.

The post only came in at 10 o'clock last night on acc^t of the floods.

On All Souls Day there were 135 persons for loaves.

Thursday
20 December

Kill'd a hog which weighd 22 score & 8lb or 448lbs.

1771

Tuesday
8 January   Killd a hog which weighd 16 score & 12lb or 332lb.

Wednesday
30 January   Killd a hog which weighd 19 score & 15lb or 395lb. Killd a cow which weighd 28 score & 8lb or 568lb, the hide was 92[lb] & the fat 55[lb] in all 147[lb].

Thursday
31 January   Sent my dun colt to Owen Wearden's of Ormskirk to be broke. His terms are 8d per night, I to find corn, to keep it about three weeks & to have half a guinea for his trouble.

Monday
11 February   This day my daughter was married, at Prescot, to Edward Standish Townley Esq., by Mr Augustin Gwin, Vicar. The bridesman & maid was John Atherton Esq. of Prescot's sister.

Saturday
23 February   Aggreed with Anne Arrowsmith to grant her a lease of 3 lives for late Ralph Brotherton's for £231. The Lord's rent to be 30s p.a. and the money to be paid the 24th June next, and if she builds a new barn or outhouses I promised to allow her 2s in the £ for the money she lays out thereon, provided it is set in lime and cover'd with slate.

Tuesday
26 February   I accompanied Mr & Mrs Standish to dinner at Standish.

Mr West's (SJ)[75] receipt for the shoote in cattle.

Red tormentil roots, wash'd clean & bruised, a good handful boiled in two quarts of small ale till the roots are soft. Than squeese the roots clean from the liquor. The quantity to be given is from half a pint to a quart, according to the strength of the beast. He don't advise keeping the beast for an nother year.

There is an apple that grows from a slip at Mr Aston's in Cheshire called a burr that is large & both a good keeper and baker.

Saturday
9 March   This day there was a blackguard cocking in the barn at the Anchor at Glugmoor.

Monday
11 March   Aggreed with Richard Sephton to change him all the lives in Mrs Mary Davenport's lease, & to put him in the three following for

---

75 Probably stands for Society of Jesus.

1771

£12 vizt. Himself Richard Sephton aged 40, his son James 15, his son Thomas 10. Davenport is to pay for the lease, which is to be ready by May Day, drawn like the old one.

Alice Wainwright came to live with me as dairymaid for £4 p.a.

Monday
18 March

The bay colt that I bought this day of Peter Moss, with two white feet behind & an open starr in his forehead, is fourteen hands & a half high & will be two years old the 17th April next. He cost me £9 19s 6d.

Friday
22 March

The bay colt that I bought of Watkinson of Scarisbrick with a white snip in his nose will be three years old in May next. He cost me twenty guineas & I gave Evan Werden one guinea more for keeping him a week & putting him on the bitts & for his trouble, so that he stands me in all in £22 1s 0d.

Saturday
23 March

There was a blackguard cocking this day at Helen Halliwell's the Red Lion.

Wednesday
27 March

There was a very hard frost in the morning east & the ground was coverd with snow, & it continued snowing & no wind, that I got the thickness of it taken in different parts of the great grass plot before the harpsicord windows, & it measured eight inches less one eight at 5 in the afternoon, when it had almost done snowing.

Friday
29 March

Killd a cow that I bought at Garswood Sale which weighd vizt. 914lb, suit 96lb, the hide 115lb, in all 1,125lb.

Monday
1 April

Mr Conyers bought a dark bay mare for £11 11s of Evan Werden.

Thursday
4 April

Begun sowing our own country oats on that side next the Avenue & went with 3 harrows in the Norley.

Friday
5 April

Continued sowing our own country oats with the harrows.

Saturday
6 April

Continued sowing our own country oats with three harrows & finished it with seventy-one bushells of oats.

Push plow'd both the Norley Acre & Kendrick's Meadow and Eliza Rigby's orchard, which cost per workman's book £4 8s 0d.

1771
Saturday
13 April   Finishd sowing ten butts next to our own country oats in the Norley below the Ha-Ha with six & a half bushells of cutts. It is rather under an acre.

Sunday
14 April   The bay colt that I bought of Watkinson of Scarisbrick was staked in leaping over the pale in the stable croft next to the barn & died this day. It hapned on Friday last.

Friday
19 April   The coal sough at my collery at the Yew Tree Farm in Sutton, work'd by Jonathan Case Esq. was finishd this day.

Saturday
20 April   Bought a bay horse riseing four with a blaze, of a man in Burtonwood, for which I paid £23 5s. I had with him a bridle, horse cloth & roller £23 5s. His fore & hind right feet whited & some white on his off foot behind.

Monday
22 April   Mr Conyers's man, Ralph, came to live with him this evening.

Thursday
2 May   Finish'd sowing & harrowing the Holland's Nooks with twelve & a half measures of barley.

Saturday
4 May   Brought half a rod of single slate from Moss Bank to Knowles's tenem^t by Catchal Moss.

Thursday
9 May   Bought of Jonathan Case Esq. the Red Lion Ale house & ground where Helen Halliwell now lives in Eccleston belonging to Robert Parker Esq., of Cuerden for £100 and the said £100 to be at Christmas next.

Saturday
18 May   Finishd sowing the Mill Meadow that were pushd & burn'd with 25 measures of Grey oats.
Finish'd sowing the Holland's Nooks with 60lb of clover seed.

Wednesday
22 May   Set off for London in a post chaise & lay at the Swan in Litchfeild where I arrived at 10 o'clock at night & got to Fenny Stratford the sign of the Stag the next night, a bad Inn. The other was not much better. And on Friday the day following 24 May I dined with my sist^r Palmes, in Green Street, Grovesnor Square.

1771
Saturday
25 May   My son arriv'd in London from Bruges at 4 o'clock in the afternoon.

Saturday
8 June   My son took Sutton's powder & salts preparative for inoculation.

Tuesday
11 June   My son took his second, and last, dose.

Thursday
13 June   My son was inoculated.

Saturday
22 June   My son was at the height of the small pox in the inoculation.

Tuesday
30 July   Begun my journey in a post chaise & lay at the Starr in Dunchurch,
                    a good Inn, & on Wednesday even^g of the 31st July I lay at Mr
                    Standish's in Shrewsbury.

Wednesday
7 August   Set off from Salop and lay at home. NB two miles on the other
                    side of Wrexham is a curious water mill called King's Mill,
                    belonging to Esq. York. It has six pair of stones, a roller for malt,
                    and a dressing mill. It hath two wheels five feet broad & twenty-
                    two round, & turns all the above with five inches of water.

Monday
26 August   Asked Owen for a full lease of his late fathr^s tenement £73 10s,
                    & Lord's rent 4s 6d p.a.

Friday
31 August   Begun reaping the few butts of Polish oats in the Norley.

Wednesday
4 September   Ned Werden came to live with me as groom for £6 p.a.

Friday
6 September   Begun cutting barley in Holland's Nooks.

Wednesday
25 September   Housed all my wheat and barley in fine order. ✝ Note. My wheat
                    in Rogerson's two Spout feilds was much blasted and what to
                    atribute it too I cannot say. The feilds being soap muck'd & the
                    corn limed when sow'd, unless it was on account of its being
                    sow'd on a barley stuble which, however, ought to be a caution
                    for the future not to sow wheat after barley. Altho' the wheat in
                    his meadow that I sow'd also on barley stubble, prov'd good and
                    was no ways blighted.

1771
Tuesday
26 November   Jonathan Case Esq. proposed to me this day that he would make a trial to dispose of the Sutton coals if I would come in for my proportion for what they should sell for less than 12s 6d per work, which I aggreed too.

Saturday
30 November   Kill'd a hog which weighd 14 score & 12lb or 292lb.[76]

Sunday
8 December   Peter Moss acquainted me that he was in Prescot yesterday & dureing the time he was there, one of my Arbell[77] trees that grows in rows on Hackley Moss, that part of one was broken down with the wind. Joseph Hewitt, the blacksmith of Prescot, came to beg it of me this day, but I refused it him, & this day, Monday 9th December I sent John Dixon to fall it, which he did, and he & William Forber, senr of Prescot helped my man Thomas Sankie to load it, & he brought it home in a cart.

Monday
9 December   Botled off a quarter cask of red port which runn 11 dozn quarts.

Friday
20 December   John Young pays for John Barnes's estate calld Burton Head £62 p.a. but does not clear it, and he is to pay for Glugsmore estate £80 p.a. and is to clear it, and besides Mr Orrill reserves to himself better than two acres of ground.

Killd a hogg which weighd 16 score 19lb or 339lb.

Killd a cow which weigh'd 590lb, fat 19lb, hide 69[lb] in all 678lb.

Andrew Valentine pays for Fenny's estate £18 10s p.a.

Take notice that if you at any time hereafter come upon any of the lands or grounds now in the possession or occupation of us whose names are hereto subscribed or any of us situate in the township of Eccleston in the parish of Prescot & County of Lancaster[78] to hunt, course, shoot, seek for, kill or destroy game there as a qualified person or otherwise and thereby commit trespass theron or on some part there of, we who sustain such trespass are determined to bring an action or actions against you in order to recover a satisfaction for the same. Dated this [...] day of [...][79] seventeen hundred and seventy one.

76 An entry of 9 lines long has been completely obliterated in the original.
77 Arbell – White poplar tree.
78 'or either of them' has been crossed out in the original.
79 Day and month not entered by BTE.

1771

> To.
> Mr Hodgkinson of Prescot notice. It cost 2s.

Monday
30 December   Begun plowing my oat stuble in the Norley with two plows.

129 measures of oats made 10 loads & 1½ windle meal and four sacks of cow meat ½ windle groats, 121 measures of oats made 10 loads, & 0½ windle meal and three sacks cow meat.

31 December   Aggreed with William Culcheth for all the Maid's Hills cont^g 23a 0r 7p for twelve years for £35 p.a. He is to allow me either coach, cart or horse road thro' them at all times, & Mr Weldon leave to drive his cow thro' them to his feild, as also liberty to cart his dung or hay thro' them. He promises to marl the three acres & Schole's Meadow & to rid all the Gorsy Hill, and the last year of his term he has liberty to have one of the closes in wheat provided it is well laid down with dung or lime. All the rest to be the green side upwards and clear of gorse &c. I am to put him up a gate next Scholes and another in the Sand Hole, they were in a poor condition, and the largest feild all coverd with gorse that I thought he paid price sufficient for them. I valued them as follows.

	a	r	p	at	£	s	d	
Maid's Gorsy Hill	7	2	34		7	10	0	clear at 15s
Four Acres	3	2	35	40s	7	7	6	the 1st hill going to Scholes
Three Acres	3	2	12	40s	7	2	6	next Wilcox's
Schole Meadow	3	1	16	40s	6	12	6	
Two Acres	2	3	22	30s	4	6	0	in the Maid's Hills
Sand Croft	1	3	8	30s	2	12	6	
[Total]	23	0	7		35	11	0	

1772

Monday
6 January   Thomas Lyon, my ten^t at Lancaster's, is for marling the Rough Hey cont^g 1a 3r 20p & putting five rods to an acre on it, and therefore I promised to put it into the cart for him, which he said would come to £7 or £8. I also allow him to push & burn it, & to summer work it this year.

1772

I planted last month in Eliza Rigby's garden

7   large fine beech[s] and
24   large middling beech[s] in the potatoe garden &
27   beech[s] same sizes in the Norley &
<u>34</u>   beech[s] in the West Norley
92   Beeches in all

The lives in Edward Wilcock's lease are to be Edward Wilcock aged 59, Eleanor Wilcock 23, Richard Goore 13, the son of James Goore.

Aggreed to give Thomas Sankie £8 5s p.a. & John Owen £8 p.a..

Tuesday
28 January   Killd a hog which weighd 20 score & 7lb or 407lb.

William Bankes came as gardener late at night at £12 p.a.

Coverd with compost &c. about five acres in the West Norley. The uper part from the pitt was coverd with what came out of the Little House Pond & the pond adjoing about two acres. The remaining three acres was earth & three kilns of lime mixt, and one kiln of lime mixt with ashes, & about six loads of hog's dung & two of horse dung, but the Slack was mostly coverd with barn dung. There remains 33 butts yet to cover, counting from the pit downwards to the Old Jones's.

Monday
3 February   Killd a cow which weighd 646lb, fat 73lb, hide 79lb in all 798lb.

Monday
16 March   There has scarcely ever been a severer season than the present continual hard frost with some snow, & very cold peirceing north east winds, in so much that no one can plow, and the ice is now so strong that one may scate upon it. Vide my almanack.

Friday
27 March   My two chestnut horses were nickd this day by Wilson of Liverpool.

Friday
3 April   I finished sowing & harrowing seventeen buts counting from the stoop below the Ha-Ha in the Norley upwards towards the gate with 9½ bushells of vetches. It is rather better than an acre & 3 rods of land.

Saturday
4 April   Finishd plowing the Pease Croft by noon & begun sowing this morning the Tuit Hill with our own country oats, & with four pair of harrows.

1772
Saturday
18 April

Killd a cow which weighd 28 score or 560lb, fat 60lb, hide 64lb, in all 684lb.

Finishd sowing & harrowing both the Tuit Hill & Pease Croft with 208 bushells of our own country oats. It is was in tolerable good order excep Slater's Croft & the brow going down to it, as likewise the hollow in the Pease Croft, from both which I cannot expect much.

Saturday
2 May

Finish'd sowing the third & fourth Old Jones's with eighteen measures of Greys.

Thursday
7 May

Finishd sowing the two Mill Meadows with 29½ bush^s of Greys, the square part at the top of the next meadow I have reserv'd to sow Siberia barley upon.

Friday
8 May

Finishd sowing the above meadows with clover.

Saturday
9 May

Finish'd sowing the top end of the next Mill Meadow, with Siberia barley & clover, and on that side next Barton's I sow'd a little old Sainfoin after the clover.

Monday
11 May

Young's mare was coverd this even^g, by Thomas Lyon's horse.

Tuesday
12 May

I believe there was seldom ever known so little grass at this time of the year.

My grey mare was cover'd this even^g by Thomas Lyon's horse.

Mr Bankes of Winstanley's receipt for a horse &c. that has lost his hair or is lousey.
Boil in one gallon of old urin a large handful of fox glove leaves, & make a strong lather with ½lb of sweet soap, & rub him stoutly all over with it against the grain, & when it is dry & the weather warm, turn him out and the hair will come surpriseingly fast again.

Friday
15 May

Numberd & markt with a T sixty stones at the Navigation and 2 others only with a ≠ + all with red paint.

Friday
22 May

Finishd sowing all my barley both in the Spout Lands & Rogerson's three feilds with 28½ bushells of our barley & 1½ of

1772

Siberia which was sow'd on the 2 head lands in the Spout Lands. It was very dry weather, which made the feilds cloddy.

Monday
1 June

The first flat came up this day thro' the Eccleston Navigation to Mr Mackay's colery fireing several Pedoreras.[80]

Tuesday
2 June

The above flat I saw return'd loaded this day.

Wednesday
3 June

My brood mare was coverd again by Thomas Lyon horse.

Wednesday
1 July

Begun mowing my clover in Holland's Nooks with two mowers.

Monday
6 July

Housed all my clover out of the Holland's Nooks in very fine order not haveing had a drop of rain on it, and it consisted of twelve large loads.

Teusday
7 July

Begun mowing the West Norley with three mowers.

Mr Denton's new sash'd house, now belonging to John Greenough is let to Mr George Drinkwater of Liverpool, broker, for £35 p.a. or if he would clear it, he might have it at £30. The bargain was broke, Mr Drinkwater would not have it.

Memorandum. The slutch that came out of the Lower Damn I laid it in 7 or 9 rows 16 August 1766, and the 11th February 1767. I mixed it with lime, & after lieing some time I turnd it and spread some five acres over with it 23[d] February 1769, & what is remarkable, the places where the slutch lay produced nothing but thistles than this year, and now it is full of red clover. What to attribute it to, I know not, for I only sow'd the places with common hay seeds that I cannot think that occasion'd it. I am rather of the oppinion it was the lime. I perceive in the same feild where I mixt lime with an old cop that it is now all red clover. All this was in the Norley, and it seems strange that if the clover proceed'd from they hay seeds how it should lye as if dead for two years in the ground & then spring up.

Monday
27 July

James Draper, of Scarisbrick, came to me this evening as cow-man for £6 p.a.

Cover'd the Slack and the thirty-three butts that were not cover'd

---

80 Pedoreras – ordnance for firing a salute; possibly fireworks.

1772

in January last in the West Norley with horse and cow dung, and put on a strong set, as likewise betwixt the beeches and the hedge.

Tickles's tenem^t, belonging to John Barnes of Sutton, is let to Platt at £54 12s p.a.

Monday
24 August   Aggreed this day to let John Sale the following lands for eleven & fourteen years vizt.

	a	r	p	£	s	d
Burrow's Lane Farm clear of all taxes cont^s	29	1	13			
But the repairs of the house I am to do for				48	0	0
Great Marld Earth demesne contains	5	2	0	8	18	6
The 3 Crow Feilds contains	9	0	13	12	7	0
[Sub total]				69	5	6
And for the last 3 years he is to pay an addition of				4	14	6
[Total]				74	0	0

He is to have liberty to reap ten acres yearly and may have four acres of wheat in the last year in any part except the feilds about the house, to allow him the first year £9 5s 6d & he to add £10 more for dung and to cart the whole.

Thursday
27 August   Begun reaping wheat in the New Close with 13 reapers.

Friday
28 August   Kill'd a porket which weigh'd 172lb besides the pluckings.

Monday
3 September   Aggreed with Richard Greenall to let him the following demesne lands from May 1773 for 14 years vizt.

	a	r	p	£	s	d	£	s	d
					at				
Rutty Park	1	0	0	2	0	0	2	0	0
Grindley Meadow	6	0	0	2	2	0	12	12	0
Further Wood	6	3	14	2	2	6	14	10	0
Middle Wood	6	0	24	3	0	0	18	9	0
Lower Wood	2	1	18	2	0	0	4	14	6
Old Lane	0	3	20	1	15	0	1	10	6
Mistress's Meadow	3	2	6	2	10	0	8	16	6
Burying Hill & Croft	10	2	27	2	2	0	22	10	6
Grange Meadow	4	0	30	2	2	0	8	17	0
[Total]	41	2	19				94	0	0

He is to cart & set upon the lands 50 loads of dung yearly, each load to be computed worth in Liverpool or Prescot 5s. I am to allow him the first year's dung on acc^t of his leaveing the same quantity on the land in his last year's term. He has liberty to reap 10 acres yearly, & have five acres of wheat in his last year. Not to push or burn; to have a road thro' the Postern Hills to drive his cattle or laid his corn or hay but for no other use. BTE to have a free road for himself & others thro' the Burying Hill, either on horse back, in a carriage or with carts. Not to cop or destroy any woods or underwoods, & to keep all the ditches & fences in repair. The wall to be repair'd by BTE & to build a shed for hay. Not to set the mills or lands to anyone without BTE's consent.

He is likewise to have German's & the Sand Hey from 1774 for fourteen years longer, paying clear of all taxes £28 0s 0d, likewise the Pigg House £1 10s 0d, likewise the mills with the water course £59 10s 5d, with the intrest of £60 laid out at 7½ per cent. £4 10s 0d, £64 0s 5d. [Total] £187 10s 5d. To keep all the water courses &c. in repair & pay the trespass where such water runs thro' and to leave them, & the mills in good repair. The rest of the mill articles to be settled by the old contract as insureing BTE from any damage from mobing &c. BTE to build a water wall.

A cart house & grainery is wanted at German's.

To leave all the lands clear of all rubish &c.

Tuesday
15 September   The names of those who have licenses to sell ale. Henry Hart, Ann Robison, John Whitlow, John Sankie, Robert Lawton, Peter Hewitt, Mary Southern, John Leland & Helen Halliwell.

Saturday
19 September   Brought home eighty-five tonns of limestone from the swivel bridge in St. Helens in seventy loads.

Thomas Owen's tenem^t, late old John Barrow's, is let to Richard Pye at £19 p.a.

I distributed the Heath coal this year to Thomas Howard, Eliza Roughley, Eliza Sixsmith & Frances Bromilow.

Sunday
25 October   Aggreed with James Clarkson, the son of Thomas, as lives with Mr Johnson of Liverpool, to come to me as groom at Christmas next for £6 6s p.a., to have a frock annually and a livery & leather breeches once in two years, and if he behaves well I promised him a pair of boots and that I would allow him something more.

I housed this year per Peter Johnson's acc^t.

1772

Out of Holland's Nooks first crop of clover		12 loads
Second crop of clover		4 loads
Fitches out of the Norley		8 loads
White hay from the Norley, West Norley, the		
Wood Meadow, Avenue and the Grange Meadow		74 loads
[Total]		98 loads

Housed all my wheat out of the New Meadow and 2^d Old Jones's 13th ulto containing 8a 1r 0p.

			Tithe			
	Th	Sh	Th	Sh	Th	Sh
The whole of the New Meadow	128	08	10	16	117	16
The whole of the 2^d Old Jones's	28	08	2	08	26	00
So I have deducting the tyth					143	16
Barleys in the Mill Meadows 0a 1r	17	16	1	08	16	08
Grey oats in the Mill Meadows	132	14	12	06	120	08
Oats in the Middle Old Jones's	31	21	2	21	29	00
Oats in the Little Old Jones's	22	00	2	00	20	00
Our own oats in the Tuit Hill	341	00	31	00	310	00
Our own oats in the Peas Croft	139	14	12	16	126	22

21 October   I finishd sowing 70 acres of wheat in the Norley with 22½ measures from Crompton & 3½ pecks of rye.

I had six acres of barley sown in Edward Rogerson's and the Spout Lands, but being so very poor and ill got in, on acc^t of the continual rains, that I had no acco^t given me of what it produced.

31 October   Killd a cow which weighd 550lb, fat 68lb, hide 71lb in all 681lb.

This year I milked thirteen cows and made no cheeses for the factor, but sold it all in butter which only made from May to the 24th instant £15 3s 11d, and in milk £2 0s 9d, so that I fancy I lost £20 by not makeing cheeses.

Monday
7 December   I planted a row of poplars in the garden about 24 or 25 years ago and five of them that grew in the onion garden I have now fallen, and them that were next the sweep & more sheltred from the west wind you will see were much the finest, as by what follows you will see their different measurements.

N^o		feet
1	stood next to the door by the sweep was	47
2	the next to it	33
3	the next to the above	28
4	the next to the above	26
5	the last in the onion garden	25
[Measur'd]		159

1773

Saturday *2 January*	John Tickle came as cowman for £7 10s p.a. Thomas Roper came as plowman for £8 p.a.

Friday
15 January

	lb
Killd a cow which weighd 518lb, suit 13½lb, tallow 21½lb	553
the hide	77
[Total]	630

	lb	at [d]	£	s	d
Value of the cow	518	3¼	6	15	5
suit & tallow	35	4½	0	13	1½
Hide	77	2½	0	16	0½
The value of the cow			8	4	7

25 January

I aggree that Thomas Pinnington, of Rainford, buys the old house & garden at the Four Lane Ends in Eccleston for the term of the lease that Samuel Ball holds of me.
Witness BTE
Peter Johnson

Tuesday
26 January

Begun stirring the Peas Croft with 2 plows for wheat.

Friday
29 January

Kill'd a hog which weighd 17 score & 8lb.

Thursday
4 February

Cover'd nigh two acres of the lower part of Holland's Nooks with run sand & lime mixed togather.

Sunday
7 February

James Clarkson came as groom for £6 6s p.a. late at night.

Friday
5 March

Killd a hog which weighd 17 score or 340lb.

Monday
8 March

Aggreed with William Pinnington & John Stannanought that the latter shall hold the farm he now lives at for seven years longer paying £50 p.a. clear of all leys &c. to go according to the old articles only he is to have liberty of reaping six acres annually. I must either mend the stable or run up two walls to enlarge it and board the grainery and assiste him in leading plat stones from the Navigation and board a room above staires, as is now laid with clay. I have given him two ashes for wheels &c. &c. NB I clear

1773

the Brook Demesne Meadow from leys & taxes, and in lieu thereof he is to clear the kiln from leys & taxes.

Friday
12 March

			£	s	d
Paid John Dickson for makeing	17	five-barrd gates			
And for	4	four-barrd gates			
And square top barrd with a spurr	2	gates			
	23	at 1s 6d	1	14	6
& for square top barr'd with a spurr	2	[at] 3s 6d	0	7	0
	25	gates cost	2	1	6

John Dickson, Crouchley a young man, & Dickson's son about twelve years of age were eight days, and Dickson & his son were another day in makeing the above three & twenty gates and Dickson & his son & Crouchly were almost 2 days in makeing the other two. NB the two square top barrd gates in the 23 above mentiond are the same as the last mention'd at 3s 6d per gate, but I had them thrown into the bargain at 1s 6d. Men's wages at this time of the year are 1s 6d & boy's 5d per day.

	at	£	s	d	
So that they were					
8 days	3s 5d	1	7	4	
And 1 day	1s 11d	0	1	11	In makeing 23 gates
[Sub total]		1	9	3	
And 2 days	3s 5d		6	10	In makeing 2 gates
So that they cleared					
by the job			5	5	
[Total]		2	1	6	

So that it just made summer's wages vizt.

	£	s	d
10 days at 3s 11d per day	1	19	2
1 day [at] 2s 03d	0	2	3
	2	1	5

Thursday
18 March

Killd a hog which weighd sixteen score wanting 1lb.

Made a sough or drain along the water course in the Paddock that runs to the house, and laid that part with alder that runs into the ditch along the garden wall, and the other part that runs into the slack is cheifly laid with horse & cow bones. This last produces but little water, the brow which this runs by I believe is very good marl.

Friday
26 March

Made a sough or drain in the West Norley quite thro' the old pit

1773

into the ditch at the head of the New Meadow, & laid it with alder, and some thro' the pit with billets of oak.

Draind the great marl pit in the Middle Wood by cuting a deep trench along the bottom of the Old Jones's to the thorough that goes under the brook into Chestford's Meadow. It lay'd it quite dry it being very full of sletch or mudd. There were two carps, a few pike and a good many eels in it. The drain was 18 rods 0 yds long & cost 18s. It was finished by Thomas Prescot in 11 days.

Monday
29 March

Sow'd about two acres of the higher end of the Pease Croft next the Postern Hills with about nine bushells of makeing pease, and put on the said two acres four kilns of lime, which I compute to be 600 bushells.

Friday
2 April

Sow'd the 2ᵈ Old Jones's with 18½ bushells our country oats.

Friday
9 April

Killd a hog which weighd 13 score & 10lb.

Killd the Culcheth segg which weighd 1,288lb vizt. fore & hind quarters 1,070lb, hide 167lb, fat 51lb.

I had this day 230 persons for peace eggs.

Monday
26 April

Finishd sowing about seven acres of the lower part of the Norley next Moss's, with 51 bushells of Greys.

Wednesday
28 April

Finish'd sowing full four acres of the New Close with oats vizt. in that part of the feild calld the Old Jones's 14 butts and the Tongue Sharps with 6 bushˢ of Peter Rostron's oats & the remaining path with 26 bushˢ Greys. Rostron does not know the name of his oat, but says it is an early sort and produces much meal.

The following trees are to be sold by auction on Thursday 6ᵗʰ May next at Thomas Westray's the New King's Arms in Leigh, belonging & growing on Culcheth estate vizt.

2,288 oaks	166 limes	35 sycamores	17 chesnuts
453 ashˢ	155 poplers	25 walnuts	8 elms
288 alders	46 withys	17 fir	7 beeches
3,029	367	77	32

In all, 3,505 trees, with all their cyphers.

Tuesday
4 May

Mrs Anne Orell junʳ Jemmy's wife was buried this day at Prescot.

1773

My good old neighbour & tenant Elizabeth Rigby died this day suddenly about 5 o'clock in the evening.

Saturday
8 May

Finishd sowing about two acres of the higher part of the New Meadow with 8 & ½ bushells good Siberia barley and with 1 bushell but ordinary not haveing a sufficient quantity of good.

Tuesday
18 May

It has been the mildest winter ever known. April was quite warm, but the begining of this month we had smart frost but now fine, soft, showers, & shews fair for plenty altho' the wheat in most places is not very promiseing.

I had ground this year, at the higher mill 19 meas^{rs} of wheat and at the lower mill 60 meas^{rs} & 24lb.

I have fix'd the following new gates which are painted white vizt.

4	in the Avenue
4	in what Mr Shaw holds in the demesne
4	in what Richard Greenall has in the demesne
2	in Peter Rostron's in the demesne
3	at German Hall
4	at Burrows Lane
2	at Stannanought's
2	at Edward Rogerson's
1	in the Maid's Hills next the Schole
1	in the hill next Schole's house
27	new gates

And I fix'd the follow^g old gates

1	at the Barn End
1	in the Little Old Jones's
1	in the 2^d Old Jones's
1	in the New Close
1	at German Hall
5	old gates
27	new gates
32	gates

Monday
21 June

Delivered Edward Standish Esq. £3 6s Halliwell's rent of 1772 to be adjusted with Robert Parker Esq. of Cuerden.

Saturday
3 July

Begun mowing the Mill Meadows with three mowers.

On Monday 21st June was married at St. Hellen's, by the Rev. Mr Berry, Mr James Dennet, of the Dog Lane in Widnes sailcloth-

1773

maker, to Miss Mary Platt of St Hellens, mantua maker,[81] an agree-able young lady with a handsome fortune. After the ceremony was over, upwards of 150 people dined after plenty of wine, beer & ale was drank, & in the evening a ball for the ladies. The Liverpool General Advertiser.

Saturday
10 July

I order'd the Heath coal to be distributed as follows being two works, vizt. to Peter Denton, George Owen's widdow of Sutton, Helen Spencer & to James Roby.

My miller Richard Greenall, marl'd the Rutty Coppy and the Burying Hill & half acre (except the cart road betwixt gate & gate) out of the old pit in the middle of the Furthest Wood Meadow and laid thereon 49½ rods. He paid for carting 32s per rod. The bottom of the pit was red rock, it did not produce much water, altho' he paid 14s per week pumping, the summer being very dry. He took all the sletch or slutch & a large quantity of crop marl out & laid it at the sides of the pit.

Saturday
14 August

I rear'd the spire at the Lower Mill.

Monday
16 August

Cost of the water wall at the Lower Mill vizt.

	£	s	d
5,000 bricks at 8s 4d per [1000]	2	1	8
63 bushells Leigh lime [at] 8[d]	2	2	0
Carriage 12s, turnpike 2s 3d	0	14	3
30 bushells common lime [at] 7[d]	0	17	6
Seting stone work 57:60 [at] 2[s] 0[d]	5	14	0
Seting of brick 22:48 [at] 1[s] 0[d]	1	2	6
Paid the surveyor	0	2	6
[Total]	12	14	5

NB the stones were what came out of the mill.

Richard Greenall marld the Sand Hey out of the Lower Damn, the marl was from 3 to 4 feet thick & they bottom'd upon a hard red sand. He put but a slender set on it.

Thursday
26 August

Begun cutting my oats & wheat in the Norley with 14 reapers.

Tuesday
7 September

The same nine ale houses that were licens'd last year have licenses this year.

81 Mantua maker – a dressmaker.

1773
Saturday
11 September   Finishd all my reaping.

One of my trees on Hackley Moss by Prescot was broke in two by the great storm this day, and the top that fell down I gave to Ellis Glover the stone cutter. Mr Atherton desired I would let the bottom part stand which I aggreed too.

Saturday
18 September   Finish'd houseing all my corn as follows vizt.

	Thr	Sh	Th	Sh
Out of the Norley wheat	104	08		
Tyth	09	11	94	21
Out of the Norley Grey oats	205	08		
Tyth	18	16	186	16
Out of the New Meadow Grey oats	183	08		
Tyth	16	16	166	16
Out of the New Meadow Siberia barley	88	16		
Tyth	8	00	80	16
Out of the 2^d Old Jones's our country oats	41	16		
Tyth	3	16	38	0

I had 19 loads of hay this year out of the Mill Meadows.

14 loads of hay out of Holland's Nooks.

34 loads of hay out of the Spout Lands & tenement.

46 loads of hay out of the West Norley. In all 113 loads.

Thursday
14 October   The late Thomas Glover's estate in Sutton is let at £10 17s 6d p.a. clear of all leys, taxes, repairs & Lord's rent.

Thursday
21 October   Dined at Scholes with mess^{rs} Weldon, Conyers, Roger Leigh, Doyle, Emmet, Nelson, Williams, Fox, Walmesley & Green, Todos de la Compania.

Friday
22 October   Aggreed with John Lucas to grant him a lease of three lives for the late Mr William Marshes belonging to mess^{rs} Barnston & Meyers for £21 p.a. clear of all leys, taxes & repairs, payable the 25th December & 25 March annually. To lay upon the premises annu- ally 17 loads of dung, to plant 12 trees p.a. and to keep a cock. To have the leases by the 2^d February the estate contains 17a 1r 20p.

Tuesday
2 November   I baked four bushells of flour, half wheat half rye, into soul loaves which made 412 loaves, of which I distributed amongst the poor

1773

276 which is more by nigh one hundred then used to come. There remaind 136 loaves.

Friday
12 November   The barometer I never remember lower. It was as low as the mark I formerly made which is a little above stormy.

Aggreed with William Makin for James Williamson's for 14 years for £28 p.a. clear of all leys & taxes. I am to have a road for carting limestone &c. & am to put the house in tenantly repair, & afterwards he is to keep it so, as well as the barn when it is new built, but till then I am to repair it. Mr Thomas Tatlaw the apothecary, & his broth^r are to be equally bound for the payment.

Tuesday
29 November   Kill'd a hog which weighd 19 score or 380lb.

Saturday
4 December   Sold all my cheeses to Jane Moss which consisted of 91 cheeses weighing 16cwt 2qtr 22lb at 28s per cwt, £23 7s 1½d. NB I this year milkd 14 cows, had little comp^y and only sold of milk & butter £[...]⁸² worth. Alice Wainwright was the dairymaid.

Wednesday
15 December   Aggreed with William Kilshaw for late William Mayor's estate contain^g 8a 1r 22p for the term he holds the Hills for, £21 p.a. clear of all leys & taxes. I to do the repairs of the house & outhouseing.

Friday
17 December   Killd a hogg which weighd 15 score & 7lb or 307lb.

Tuesday
22 December   Killd a cow which weighd 617lb, fat 50lb, hide 103lb.

1774

Monday
3 January   The following servants came in the evening to live with me: Helen Houghton as dairymaid at £4 p.a., John Mundus as plowman at £8 5s p.a., Joseph Howard as plowman at £8 0s p.a.

Monday
17 January   Killd a hogg which weighd 17 score.

Tuesday
18 January   Aggreed with Joseph Smith to grant him a full lease of late

82 Amount not entered by BTE.

1774

Foster's now tenanted by Burrows for £130 to be paid the first day of May next, and I have promis'd to allow him the last half year's rent now comeing due from Burrow's in lieu of wood, as he is to repair the house. The Lord's rent is 15s p.a.

Saturday
22 January   Promis'd John Sale of Burrow's Lane to mend the house this spring, and pave the cart house, & either mend, or make new barn doors & doors for the cart house.

Made 186 bush⁵ of oats at the mill which produced 15 loads of meal and 3 sacks of light for the horses, cows, piggs and dogs.

1774[83]   Cost of the spire at the lower mill, vizt.

	£	s	d
25 yards of oak at 5d £0 10s 5d, 234 feet dale £1 19s	2	9	5
Iron work per bill 11s 9d, nails 4s 10d	0	16	7
Lead 1cwt 3qtr 23½lb, £1 16s 7d, carpinter's work £2 0s 8½d	3	17	3½
A copper weather cock £1 5s, leaden ball 3s	1	8	0
Gilding 15s, four times painting £1 1s 7d	1	16	7
[Total]	10	7	10½

Wednesday & Thursday
2 & 3   I had 2 flatt loads of limestone unloaden at my landing place in
February   Williamson's tenement these two days, which was the first kind of goods of any sort that ever came by water and were landed in Eccleston before.

Tuesday
8 February   Killd a cow which weighd 592lb, fat 57lb, hide 85lb.

Aggreed with the Makin's that for the first seven years they might plow four acres and the last seven only three, and that in the last year they might have one acre of wheat. I am to allow them £4 towards ditching and for dung in consideration of their leaving all their dung upon the premises as they are to consume all of the produce therof thereupon.

Friday
18 February   Ralph Ashton told me this day that he is to pay for Denton's £30 p.a. and clear it all leys and taxes except the Lord's rent.

Friday
4 March   The ground was cover'd this day three to four inches thick with snow, and it froze. The wind was in the east.

83 No other date given.

1774

For some months past all guineas were weighd, & none would pass curr[t] that wanted six grains, the Portugal peices they would not receive, which caused a great stagnation in trade, & no new guineas were coin'd, but from those that were sent up short in weight, and the government only allow'd £3 17s 10½d (per oz) for them, whereas I remember nigh forty years ago when the broad peices were calld in they, allow'd £4 (per oz) for them at the Tower.

Friday
1 April

Killd a pigg which weighd 12 score & a half at 4d per lb.

I had this day 286 persons for peace eggs.

Thursday
7 April

I paid half the expences makeing the bridge at late Lancaster's, the other half was defray'd by the trustees of Sir Thomas Gerard.

Monday
11 April

Cost of rebuilding a water or nable wall at the Higher Mill

	£	s	d
2,300 bricks £1 3s, 25 bushells lime 24s 7d and			
12 bushells Sutton lime at 10d are 10s	2	17	7
To nable wall 3,745 yards at 2s 1d	4	1	1½
Head Stock wall within the mill 2s, two arches 4s	0	6	0
To carting the brick lime and	0	6	3½
[Total]	7	11	0

Thursday
14 April

Prickled 31 horse beans in the west border by the Ha-Ha.

Thursday
28 April

My black mare that was covered by Lythgoe's brown horse Champion the 19th of May last foal'd a colt[84] this last night and it died the day following.

Monday
9 May

Sold to Mr John Chorley of Prescot 1,075 oaks with 695 cyphers with their bark, half to be paid for the 29 September next, the other half on the 29th September 1775, for the sum of £322, & sold to John Whitlow of Eccleston 199 ashes with 40 cyphers, 210 alders with 53 cyphers, 4 poplars, 6 withy & 4 sycamores to be paid for at the same time for the sum of £100 19s 0d.

Wednesday
1 June

Ask'd Thomas Owen for adding two lives to the late Barrow's in which his son John is the only life, seven year's vallue. It is now let to John Dunbill for £19 p.a.

84 Original entry, 'filly' crossed out and replaced with 'colt'.

1774

He sets his other estate on Catchall Moss[85] to Michael Bibby for £10 10s clear of all taxes except the Lord's rent.

Wednesday
22 June

	£	s	d
My new hogg house and the walls with the stones and workmanship cost	8	14	5½
35 bush^s of lime £1 5s, leading the stones 17s 6d	2	2	6
Timber, 2 new gates and carpinter's work	4	15	11
¾ of a rod slate & leading £1 7s, slateing & laths 13s 6d	2	0	6
[Total]	17	13	4½

Monday
29 August   John Davis came in the even^g as groom for £10 10s p.a.

Monday
19 September   Finish'd all my reaping.

Begun sowing wheat in the Norley with three plows.

My tenant John Stananought told me that Mr Wilson of Appleton last year from an acre & one quarter of land kept two horses & four cows, and that he made from the cows 17cwt of cheese, and that this year from an acre & quarter of land he had 110 threaves of barley, & that he had threshed out that as was laid & it produced 1¼ bushels per threave, and that he thought the rest would produce 1½ per threave.

Cost of my new stables at the late William Mayor's vizt.

	£	s	d
48 yards of brickwork of brick & a half [at] 2s 6d	6	0	0
129 yards brick length 1s 9d	11	5	9
1 rodd slate 30s, carting 7s 6d, slating 10s 6d	2	8	0
Ridgeing stone and carting	0	5	4
Timber and carpinter's work	9	0	0
Nails & iron work 10s, three locks 3s 10d	0	13	10
The grainery steps and swine coat	2	10	0
Paveing & laying the ground work 5s 6d, 150 laths 4s 6d	0	10	0
[Total]	32	12	11

Friday
7 October   Aggreed with Helen Halliwell for the Red Lion the house she now lives at, for £8 p.a. she to pay all leys and taxes.

---

85 Catchall Moss now known as Catchdale Moss.

1774
Wednesday
2 November

Told James Greenhough's son-in-law that if he builds a house the size of Peter Johnson's of brick & set in lime and slates it, I will allow him the roofe timber, joices & sparrs. I ask'd him £12 to change a life.

I had ground three bushells of wheat, rye & barley which was made into 305 little loaves which were to be given to the poor. There were 259 distributed so there remained 46.

	Loads
I had this year clover out of p^t of the New Meadow	14
The 2^d crop of clover (a very wet time) I housed only	2
Hollands Nooks	12
West Norley	38
Mill Meadows	25
[Total]	91

Housed my corn as follows vizt.

	Th	Sh	Th	Sh
Oats of the Peas Croft	125	8		
Tyth	11	12	113	20
Pinfold Meadows oats	84	3		
Tyth	7	16	76	11
Old Jones's oats	69	9		
Tyth	6	8	63	1
Old Jones's barley	124			
Tyth	11	8	112	16
Middle Old Jones's wheat	22	12		
Little Old Jones's wheat	17			
[Total]	39	12		
Tyth	3	12	36	0
Pease Croft wheat	37	1		
Tyth	3	1	34	00
Pease Croft rye	3	1		
Tyth		1	3	00

Wednesday
16 November

	lb
Kill'd a cow which weigh'd	668
Tallow 49lb, suit 31lb hide 79lb	159
[Total]	827

Tuesday
22 November

	lb
Killd a cow which weigh'd at 3d per lb	624
Tallow 30lb, at 3¾d, suet 24lb at 4d, hide 90lb at 2½d	144
[Total]	768

1774
Friday
25 November   Kill'd a hogg which weighd 16 score 15lb, 335lb.

Friday
2 December   The following prices of coals was advertis'd this day in the Liverpool paper to be deliverd at the people's doors for ready money by the following propieters vizt. 20cwt each hundred containing 120lb.

	To house keepers per ton			To shipping per ton		
	£	s	d	£	s	d
Peter Leigh Esq.	0	7	2	0	6	6
John Mackay Esq.	0	7	0	0	6	4
Thomas Case Esq.	0	6	10	0	6	2
Sir Thomas Gerard	0	6	6	0	5	10

And to poor people they will deliver them at the yard at 4½d per hundred containing 120lb.

Wednesday
7 December   Sold & deliver'd the following cheeses to Thomas Greenall's order

	Weight			Weight			Weight	
	Cwt	lb		Cwt	lb		Cwt	lb
7 cheeses	1	13	32 cheeses	5	51	63 cheeses	10	118
7 cheeses	1	13	6 cheeses	1	9	7 cheeses	1	5
6 cheeses	1	13	6 cheeses	1	15	7 cheeses	1	6
6 cheeses	1	12	6 cheeses	1	8	6 cheeses	1	0
6 cheeses	1	0	6 cheeses	1	81	6 cheeses	1	1
			7 cheeses	1	14			
32 cheeses	5	51	63 cheeses	10	118	89 cheeses	15	10

[Total 89 cheeses 15cwt 10lb] at 27s per cwt £20 7s 3d.

NB my cheese were very ill made this year several of them were hoven[86], and due care was not taken of them, in so much that about seven hundred were left as not saleable. I milk 13 cows but two of them were only calves of two years old & a third was barren.

Friday
16 December   Kill'd a hogg which weighd 20 score & 11lb or 411lb.

1775

Friday
20 January   Kill'd a hogg which weighd 16 score & 3lb or 323lb.

Friday
10 February   Killd a hogg which weigh'd 19 score or 380lb.

86 Hoven – swollen or bloated.

1775

NB I made for the Mill Lane last year 1 gate, 2 gates for the hogg house, 1 gate for Burrow's Lane.

Thursday
23 February   John Dickson's acco^t for makeing the follow^g gates vizt.

		£	s	d
25 five-barr^d gates				
3 four-barr'd gates	} 31 gates at 1s 6d with spurrs	2	6	6
3 with strong top barrs gates				
1 gate strong top barr with spurrs		0	3	0
1 gate repair'd all the barrs new		0	0	9
37 new gates made this year & the last year		2	10	3

Monday
13 March   ✝ Begun wearing my new nightshirts of which I had fourteen.

Saturday
18 March   Agreed with Mr John Robison for five years for late Peter Denton's containing 3a 1r 36p for £12 12s p.a. clear of all leys, taxes & repairs. He may lay down the feilds, but to plow none in the last year, and to manure it with as much dung as such an estate would produce if well stockt. I am to white wash it & put it into repair.

Thursday
30 March   At night. About half an hour past nine o'clock this evening there appear'd in the sky very luminous lights that were form'd into a very large bow from east to west and as large as ever I saw a rainbow.

Thursday
6 April   Agreed to let Ralph Cook, butcher of Prescot, late Green & Faulkner's tenem^t containing 9a 0r 3p for 14 years to commence in May 1776 for £28 p.a. clear of all leys & taxes, but am to make him an allowance the first year of £14 on acco^t of puting the land into condition.

Saturday
15 April

	lb
Kill'd a segg which weighd	884
Tallow 56lb, suet 26lb, hide 125lb	207
[Total]	1,091

14 & 15 April   Gave to 313 poor persons these two days £0 13s 0½d.

Friday
28 April   My worthy freind William Bankes, of Winstanley Esq. died this day about one o'clock aged 66.

1775
Wednesday
3 May   My above freind was buried this day at Wigan. The bearers were,
                   Mess[rs] Bob Gerard, Tom Cholmondeley, Doc[r] Masters of Croston,
                   Parker, self, Hearn jun[r] of Cheshire, Holt Leigh & Parson Low of
                   Winwick.[87]

Friday
12 May   Every one agrees that this is the forwardest spring rememberd,
                   except Edward Rogerson, a man about 74 years of age, who told
                   me he remember'd when a boy in the spring seeding that it was
                   so warm that they went to plow early in the morning & work'd
                   then about nine o'clock and yoak'd to again at 4 in the afternoon
                   and that they work'd in their shirts.

26 May   The Slater's Crofts, the bottom of the Tuit Hill that I have enclos'd
                   were measur'd this day by Mas[r] John Ainsworth to 1a 1r 0p land.

Saturday
10 June   Jonathan Greenall & George Rice of Eccleston haveing aquaint-
                   ed John Mackay Esq. of Ravenhead in Sutton, a Justice of the
                   Peace, that the lane leading to the house in Eccleston where
                   Thomas Mather now lives was a path road, they appeard before
                   him this day in the company of the said Mather, James Yates, Mr
                   Mackay's agent, John Balert, carpinter & his wife, my son & self.
                   Greenall swore he had known it so for 45 years and Rice swore
                   he had known it for 30 years. I produced the handwriting of the
                   following persons who said it never was a road otherwise then to
                   the house: Charles Dagnall aged 76 years, Jonathan Tyrer aged
                   75 years, William Sadler 60 years, all of Eccleston. Which writ-
                   ing will be found in a drawer of my bookcase, and it was agreed
                   before Mr Mackay & the above mentiond people that appeard
                   before him, to be no road & that he might stop any person for
                   going through. The estate formerly belongd to the late Mr Daniel
                   Lawton of Prescot.

Wednesday
5 July   I agreed to allow Peter Johnson £15 15s p.a. as in future he is to
                   have no livery.

Monday
14 August   John Molineux came to me this morning as cow man at £7 10s p.a.

Tuesday
15 August   θ θ θ θ I disposed of the 2 works of coals allowd by John Mackay
                   Esq. for the Hatwell stream of water to Peter Gerard of Prescot,

---

87 Doctor Masters was the rector of Croston, and Holt Leigh a Wigan lawyer.

1775

James Foster of Windle and John Pike & Thomas Howard, both of Eccleston. Each to receive 30 baskets.

Monday
21 August

	Th	riders
I had in the Norley of wheat	271	0
Of rye	3	2
[Total]	274	2

So that it only wants 5 threaves & 1 rider to make it 20 threaves to an acre.

Friday
25 August

Housed the above wheat in my nearest barn and over the cart house, and there was room enough left to receive 2 acres of barley out of the Pinfold Meadow. NB the rye was in the other barn. The straw was short this year occassiond by the dry months of May and June.

	Th	riders
Our country oats in the Postern Hills were	348	2
Tyth	32	0
[Total]	316	2
Barley in the Pinfold Meadow was	138	

I finishd houseing the 1st September all in good order, and the harvest was forwarder by 3 weeks or a month then ever was rememberd.

29 September I hous'd out of the 2d Old Jones's, of the 2d crop of clover 10½ large loads, all in fine order, which is the first of a 2d crop that I ever had good fortune with since I liv'd here.

My barns contain the 30 acres of corn & 24 & ½ loads of hay which filld them compleatly.

I agreed with Richard Greenal for the tyth of the Norley in £21 0s 0d and for the Pinfold Meadow Barley in £2 8s 0d.

Friday
27 October Kill'd a pig which weigh'd twelve score.

Thursday
2 November I ground 1½ bushells of wheat, 1 bushell of rye & half a bushell of barley, in all 3 bushells, & made it into 233 loaves all of which were distrubted to the poor, except two which are intended for old Thomas Tarbock.

1775
Wednesday
8 November

Sold to Messrs Nathan & Samuel Macknight of Moor Street, Liverpool the following cheeses for which they paid £22 4s 9d.

	Cwt	qtr	lb		Cwt	qtr	lb
8 cheeses	1	0	5	83 [cheeses]	12	3	26
7 cheeses	1	0	7	6 [cheeses]	1	0	08
7 cheeses	1	0	2	6 [cheeses]	1	0	07
8 cheeses	1	0	15	6 [cheeses]	1	0	02
7 cheeses	1	0	5	6 [cheeses]	1	0	08
7 cheeses	1	0	16	7 [cheeses]	1	0	20
7 cheeses	1	0	0	1 [cheeses]	0	0	23
7 cheeses	1	0	10	115 cheeses	18	2	04
6 cheeses	1	0	16				
6 cheeses	1	0	12				
6 cheeses	1	0	12				
7 cheeses	1	0	16				
83 [cheeses]	12	3	26				

at 24s per cwt, £22 4s 9d.

NB both this & last year's make were very ordinary inclined to heave, the maid Helen Houghton, not understanding the buissiness so well as she ought to have done.

NB I had 38 large cheeses left which would be about 6cwt.

Saturday
11 November

The township was fined in £300 for the lane by the finger post by the Lower Mill to Dagnall's comb shop at the turnpike and it was paved with Moss Bank stones, only the side ones were from Seddon's Delf (which I gave to the town). It was compleat'd in this one season by Richard Greenall the miller, and the assesm^t for Scholes End was £153 14s 9½, the assesm^t for the Hall End £154 4s 11½d. I paid for the demesne & Spout Lands at 2s 5d per £, £46 6s 9½d.

Friday
1 December

I killd a cow which weighd 722lb vizt.

	lb		£	s	d
The quarters	566	at 3[d] per lb	7	1	6
The hide	94	at 3½[d]	1	7	5
Tallow & suit	62	at 3¾[d]	0	19	4½
Tongue 1s, head 2s	0		0	3	0
[Total]	722		9	11	3½

9 December

Paid Richard Ellison for 771lb ox beef at 3d, £9 12s 9d.

Tuesday
12 December

Killd a hog which weigh'd 16 score 10lb or 330lb.

1775
Tuesday
19 December   Killd a hog which weigh'd 15 score 2lb or 302[lb].

22 December   Paid Richard Ellison for 662lb cow beef at 3d per lb, £8 5s 6d.

Settled accounts with Jonathan Case Esq. on Thursday the 14th ins^t at Redhasells, and there is due to me as follows

	£	s	d
From Sutton collery as per acc^t	242	15	3½
From Eccleston collery for quarterly rents			
1¼ years settled to the 15th October last	243	10	0
2 year's rent of lands due 25th ins^t December	48	0	0
[Total]	534	5	3½

NB he is to pay sixty guineas quarterly & the coals he is to raise annually for that sum at 2s 6d per work will be 2,016 works yearly so for one year & one quarter the get will be 2,520 [works]. Coals got in the said time to 16 September as per his account 1,390 [works] 28 [baskets].

So he has to get to make up £243 10s as yet 1,129 works 32 [baskets].

1776

Tuesday
16 January   The Tuesday's London Mail of the 9th & Friday's of the 12th did not arrive then this morning, occassion'd, as they say, by a large quantity of snow having fallen on the other side of Coventry.

Friday
19 January   Sunday's mail of the 14th & Tuesday's of the 16th did not arrive then this afternoon.

Sunday
21 January   Friday's mail of the 19th arriv'd last night.

Monday
22 January   Sunday's mail of the 21st arriv'd this morning.

Wednesday[88]
24 January   Yesterday's mail arrivd this morning. NB the days of the month that I have mentiond, are the days the mails shou'd have come into Prescot.

Killd a hog which weighd 14 score 19lb or 499lb.

Friday
26 January   This day's post came in as usual.

---

88 'Friday' crossed out and replaced with 'Wednesday'.

1776
Saturday
27 January   I never have known it freeze so hard. It has froze upwards of two inches in the night & the watering pool that was broke for the horses to drink at, at noon, bore my butler Peter Johnson at 5 in the afternoon. The brook in the garden was cover'd with ice, and my water bottle was filld at 10 o' clock at night & put in the window seat & the frost broke it & the water that was spilld was all ice before I got up.

Monday
29 January   The water in my bottles in the window seat in my room froze in less than two hours, & the ice broke in the current in the garden that runs to the fountain froze in less than half a miniute.

Thursday[89]
1 February   The water in the cruet this day in time of prayers was so frozen that it was taken out to be thaw'd. There was a little rain which froze as it fell & from this to Liverpool was one continu'd sheet of ice. There were 40 waterside carts coming to load at my pitts but the ice hinder'd them proceeding, & all along the road to Liverpool there were loaded carts left which coud not proceed for the above reason.

Friday
2 February   There was a little rain in the night & now it seems to be a thorough thaw.

Tuesday
6 February   Killd a hog which weighd 14 score or 280lb.

Shroves Tuesday
20 February   My great Damn head brook down this day about 3 o'clock in the afternoon in the deepest place above the last breech nigher to Rushy Park. It made an opening of about 14 yards (and the damn being quite full) it forced its way with very great impetuosity & burst the higher damn head by the stile, swept away or destroy'd all the corn in the mill, enterd the south end of the kiln, broke down the wall, forced up part of the tiles & almost destroyd the inside. It demolish'd the mill bridge, & not being able to carry away the water, either below or above the bridge, it forced down part of my Norley hedge & cop (and my horses that were plowing narrowly escap'd) & then provedentialy broke the Lower Damn Head by the middle stile (which saved the mill) and carry'd away or destroyd all the corn & flour in the 1st & 2^{d} stories. Some of the sacks were carryd to the pig-house & into other feilds. The old building that coverd the wheel fell upon it & the road

89 'Saturday' crossed out and replaced with 'Thursday'.

1776

opposite to it was cut quite cross over it about 5 feet deep, & the sluice from the wheel was so fill'd up that I rode over it. The lower bridge was so demolishd, that I fancy it must be repaird by a new one. Gracious Street escap'd pritty well, except Randle Lygo's, for it was a yard high in the house & cover'd his calfs' heads in the cow house. He had some corn wash'd away from the floor & his mow damag'd. It likewise much hurt the wheat land in Joseph Houghton's, Stannanought's & Thomas Lyon's lands. From the Ha-Ha it was a perfect sea, but mostly to the right hand. All night long there were hundreds of people dispers'd all the feilds over catching of the fish and looking for plunder the same as after a ship wreck.

Wednesday
21 February

I fishd the Great Damn, it now being empty, & caught
206   carp which I put into the Little Damn &
313   carp put into the recevoir, &
  6   carp into the stews
525   carps and 12 fine pikes

There were a parcell of small bream which I gave to the people, there were neither tench, perch nor trouts, & only some 20 ells as coud be caught, the weather being cold they cou'd not stand in the mud.

Helen Fazakerly came to me this day as dairy maid at £4 p.a.

⊗⊗*Tuesday*
5 March

Commissioners to be appoint'd for the fine & recovery are Jonathan Case Esq., John Atherton Esq. of Prescot, the Rever^d Mr William Johnson Clark of Prescot, Mr John Chorley Gent^m of Prescot, & Mr Thomas Maddock clerk to Mr William Law attorney of Ormskirk.

Friday
15 March

My poor chambermaid Mary Talbot died this day about four o'clock in the afternoon. She took to her bed the 8th December 1774 being ill of a consumption & rheumatism and kept lieing being only remov'd now & then into a chair whilst the bed was made. But within these 8 or 10 weeks last passed, she cou'd not be moved at all. Both her legs were sinew grown, & her back was raw. About a month ago she filld with a dropsy, and this day about 10 o'clock she was seized with a bleeding at the nose which continued, then she expir'd. She bore all her great sufferings with the greatest resignation to the divine will of Almighty God & never complaind. She kept her bed 464 days or 66 week & 2 days. R.I.P.

1776
Good Friday
5 April   I had this day for peace eggs 336 persons which exceeds last year by 106.

18 April   The famous Doct[r]. Elliott's eye wash.✝✝✝✝✝
Rosmery flowers, lavender flowers of each three drams. Infuse these in a pint of the best old coniac brandy for about thirty hours, squeese the ingredients every day then filter the infusion and dissolve in it one dram & a half of campher cut small. After shaking the bottle for a day or two.
Wash the eye lids, brows & temples with a fine rag dipt in it every morning for ten or twelve days, interupt, and use it again as occassion serves. It strengthens the eye and sight exceedingly.

26 April   Sow'd in the Norley 47 measures Scotch White oats, 21½ measures Greys, & 24 measures barley.

15 May   Aggreed with Mr [...][90] Cross of Denton's Green that he may hold the late Ned Rogerson's another year paying £1 11s 6d advanced rent.

Saturday
18 May   Mr William Meynell came to live with me this evening.
Particulars of repairing my damns &c. &c. &c.

	£	s	d	£	s	d
Mending the lower damn head per Mr Carr	29	6	10			
Carriage of barrows to & from Wrightinton	0	10	0			
Half a barrell of ale	0	16	0	30	12	10
The Great Damn:						
Getting 23 rods 28 yds of earth on the north side of it and 16 rods 21 yds of earth out of the west side at 22s 6d per rod	44	14	8½			
Paid day wages prepairing things	0	6	5			
Mending barrows 5s, carting barrows and planks to & from the Navigation 10s	0	15	0			
Carting wood, brick, stone & lime	0	9	0			
1,200 new bricks 10s, 1,500 old bricks 10s, lime 5s 3d	1	5	3			
Dickson & Forber's work at ditto	1	13	0			

90   Forename not entered by BTE.

1776

	£	s	d	£	s	d
Robert Myers for iron work at the clough	0	3	6			
Measuring iron 10s, a cask of ale 16s	1	6	0	50	12	10½
Repairing the Little Damn per Bill				3	3	8
Clearing the Mill Brooke	2	10	4½			
Soughing part of the Mill Brooke	0	7	3	2	17	7½
Lower Mill Damn Head Road & Broad Well Lane				5	9	2½
Repairing the Mill Bridge £1 15s 7½d, stones 8s 2d				2	3	9½
[Total]				95	0	0

Stones for the sough for coverings.

Richard Greenall d^r for three oaks sold him 27th ulto & measur'd by James Gardner & William Moss to 115 feet at 1s 6d per foot is £8 12s 6d. Paid.

Saturday
3 August

Burtonhead Barn tenem^t valued by Richard Greenall

	a	r	p	at (s)	£	s	d
Barn Hey	3	1	02	55	8	14	10¼
Higher Wood	4	2	18	55	12	13	8¼
Lower Wood	2	2	04	50	6	6	3
Coal Pit Meadow	1	3	26	50	4	15	7½
Further Coal Pit Meadow	2	2	18	60	7	16	9
Brick Hey	3	3	24	55	10	14	6
New Year's Clough	2	2	17	60	7	16	4½
Alder Hey	3	0	18	52	8	1	10
Great Meadow	4	0	27	60	12	10	3½
House, barn, fold, croft & garden	0	3	09				
[Total]	29	2	03		79	10	2

No valuation taken of the croft & garden as we cou'd not exactly fix any for them, as we did not know the areas thereof. The tenant to have the house, buildings and fold and the leys & taxes to be deducted out of the above valuation. The above is rated for a term of fourteen years. If you please to let it for a shorter time you may deduct therefrom what you think proper.

Tuesday
6 August

Agreed with Richard Johnson for late Ned Rogerson's, the Spout Lands and Holland's Nooks containing 15a 2r 21p for 14 years for £50 p.a. he to pay all leys & taxes except for the Holland's Nooks. To plow 4 acres the first 7 years & 3 the last seven, to have a calf or heifers summers run for the first 7 years if there is room in the score.

1776
Wednesday morn^g

14 August   Call'd on Mr Mackay & shew'd him the valuation of Burton Head Farm amounting to £79 10s 2d, which he objected nothing too, only ask'd if I wou'd secure it to him for fourteen years after Barnes's death to which I answer'd no, but only for fourteen years from this time.

Gave the Hatwell Heath coal allow'd for the water to [...][91].

Saturday
17 August   The Mill Meadows measur'd by Mas^r Lyngart.

	a	r	p	
That next to the Avenue	2	1	16	
The other by the Lower Damn	1	2	29½	
[Sub total]	4	0	5½	
Deduct the potatoe ground	0	0	5½	in this last meadow
				in the old pit
[Total]	4	0	0	

Monday
19 August   Begun mowing my barley in the Norley with four mowers.

Wednesday
21 August   James Wilson came to live with me for £6 6s pa.

Thursday
22 August   Finish'd mowing the five acres of barley in the Norley.

Monday
26 August   Begun mowing the 9 acres of oats in the Norley.

Saturday
31 August   Charles Dagnall died about one o'clock this day aged 76.

Saturday
7 September   The valuation of Late Charles Dagnall's by Richard Greenall.

	a	r	p	at per acre	£	s	d
House barn, stable, shop, fold, orchard and garden	0	2	28	£4	2	14	0
Little Mead	1	3	16	£2 15s	5	1	9
Little House garden, gin Croft & Comb shop adjoining	1	0	05	£4	4	2	6
Old Meadow	2	2	23	£3 15s	9	18	3
Pasture Feild	2	0	10	£2 15s	5	13	5
Furry feild and croft	4	1	06	£2 10	10	14	4
[Total]	12	2	08	value	38	4	3

91 Detail not entered by BTE.

1776

> The tenant to have the house and offices adjoining & all the barns, stables &c. at the above valuation. The tenant to clear the above premises from all leys & taxes & the land owner to keep all buildings, gates, walls, pails, stiles, plats &c. in sufficient tenantable repair of his own charge.
>
> NB there is some lands where Rachael Dagnall's house & garden & the comb shop & garden are, which you may deduct or otherwise as you please, as they are estimat'd in the within valuation, & I did not know the breadth thereof

	£	s	d
The house where Rachael Dagnall now lives	5	10	0
The comb shop and house adjoining	2	10	0
The cottage adjoining the stable	1	15	0
[Total]	47	19	3

> The tenants to pay all leys and taxes over and above the rents & the buildings to be kept in repair by the landowner.

Wednesday
11 September   Finishd houseing my 5 acres of barley out of the Norley.

Begun houseing my oats out of the Norley with three carts.

Friday
13 September   Housed all my wheat.

Saturday
14 September   Housed all my oats & finish'd my hervest.

Monday
16 September   Begun mowing the 2ᵈ crop of clover in the New Meadow.

Monday
10 October   Agreed with Henry Ascroft of Parr to let him the late John Wilcock's tenement for nine years for £30 a year clear of all leys & taxes. To have liberty to plow three acres p.a. the first six years but only two the three last years. To have no stubble wheat nor none to be left with wheat the last year, to leave his dung on the premises, the canal cut to be my property, he is to have into his bargain the cottage adjoining late Ned Wilcock's for keeping it in repair. He is also to have the cottage & the stable in the lane by Dagnall's fold which I must keep in order. To have free liberty of coaling paying trespass. Rent days 29ᵗʰ September & 2ᵈ February.

Saturday
19 October   Agreed with Rachael & Anne⁹² Dagnall to let them their late

---

92 'Eliza' crossed out and 'Anne' inserted.

1776

father's estate for seven years with all the houses and outhouse-ing except the cottage & stable next the lane for £45 p.a. clear of all leys & taxes except repairs. To have liberty to plow 1½ acres except in the meadows, and may let the Furry feild for pasture only. To have no stuble wheat nor any wheat at the end of the term. To leave all their dung upon the premises & BTE to have liberty of coaling paying trespass.

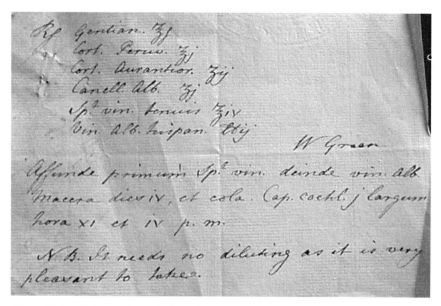

Figure 10 Medicinal recipe including 'Peruvian bark' (Cort[ex] Peruv.), almost certainly quinine.

Friday
25 October　　Kill'd 2 hogs which weighd 27 score & 12lb.

Thursday
31 October　　My son went to travel in foreign parts.+ + + + + +

Saturday
1 November　　I ground 3 measures of corn, half wheat, half barley, and made it into 252 loaves whereof 247 were distributed & the remaining five gave to my poor neighbours. NB there were 16 more poor this year than the last.

Monday
4 November　　Agreed with John Liptrott to let him Woods's estate in Sutton for eleven years for £28 p.a. clear of all leys & taxes. To be allow'd

1776

£5 out of the first year's rent towards ridding & ditching the estate. To have liberty to plow 5 acres the first 5 years & only 3 in the last six years. Not to plow the old meadowing nor push plow any. The house to be put in tenantable repair, to leave all his dung on the premises & for every load of hay he sells of the estate to buy & bring to and set on the estate two loads of good dung & for every load of straw one good load of dung. BTE to have liberty of coaling paying trespass.

Tuesday
5 November   NB the bond which my son gave to Mr Thomas West the 30th ulto for £450, the intrest only commences as this day having only just now receiv'd the capital. NB he has mark'd it on the bond.

Saturday
9 November   Killd a cush which weighd 423lb, hide 54[lb], tallow 27[lb], suit 13[lb] in all 526lb at 3¼d per lb £7 2s 5½d.

Wednesday
13 November   Sold to Mr Matthew Ellam[93] the following cheeses vizt.

N°	Cwt	lb
7 weighd	1	13
6	1	4
6	1	13
6	1	0
6	1	0
6	1	15
6	1	0
6	1	7
6	1	12
6	1	6
6	1	9
6	1	9
73	12	88 at 34s 6d per cwt £21 17s 6d.

I milkd this year 13 cows, but some of the cows calv'd very late & the year did not turn out either to milk, butter or cheese, as being a very poor grass year.

Wednesday
27 November   Killd a cush which weighd 444lb, hide 63 pound, tallow 29[lb], suit 14[lb]. In all 550lb at 3¼d per lb, £7 8s 11½d.

Mr Mackay is assess'd in Sutton in £194 out of which deduct for cottages £24 Gascoine in £190, BTE in £160.

---

93 Matthew Ellam – agent to Jonathan Case.

1776
Tuesday
10 December   Killd a hog which weighd 13 score & 14lb.

Wednesday
18 December   Kill'd a hog which weighd 15 score & 1llb.

Monday
23 December   Killd a cush which weighd 520lb, hide 61lb, tallow 36lb, suit 19½lb in all 636½lb at 3½d per lb, £9 5s 7½d.

1777

Wednesday
1 January   Anne Fogg came in the evening to live with me as dairy maid for £5 pa.

Friday
3 January   Margret Hewitt came in the evening to live with me as chamber maid for £5 pa.

Thursday
9 January   Jonathan Case Esq. sent me on acco^t of my son's bill on Mr Matthew Ellam's for £63 & charges of protest &c. four bills amounting to £65 10s.

Saturday
11 January   Peter Johnson agreed with Thomas Makin & set him the late Lawton's tenem^t for eleven years for £16 p.a. clear of all leys & taxes. He has the house for keeping it in repair but I may take away the barn.

16 January   I also agreed with him to have the priviledge the [*sic*] for six years to plow what he thinks proper, but the last five years only to plow two acres & to have the liberty of haveing one acre of wheat in the last year. To push or burn none, onely one acre this year, & for every load of that hay he sells to bring three good loads of dung to the ground for it. There wants some gates & platts.

Saturday
31 May   Mrs Palmes of London's receipt for Scotch Collops.[94]
Take a filet of veal, cut thin cutlets of it, then take all the skin & fat of it, beat it very well, then fry it in some fresh butter, a little brown. Then thicken the butter you fry it in, cover it well in gravey or strong broath, season with salt, nutmeg, cloves and mace to

---

94 Collops of beef – a Scottish dish traditionally served on Burns Night.

your taste, then set your stewpan over a slow fire, stew it to a proper thickness.

Mrs Townley of Chiswick's receipt for gingerbread.

A pound of treacle, a quarter of a pound of brown sugar, a quarter of a pound of butter, an ounce & a half of ginger powder'd, seeds to your taste. Mix it up with flower, and roll it out into thin cakes. When baked put it into a tin box which will keep it always crisp.

Mrs Townley's of Chiswick's receipt for Yellow Mange.

Take 2oz of isinglass & a pint of spring water, half the peal of a fresh lemon, a stick of cinnamon bruis'd. When it is melted, strain it thro' a lawn seive into a bowl, put to it half a pound of double refin'd sugar and the juice of a large lemon or two little ones. Let it stand till almost cold. In the main time take six yolks of eggs, well beaten, mix them with a pint of white Lisbon wine. Then put it all together in a clean sauce pan upon a clear fire, turn it always one way till it boils up, then put it into your tins.

Mr T. Chadwick's receipt for sucking calves.

Give it as soon as calv'd a glass of gin for 3 mornings succesivly & keept it low for 8 or 10 days. Near Michelmass take a handful of hen's dung, a pint of old lant & 2 or 3 spoonfuls of salt. Mix them all well togather & strain it thro' a cloth & give it the calf fasting, and bleed the night before.

		lb
Kill'd a pig the 31st January which weigh'd		310
Kill'd an nother the 7th February weigh'd		329
Killd a cow the 28th March the quarters weighd 676lb,	676 }	
Hide 78lb, tallow 48lb, suet 35[lb]	161 }	837

Saturday
5 July

I told Heaton that I had orderd Mr Mackay to get no more coals. He ask'd in his master's name, Mr Jonathan Case, whether he might not get them. I told him he shou'd not.

Monday
7 July

Begun mowing my first crop of clover in the Norley.

Friday
18 July

Bottled off a quarter cask red port which run 11 dozⁿ & 2 bottles which cost £8 10s & at 1s 3¼d per bottle comes to £8 10s 3½d.

Saturday
19 July

Hous'd all my clover out of the Norley, without any rain, in the finest condition imaginable vizt. 57 loads of red clover 13 loads of Dutch or white clover all large loads. In all 70 loads.

1777
Saturday
16 August   I am accountable to Richard Greenall for 33 tonns of lime stone. I this day weighd of his at my quay at 5s 6d per tonn, £9 1s 6d.

Saturday
23 August

	£	s	d
Contract for my new house in Sutton was for	80	0	0
Swine coat & little house £3 13s 11d, stubs & rails 14s 11d	4	8	10
Paveing & clearing £2 1s 0d, paleing, stones & iron work	3	4	2
Materials of the old house £8, whitewashing	9	0	0
[Total]	96	13	0

Thursday
28 August   Messrs James Orrell & John Chorley valued the thirty oak trees and six ashes growing in Broad Fenny Wood and damag'd by the water in the resevoir by the proprietors of the Sankey Brook Navigation to £21 0s 0d, and to be paid on Candlemass Day next. 30 oak trees & 6 ash's.

Monday
15 September   Told Thomas Holland he might hold the grounds he now has of me for £21 p.a. for a term of years to be agreed on by my son.

Friday
19 September   The value of Scarisbrick estate was deliver'd to me this day by Mr John Formby the steward & is as follows vizt.

	£	s	d
The Hall Farm	215	0	0
Gorsuch	92	10	0
Parks	70	0	0
New Hall	90	0	0
Wyke	56	10	0
New House £25, Escowood £12	37	0	0
The Mills	38	0	0
The Woods let to sundrys	72	8	0
Part of Gorsuch ground	25	18	6
Lord's rents & boons	158	9	8
Biscar Meadow Hay	78	10	0
Biscar Meadow yearly score	20	0	0
Delf Hey	5	0	0
Cheifs £1 6s 1¼d } Seats church £4 3s 0d	5	9	1¼
Part of the Parks, Garden & Grey Field	35	0	0
[Total]	999	15	3¼

1777

In the aforegoing valuation he does not account for the Lord's rent of Martin Mair which is about £26.

The outgoings of Scarisbrick estate are as follows vizt.

	£
To Mrs Scarisbrick p.a.	200
To Mr Edward	60
To Mr Francis	40
To Mrs Mary Scarsbrick	40
To B. Thomas Eccleston	30
To Mrs Palmes in^t on £2000	80
To Fazakerley Esq. in^t on £1000	40
Leys, taxes, repairs & 20s cheifs workman's wages &c. about	110
Joseph Scarisbrick Esq. reserves to himself	300
The whole outgoings are	900

Bought the following books at the sale of J.P. Coghlan, London.

	Vols	£	s	d
Haylin's History	1	0	5	0
Pole's Life	2	0	6	0
Ellis's Husbandry	2	0	6	0
Ganganelli	2	0	12	0
Hume's History Eng^d	8	2	8	0
Gulliver	2	0	6	0
English Martyrology	1	0	3	6
Roman Martyrology	1	0	2	6
Hudibrass	1	0	2	0
Gother's Cathecism	1	0	1	6
Gother's Afternoon	2	0	2	6
Way to Happiness	1	0	2	6
Catholick Christian	1	0	1	6
Spectators	16	1	18	0
English Poets	42	6	6	0
Glass on Cookery	1	0	5	0
Jus. Regium	1	0	7	6
History of Japan	2	0	12	0
The whole amount of books bought		14	7	6

Saturday
4 October   My son return'd from Paris about 8 o'clock in the evening.

Saturday
1 November   Left at the Yew Tree House in Sutton 6,570 bricks. Brought home for which I paid 7s 6d per M[95] 1,630, in all 8,200 £3 1s 6d.

95 'per M' = per thousand.

1777

    Kill'd 2 pigs which weigh'd 276lb.

Tuesday
4 November

	lb	at	£	s	d
Kill'd a cush which weigh'd	444	3¼d	6	0	3
Tallow 40[lb], suet 20[lb] in all	60	3½[d]	0	17	6
The hide sold at 3½d per lb, 14s 3½d	49	3d	0	12	3
[Total]			7	10	0[96]

Friday
7 November   The Wall Pond was fish'd and let off.

Henry Lyon proposes building a barn 10 yards long, 7 yards backwards & 5 yards to the square to hold 4 cows & 2 horses, to be of brick and set in lime mortar & cover'd with slate, if I will add him a life gratis to the two he has in his lease.

Cost of the 2 spires at the mill vizt.

	£	s	d
12 M[97] brick at 7s 6d, £4 10s 0d, 36 bushells lime [at] 6½d, £0 19s 6d	5	9	6
20 bush[s] Sutton Lime 13s 4d, 5 bush[s] hair at 5s	0	18	4
Bricksetters & carpinter's work	11	11	9½
Stone & stone work per Elias Glover	9	12	3
Iron work for vanes & rails	1	13	11½
A new copper vane £1 5s, use of scaffolding boards 2s 9d	1	7	9
Two new leaden balls, gilding them and the vanes, painting the rails & drawing lines on the spires per John Hatton	3	8	11
A rope to hold the scaffolding togather 17lb at 7½d	0	10	6
The whole cost amounted to	34	13	0

Wednesday
26 November   Lancaster's tenem[t] valued by Thomas Greenall as follows vizt.

	a	r	p	at	£	s	d
Coal Pit Hey	2	0	01	70s	7	0	5¼
Outlet	1	0	05	60s	3	1	1½
Higher Lee	1	1	23	70s	4	17	6¼
Lower Lee	1	2	08	50s	3	17	6
Fish Yard	1	3	20	60s	5	12	6
Brook Meadow	1	1	35	50s	3	13	5¼
Rough Hey	1	3	20	60s	5	12	6

96 It would appear that BTE changed his mind about the price of the hide from 3¼d to 3d per lb. His total of £7 10s 0d is based on the latter.
97 '12 M' = 12 thousand.

1777

	a	r	p	at	£	s	d
Cow Hey	2	3	21	40s	5	15	3
Little Hurst	1	3	11	35s	3	3	7¾
Great Hurst	2	3	36	80s	11	18	0
Further Hey	1	3	15	40s	3	13	9
Three Nook'd Hey	2	0	27	60s	6	10	1½
Sand Hey	2	2	35	60s	8	2	6
Well Croft	0	3	13	60s	2	6	1½
Old Orchard	0	1	20	60s	1	2	4
Barn Meadow	1	1	05	70s	4	9	8¼
[Totals]	28	0	15		80	16	7¾
House, barn, malt kiln, fold, orchard and garden	0	3	15				
	28	3	30			£ [...]⁹⁸	

At the above valuation BTE to pay the leys.

NB Thomas Greenall advises to have a clause in the lease to reserve to myself a power to divert any brook or spring to my own use, as he says it may be of consequence hereafter.

Saturday
29 November

	£	s	d
Kill'd a cush which weigh'd 479lb at 3¼d	6	9	8¾
Tallow 18lb, suit 14lb in all 32lb at 3½d	0	8	11
Hide 65lb at 3½d	0	18	11½
[Total]	7	17	7¼

Saturday
6 December   Mrs Eliza Rigby died this day at Cowley Hill. She had scarcely breathed the fresh air for these 30 years last past. R.I.P.

Monday
15 December   Kill'd an old sow which weigh'd 23 score & 5lb.

Thomas Poole's of Scholes's receipt for touls in cattle.

Take oil of vitriol six pennyworth & ten pennyworth of oil of turpentine. Mix them togather their feet therwith.

Monday
22 December   Mrs Townley of Standish died this morning about half an hour after eight o'clock R.I.P.

	£	s	d
Kill'd a cush which weigh'd 470lb now at 3½d per lb	6	17	1
Tallow 26[lb], suit 23lb in all 49lb at 3½d per lb	0	14	3½
Hide 59lb at 3½d	0	17	2½
[Total]	8	8	7

98   Amount not entered by BTE.

1778

Sold all my cheese to Jane Moss which she begun taking away the 1st August last & continued so doing the 16th & 21st, the 2^{d}, 8th, 16th, 22^{d} & 27th September, the 3^{d} & 15th October, 10th December as follows vizt.

	Cwt	qtr	lb		Cwt	qtr	lb		Cwt	qtr	lb
6 cheeses	1	0	5	6 cheeses	1	0	17	7 cheeses	1	1	13
6 cheeses	1	0	13	6 cheeses	1	0	24	25 cheeses	4	0	23
6 cheeses	1	0	14	14 cheeses	2	1	26	36 cheeses	5	0	14
6 cheeses	1	0	10	6 cheeses	1	0	28		10	2	20
	4	1	12		6	0	5				

The aforegoing 122 cheeses weighed 21cwt 0qtr 7lb and were sold

		£	s	d
10cwt 0qtr 0lb	at 30s per cwt	15	0	0
11cwt 0qtr 7lb	at 36s per cwt	19	17	9
[Total]		34	17	9

and paid for.

Kill'd a hog which weighd 17 score 17lb or 357lb.

The following roads were measur'd by my son & Mr Meynell

	Miles	Furlongs
From Eccleston Hall door to the Broad Well Lane spring	0	2
To the 3^{d} post past the mill gate, going towards Peter Moss's	0	4
To the door of the kiln at the lower mills	0	6
To James Barton's barn	1	0
To the gate by Anne Arrowsmith's	0	2
To the 2^{d} fir tree by Davenport's large house & gate	0	4
To Sixsmith's cottage	0	6
To Kewquick's cottage, Gillars Green	0	7
To the gate by Burrow's lane facing Parkside stile, right hand	2	0
To the 3^{d} tree before Roughly's Brow House, next Holden's left hand	0	2
To the 2^{d} tree before the Tyth barn, right hand	0	4
To the further end of the Round Croft joining to New House	0	6
To the left hand tree before Ralph's Cook's first gate	3	0
To the 1st right hand hedge, dividing Mr Chorley's feilds after Pitman's	0	2

1778

	Miles	Furlongs
The corner of Ellis Glover's croft left hand	0	4
The first right hand tree school lane	0	6
A little past the Hill gates	4	0
Edward Rogerson's house gate	0	2
Mr John Travese's house	5	0
Peter Barrow's first gate on the right hand	0	2
Thomas Lyon's house gate (Lancaster's)	0	4
Entrance into William Moss's coal pitt or Wood feild or clough	0	6
The hedge that divides Gillibrand's crofts left hand	6	0
The Damn Head in the hollow of the inside of the Paddock	0	2
To Eccleston Hall door	0	4
Ditto in short		
From Eccleston Hall door to Barton's barn	1	0
To the gate facing Park side style	2	0
To the left hand tree before Ralph Cook's first gate	3	0
A little past the Hill Gates	4	0
To Mr John Traveses's house	5	0
To the hedge that devides Gillibrand's crofts left hand	6	0
To Eccleston Court gate	0	4

Kill'd a hog which weigh'd seventeen score or 340lb.

Tuesday
× *3 February* × The resevoir made in Hum Wilson's now Hunt's tenement measures 0a 3r 30p for which the proprieters of the Navigation pay at 30s per acre, £1 8s 1½d.

Henry Lyon of Eccleston agrees to build a new barn of brick set in lime & slated to be 10 yards long, 7 yards backwards & at least 5 yards to the square. The outheel to hold 4 cows & 2 horses on condition that I add him one life Gratis to his tenem^t which is to be William Hixson, his grandson, aged 5, January last eight months, he is son of William and Helen Hixson of Derby farmers.

Friday
6 February Michael Bibby informs that at the bottom of Thomas Butchard's marl pit which he made 2 years ago, they came to the crop of coals.

1778

	lb
Kill'd a cush which weigh'd	552
Tallow 22lb, Suit 12lb	34
Hide	54
[Total]	640

Saturday
28 February   Henry Kunzen perfumer, N° 4 Vere Street, Oxford Chaple the end of New Bond Street, sells the best tooth powder at 1s per box, Miss Dicconson.

Tuesday
7 July   My dear bro^r Edward Scarisbrick died this evening at nine o'clock as he was going to bed, without any agony, aged 81. Requiescat in Pace.

Mr Flask of Reading's receipt for cleaning tables & makeing them have fine glose.
2 pennyworth of alhanett root, 2 pennyworth rose pink, 1 quart of cold drawn linced oil. Mix the above together & let it stand for three days before you use it, then with a clean linen cloth rub a little over the table & let it lay for about 3 or 4 hours then rub it dry with a linen cloth.

Monday
20 July   I this day took the Oath of Allegiance at the Quarter Sessions at Prescot (being the first ever held there) before Doc^r Maisters Rector of Croston & Thomas Seal Esq. of Liverpool the 2 Justices, & it was administer'd by Mr James Taylor of Leigh, Deputy Clerk of the Peace.

Wednesday
22 July   Lent Mr Standish the 1st & 2^d vol. of Ellis's Husbandry.[99]

The dimensions of 3 rooms at Wootton belonging to Peter Holford Esq. of Warwickshire. The parlour of the inside is 10 yards & 4½ inches long, 7 yards & 4½ inches broad, the hall is 12 yards & 4½ inches long, 7 yards & 30 inches broad, the drawing room is 10 yards & 6 inches long, 7 yards & 4½ inches broad, the height is 16 to 17 feet. The walls are a yard thick.

Wednesday
19 August   The 2 works of coals given from Hatwell Heath this year were to the two widow Traveses, William Dennet & James Arrowsmith with 30 baskets each.

99 William Ellis, *Ellis's Husbandry: Abridged and Methodized: Comprehending the Most Useful Articles of Practical Agriculture* (London, 1772).

1778
Friday
2 October

Mrs Standish's receipt to make lavender water vizt.

Put 1oz of spirits of lavender, & six penyworth of amber grease to one quart of rectified spirits of wine, shake it well together keeping it warm.

Monday
5 October

This day was intirely calm & a very warm sun in so much that the cows run a gadding the same as in summer, & both them and the horses run into the water for shelter. I saw many gad flies, the wind was very nigh due North at 11 o'clock the thermometer was 5 degrees above temperate, the barometer at chang'able.

⊕ The cost of the new works at Gracious Street kiln vizt.

	£	s	d
14,200 bricks and carting	10	9	4
125 measures of lime & carting	4	3	4
4 measures Leigh at 10½d	0	3	6
10 measures hair	0	11	8
Two rods of slate and carting	3	16	0
Nine yards of ridging stones	0	7	6
Paid John Dickson carpenter	5	2	1
Carting sand & sleck	0	15	0
102 feet balk & 400 foot laths	7	12	3½
Carting of balk & laths at 1½d per foot	0	12	9
Old oak timber valued by John Dickson	9	6	0
Nails & ironwork	0	18	10
Lead	2	4	10½
William Forber's work	6	8	0
£52 11s 2d at 10 per cent is £5 5s 1d			
[Sub total]	52	11	2
Repairing & slating the old part came to	7	3	8
[Total]	59	14	10

21 November

Mrs Townley's of Chiswick's receipt for a cough vizt.

Take a piece of Burgundy pitch, the size of a nutmeg, mixed with a little peice of bee's wax and spread cold on a peice of leather the size of your hand, and place it between your shoulders and when the plaister is taken off, wash the place with warm milk & water.

Monday
23 November

My sister Mrs Palmes advis'd me the 19th instant, that she had sent by Mr William Neville £28 13s 6d of my late bro[r] Edward Scarisbrick's money to my br[r] Francis Scarisbrick of Leige.

1778

Mr Turner of Warrington's receipt for a spavin[100] vizt.

Take four pennyworth of the oil of bays, the same of the oil of swallows, the same of the oil of origanum, the same of french flies (or two pennyworth according to D[r] Tatlaw). To be made into an oinment. Let the part be well rubb'd with a roller, & the size of a nutmeg be rubbed into it every morning for eight days together, then it may be disused for four or five days and the remainder of the pot may be used.

Monday
30 November   Kill'd a hog which weigh'd 14 score 10lb besides the pluckins.

Tuesday
8 December   Kill'd a hog which weigh'd 14 score 14lb with the pluckins.

I was told by Mr Bishop at Mr Holford's Thursday 11th June last that there was a son of one N. Sherburne near Stow in the Woold, nine years of age, who weighs 15 stone 8lb and is four feet & ten inches high.

Sunday
27 December   For these five or six days past the weather has been remarkably calm & warm sun, and the barometer in the harpsicord parlour was a degree above settled fair, & that in the hall three degrees lower than very dry, which is both lower & higher than I have ever remberd before.

My son's eye water is brandy, elderflower and rose water, of each an equal quantity, mix'd, & shaked up & rub your eyes with it.

Thursday
31 December   Mr Weldon's butler came to live with me as plowboy.

1779

Saturday
2 January   Margret Lyon came to live with me as dairy maid at night.

Friday
8 January   Kill'd a hog which weighd 17 score and 2lb.

Monday
11 January

	at	£	s	d
Cost for 62lb of twine for a fish net	1s per lb	3	2	0
Paid James Dennet for kniting				
52½ yards	8d	1	15	0
Making a cod 6s, 2 lbs more twine 2s 4d yards of cord				

100 Spavin – a swelling or enlargement of the hock joint in horses.

1779
Saturday
23 January   Kill'd a hog which weighd 16 score.

	£	s	d
Wednesday			
3 February Sent to my son a six inch cart & wheels cost	18	0	11½
One double coulter'd plow on wheels	5	18	6
One large harrow & gears £9 19s 11d, 10 bushells			
small wheat £1 5s 0d	11	4	11
Un pernil de tocino, medio cochino y un Queso	35	4	4½
[A leg of pork, half a pig and a cheese][101]			

Sunday
28 February   James Arnett came at night as cowman to serve me for £8 p.a.

	£	s	d
I paid John Whitlow for the above cart	9	0	10
3cwt 3qtr 19lb iron at 17s, £3 6s 7½d, & 0cwt 3qtr 5lb			
& carriage 1s 6d at 22s per [cwt], 18s 11½d	4	5	7
More iron per Patrick & his work per bill			
31ˢᵗ October 78	4	0	11
Two pair of chains 29¾lb at 5½d per lb	0	13	7½
One double plow per bill	5	18	6

Wood for a harrow 8s and making						
a harrow 6s	0	14	0	⎫	1 17 8	
109lbs iron for [a harrow] at 22s	1	3	8	⎭		

	£	s	d
John Barlow's bill for geers			
27ᵗʰ January 1779	8	2	3
[Total]	33	19	4½

NB. As there is no particular charge in Patrick's bill for the work of the harrow, he must have charg'd it in that of the cart.

Tuesday
25 May   Poor, honest, William Forber died this day about two o'clock.

Copy of the note I sent to the Justices of my servants. Peter Johnson the steward, Joseph Howard plowman, James Wilson the groom, Jack Ashton plowboy, William Bankes that works in the garden, James Arnet cowman, John Patrick blacksmith, denominated gamekeeper.

Monday, St. Bazil
14 June   John Dickson begun pulling down the chapple end of the house.

Saturday
19 June   Stored the engine warm water pit in Dagnall's from the pit in the lane opposite James Alcock's with 1½ brace large carp and 41½ brace small carp.

101   Translation by the editors.

1779
Thursday
24 June   The foundation of the chapel end is on a sandy clay on which I put rock stones & rammed them hard down, then brick batts which were likewise beat hard down, then two rows of double ashlers, then 1 row of ashlers & the inward part next the house with bricks & both set in lime mortar.

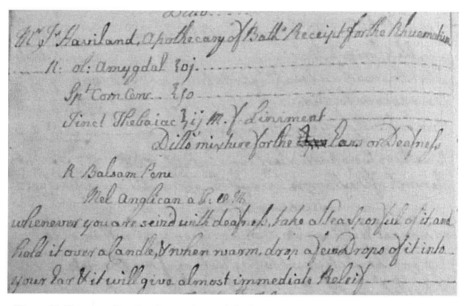

Figure 11 Two remedies, for rheumatism and deafness respectively. 'ol Amygdal' is probably almond oil. 'Thebaic' is defined in the Oxford English Dictionary as 'of or derived from opium'.

Friday
17 July   Housed all my hay being 8 loads in the very finest order without rain.

Saturday
18 July   Kill'd a pig which weighd 89 pounds, sent a side of it to Scarisbrick.

Wednesday
21 July   Found a painting on copper of the B V Mary & the infant Jesus upon the crook in the hall next to the great door which was cover'd with mortar and lay on the beam which I conjecture was put there when the house was built. × × ×

1779
Monday
26 July

The value of the bark sold to Mr John Chorley of Prescot this year was given me this day by William Moss and it amounts to £6 8s 6d.

The mare I bought of James Glover of St Helens foal'd this night a colt.

Monday
9 August

Begun cuting my wheat in the West Norley with 12 reapers & begun in the Copy Part.

Sarah Shaw came to live with me as chamber maid on Sunday 25th July.

Saturday
14 August

	Th	H	Sh
Finish'd cuting my wheat in the West Norley without a drop of rain & it contain'd	191	0	8
& I hous'd this day	47	0	0
And the tithe	19	0	0
In all	210	0	8

Thursday
19 August

Hous'd all my wheat out of the West Norley, almost without rain, there being only a kind of a dew that fell the 14th & 15th & it was all hous'd in the afternoons, & so dry that it was ready to be thresh'd out immediatly. The crops of wheat & barley this year were very great, also potatoes & the oats were tolerable.

Sunday
29 August

Had prayers in the chaple for the first time since it was altered.

Friday
3 September

The quarter cask of red port that I had from Capt Holme run to 11 dozn and 3 bottles, which I begun drinking of this day.

Tuesday
7 September

Went to Prescot to the sale of part of the Scholes's estate & John Williamson Esq. of Liverpool bought Scholes's estate contg 62 acres & let at £132 10s. The landlord paid the taxes, togather with the old mansion house & croft let for £13 0s for the sum of £4,500. I bought Giller's Green estate contg 21a 1r 29p let clear £30 for £1,120. Both the purchasers paid the new tax on auctions.

Friday
10 September

Giller's Green House measures in front 36½ feet, backwards with the downheel 38 feet and clear of it only 26 feet so it is computed to be 12 yards & 6 inches in front and 11 yards backward.

1779

Distributed this year the two works of coals from Hatwell Heath equally to Helen Hawarden, William Rigby's wife, Thomas Gower and widow of William Kilshaw.

Friday
17 September   Begun sowing wheat with two plows in the New Close.

Friday
8 October   Finish'd sowing the above feild in excelent fine order with 17½ bushells.

My son's receipt for the grease in horses, given him by Col. Stanley of Chester.
4oz rosin, 3oz saltpetre, 3oz diapente, 3 drachms of salt of tartar, powder'd & mixed in three pints of forge water, to be given fasting. If it does not move the swelling give a second.

The sweet scent'd shrub on the mosses, vulgarly call'd Heath Gale, is Candle Berry Myrtle, and call'd by Mr Leigh M.D. that writes on Cheshire, Lancashire & Derbyshire, Dutch Myrtle.[102]

Friday
15 October   The Rever^d Mr Sewell of Prescot, call'd on me this morning & said he would have the following words inserted in his own writing to the receipt he gives me for the tithes vizt. Rec^d the above sum for small tithes of the demesne that respect not articles of modern introduction or cultivation & for such tithes only as are above expressly specified in respect to the Lordship & Manor.

The Rever^d Mr Sewell's receipt for making Norfolk or milk punch. Take 20 quarts of best brandy & put into it the peels of 30 Seville oranges & 24 lemons pared very thin. Infuse them 24 hours of water that has been boiled & stood till it is cold, 30 quarts. Put into the water 15lb of double refin'd sugar, & when it is dissolved mix the water and brandy together, having first strain'd it from the peels of the oranges & lemons. Then put it into a cask having first rinced it with the brandy then put in one quart of orange juice & one quart of lemon juice, & stir it well. Lastly put in one quart of new milk, as warm as when taken from the cow, stir it well & stop it close, & let it stand six weeks in the cask. Then bottle it & it will keep many years, the older the better it is. NB the later end of February is the best time to make it.

The late Mrs Astrea Hill's receipt for to dry ripe morella or other quick tasted cherries without sugar, so as to retain their own natural relish.

---

102   Charles Leigh, M.D., *The Natural History of Lancashire, Cheshire, and the Peak in Derbyshire* (Oxford, 1700).

1779

Put them into a tin plate made in the shape of a brass scale, & full of holes, like a cullender, let them down by the strings into a fine serving pan full of boiling water, & keep them there for a minuet or two, or till the skins begin a little to crack, & then lift them out at once. Note the skins, by being a little broken or shrivell'd, make such way for the moistures exhaling as prevents any danger of mouldiness in the course of their drying. As soon as the hot water is drain'd back, place the cherires (not to toutch one another) upon tables, or small wicker frames, to be set out to the sun & wind. They should be turn'd once a day, & taken in before sunset, or against rainy weather. It wou'd be (tho' not absolutely necessary) to hang net work flat over the frames, within an inch or two of the fruit to keep flies &c. away. And when the cherries are shrunk into the dryness of a raisin, they are in order for puting up, which will be in 3 or 4 days, or a week, as the sun shines hoter or fainter. They shou'd be kept in glasses, paper'd over, & if press'd down closely together they will hold good for years in perfection. Two days before they are to be used, they must be steep'd in as much luke warm water as they will suck up at two or three times, till it covers them and then baked, with that liquor amongst them. NB Peaches, apricots, plumbs, grapes, or any other sort of fruit may be managed & preserv'd the same way without the smallest assistance of sugar.

Friday
15 October

To salt a hog.
Take a stone of salt, half a stone of course brown sugar, 6 ounces of salt prunella, a quarter pound of salt petre, take the half quantity & rub it well on & let it lye a week, then turn it, & at a fortnight's end, rub on the remainder. Let it lye a week, then turn them again, and let them lye a month or five weeks, keeping them frequently rubing with the brine.
For beef, rub it over with brown sugar, let it lye two days with the sugar only, then take 1oz saltpetre, 3oz salarmoniac, 1oz common salt and mix them all together & let them lye before the fire, & rub the beef with them, when they are hot.

2 & 7
November

I saw a swallow fly merrily about this day Tuesday.

Tuesday
2 November

I ground 4 bushells of wheat, out of which was taken some fine flour about a load & the rest made 207 loaves & gave beside 4s 10d to 58 persons in all 265 persons.

1779
Monday
8 November   Deliver'd Robert Moss Esq., Mr Tomkinson's oppinion concerning small tithes.

Friday
12 November   Killed a hog which weigh'd 19 score & 12lb.

Friday
26 November   Killed a hog which weigh'd 16 score & 12lbs.

Saturday
11 December

	£	s	d
The stone drains in the 1st & 2d Old Jones's are 190 rods of spit drains at 4d, & seven large drains at 8d cost	3	8	0
In the West Norley 64 small & 30 large at 4d & 8d cost	2	6	8
Besides 3 men 4 days at 1s 4d in the old pitt sough	0	16	0
In the Stable Croft 33½ & 1 yard small & 2 large at 4d & 8[d]	0	12	6½
In the Cow Pasture 12½ small 11½ large & 6 very difficult 10d	0	16	10
Besides 1 man 11 days in very difficult work at 1s 4d	0	14	8
In the bowling green in the garden 27 small, supervisor 6s	0	15	0
The cost besides the stone & carting	9	9	8½

The valuation of Gillar's Green Estate per Richard Greenall

	a	r	p	at	£	s	d
Further Long Hey	1	0	31	23s	1	7	3
Nearer Long Hey	0	2	22	23s	0	14	8
Further Hill	2	0	14	27s	2	16	3½
Spring Croft	0	3	17	30s	1	5	8
Further Meadow	2	2	04	36s	4	10	10½
Nearer Hill	2	3	04	22s	3	1	0
Nearer Meadow	2	1	20	40s	5	5	0
Feild below the Wood	1	1	16	21s	1	8	4
Wood	1	1	37				
Fern Croft	1	0	25	22s	1	5	5½
Hurst Wood Meadow	1	1	03	25s	1	11	8
Brick Kiln Croft	1	1	05	30s	1	18	5
Meadow at back of the house	1	3	19	45s	4	4	0
House, housing & Lane	0	1	32				
Barn Croft	0	0	18				
[Total]	21	1	27		29	8	7½

The tenant to pay the leys & taxes & keep it in repair.

1779
Friday
17 December   Killed a hog which weighed 17 score & 16lb.

Wednesday
22 December   Kill'd a cow which weighd 884lb vizt. the quarters 712lb, tallow
27[lb], suet 28lb hide 117lb in all 884lb at 3½d per lb, £12 17s
10d.

1780

Monday
17 January   Kill'd a hog which weighed 18 score & 12 pounds.

Sold to Jane Moss, last week my cheese which weigh'd as
followeth vizt.

	Cwt	qtr	lb
7 cheeses weigh'd	1	0	15
7 cheeses weigh'd	1	0	17
7 cheeses weigh'd	1	0	17
7 cheeses weigh'd	1	0	20
7 cheeses weigh'd	1	0	16
7 cheeses weigh'd	1	0	15
7 cheeses weigh'd	1	0	12
7 cheeses weigh'd	1	0	10
4 cheeses weigh'd	0	2	16
60 cheeses weigh'd	9	2	13
7 cheeses weigh'd	1	0	17
8 cheeses weigh'd	1	0	24
7 cheeses weigh'd	1	0	15
7 cheeses weigh'd	1	0	8
7 cheeses weigh'd	1	0	8
7 cheeses weigh'd	1	0	10
7 cheeses weigh'd	1	0	18
7 cheeses weigh'd	1	0	19
3 cheeses weigh'd	0	2	2
60 cheeses weigh'd	9	1	29
[Total]	19	0	12 at 25s per cwt £23 17s 6d

Richard Greenall's valuation of Edward Rogerson's

	a	r	p		£	s	d
House, barn, fold, orchard							
& garden	0	1	0		0	10	0
Barn Hey	1	2	30	[at] 75s	6	6	6
Smithy Hey & Smithy	1	1	12	[at] 60s	3	19	2

1780

	a	r	p		£	s	d
Higher Meadow	1	1	26	[at] 37s	2	12	2
Lower Meadow	1	0	37	[at] 55s	3	11	6
Higher Feild	1	2	08	[at] 38s	2	18	11
Lower Feild	1	0	0	[at] 42s	2	2	0
Spout Feild & Entry	1	2	14	[at] 40s	3	3	6
Spout lands in two parts:							
Higher feild	1	0	09				
Middle feild	0	2	02	[at] 48s }	5	3	10
Meadow	0	2	15				
[Sub total]					30	7	7
Hollands Nook's, demesne	3	0	0	[at] 45s	6	15	0
Clear yearly rent					37	2	7

The Landlord to keep the buildings in repair & the tenant to pay the taxes.

Monday
24 January

Agreed to allow Richard Greenall an abatement of £14 in his last year's rent & to continue the same to him if markets doth not rise p.a., & when they do he is to pay the old rent of £94 instead of £80.

Saturday
5 February

My son & I drew this day on Messrs Arthur Haywood Sons for £830 upon demand to cary 5 per cent. No time mentiond when we are to refund it.

Friday
24 March

Kill'd a cow which weigh'd 922lb, Dick Downal said she was the fatest he had ever kill'd & that she wou'd sell in Liverpool at 5d per lb. The tallow was 46lb, suit 60lb, hide 94lb, the quarters 722lb in all 922lb.

Tuesday
28 March

The measurement of the roof of my house by John Dickson.

	feet	by	feet	feet	Rod & ¼	feet
Over the chapel	41		21	1,722	4¼	22
The hall	36		15	1,080	2½	80
Mr Meynell's	51		18	1,836	4½	36
The study	61		13	1,588	3¾	88
My room	27		18	972	2¼	72
The staircase	16		13	208	0½	08
The laundry	24		16	768	1¾	68

You multiply as followeth, example 41 by 21 makes 861. You double that to make good both sides, which produces 1,722 feet which devided by 400 makes 4¼ rods & 22 feet.

1780
Thursday
30 March   John Liptrot, of Sutton, came to aquaint me this day, that he will give up both the estates he holds of me in Suttton, May come 12 months 1781.

Friday
31 March   Kill'd a hog which weigh'd 12 score & 16lb.

Friday
7 April   Put into the Great Damn 128 brace of small carp that came from Aston.

Saturday
8 April   Put into the Great Damn 177 brace of same sized carp and from Aston.

Thursday
20 April   Agreed to take of Richard Greenall 100 measures of malt at 5s per meas^r, and he to keep it, then I have occassion for it.

               Poor Mr Thomas Conyers died this afternoon about 6 o'clock R I P.

Monday
24 April   And he was buried this morning at Windleshaw Chappel.

               Sent 5 new gates with stoops to Giller's Green estate, one of the best & four of the common sorts. NB there are 13 gates in all.

Friday
28 April   Bottled of a quarter cask of red port which run to 10 doz^n & 3 bottles. NB I had made use of some of it when in the cask as my wine was out.

Wednesday 3
Thursday 4
May   My bay cart mare was cover'd both these days by a bay horse with a star in his forehead & one white leg behind, 15 hands high & 15 years old, an old hunter bred on Martin Muir, & now comes from Longridge Fells. ⊕

               I made the following stone drains at the top of the Middle Crow Feild & some three in the feild above it vizt.

	£	s	d
30 rods large at 8d & 116 rods small at 4d	2	18	8
In Ned Rogerson's old Meadow & Smithy Hey	2	8	4
58 rods large & deep at 10d			

Saturday
13 May   I bought & paid for the following at Mr Thomas Conyers's sale this day vizt.

1780

	£	s	d
A punch bowl	1	3	0
Japan'd bread basket	0	3	6
White snap table	0	3	4
1¹⁹⁄₄ sqr D. table cloth	0	10	0
[Sub total]	1	19	10
2¾ table cloths	0	10	0
6 breakfast table cloths Huch	0	5	0
2 pair fine sheets	2	7	0
1 pair steps or cricket	0	0	9½
[Sub total]	3	2	9½
1 large step ladder	0	6	6
1 large step ladder less	0	2	2
1 saddle & cloth	0	16	0
[Sub total]	1	4	8
Brought over the amount of Mr Conyers's sale	6	7	3½
I bought a dresser, which when deliver'd, I must pay for it	0	14	0
A marble mortar	0	6	0
[Total]	7	7	3½

Tuesday
20 June

I begun striping my room to the court side, in order to new slate the whole house. The people employ'd were John Dickson & his three sons, William Forber, his son George and his apprentice.

My bay cart mare was cover'd again by the same horse.

Sunday
25 June

My bay cart mare was cover'd again by the above horse.

Friday
30 June

The leaden cistern sent to John Hatton's weighed 1cwt 3qtr 1lb.

Wednesday
5 July

Begun mowing the Avenue, & then shall go on mowing the rest.

Monday
31 July

Drew the Horse Pool & stored from thence the following waters vizt.

Great Damn with	100 brace small carp
Higher Crow feild	5 brace small carp
Greenall's Furthest Wood	6 brace small carp
Wall Pond	17½ couple of tench^s
Tench pond in the garden	10 couple of tench^s

1780
Monday
17 August

Fish'd & emptied the Little Damn & took out
of it carp   161 brace
and sent to Scarisbrick 20 brace, Cowley Hill ⎫
1 Mr Shoare 1 two eels Messrs Orrell 1 B W ⎪
ditto Parson Johnson 1 ditto Parson Sewell ⎬ 30 brace
1 ditto Atherton 1 ditto Makin 1 ditto Chorley ⎪
1 ditto Weldon and R^d Greenall between them ⎪
1 ditto in all 30 brace[103]   ⎭
_____
120 brace remain

There was a large quantity of eels, some I took for the house use
and gave others to the fishers, the rest I sold at 3d per lb which
made £1 3s 5½d.

Thursday
31 August

I begun reaping the following feilds of wheat, barley, & oats on
Wednesday 23^d ins^t and hous'd them all in the finest condition
this day vizt.

	a	r	p	threaves	sheafs	Tythe threaves	Tythe sheafs
New Meadow wheat	6	1	38	202	13	18	13
				18	13		
[Sub total]				184	0		
West Norley: barley	2	0	0	104	04		
West Norley: oats	5	1	38	240	16		

Distributed the 2 works of coal from Hatwell Heath equally to
Isabel Knowles Prescot, Robert Dicconson Brown Edge, Widow
Howard Eccleston, Widow Bromilow Thatwell Heath.

23 September

Settled as under with Richard Johnson for 3 years value £150

	£	s	d
Receiv'd at his 1st sale in cash	36	19	5
A pair of wheels & an iron axle tree	7	0	0
Work done as per bill	1	0	0
Allow'd him for building & repairs	31	0	0
Receiv'd cash at his 2^d sale	15	3	4
Allow'd him for marling	32	0	0
Wheat, barley, & oats per bill	11	7	0
Straw 13s 6d work & carting per bill 13s	1	6	6
Wheat valued on the ground to	10	10	0
[Total]	146	6	3
Due from William Wilcock paid 2^d December ditto	1	4	0

103 The meaning of this entry is unclear therefore transcribed verbatim.

1780
Saturday
30 September　Sold to Richard Greenall 12 threave of wheat, which produced £7 10s 2d & of light about 2 measures for which he has paid.

Monday
16 October　Robert Moss Esq. of Sanhills receipt for the tread of a horse. Take Roman vitriol & pound it to a fine powder, then boil some buttermilk, & take of the head of it & mix it with the powder & make a pultass of it, & apply it to the place effected & tie a flannel round it, & repeat it then it is well, which will be in a short time.

Monday
30 October　I put into the Little Damn 49 brace of carp, about seven inches long.

Thursday
2 November　Ground three bushells of small wheat which were made into 343 loaves & given this day to the poor & a measure of flour to Peggy Bankes.

Saturday
4 November　Kill'd two hogs one was 14 score 2lb the other 12 score 11lb in all 26 score 13 pounds.

Tuesday
14 November　Sold my dairy of cheese of thirteen cows to Jane Moss, which weigh'd as follow'ths.

Cheeses	Cwt	qtr	lb
7	1	0	19
5	1	0	6
6	1	0	11
6	1	0	24
6	1	0	20
6	1	0	7
6	1	0	10
6	1	0	16
6	1	0	2
6	1	0	22
60	11	0	17
7	1	0	11
7	1	0	19
7	1	0	3
6	1	0	10
6	1	0	24
6	1	0	4
7	1	0	13

1780

Cheeses	Cwt	qtr	lb
6	1	0	9
6	1	0	6
5	1	0	9
63	10	3	9
123 in all	21	3	26

at 25s, £27 9s 2d

NB 6 weeks at the end of summer proved very hot & sultry & burn'd up the grass which made the cows go much of their milk. The begining of the year was very cold, & scarcely any summer, then the hot weather came, tho' the cows during that time gave very well of milk.

Saturday
25 November   Kill'd a pig which weigh'd 64lb, the head 7lb, in all 71lb.

Saturday
9 December   Kill'd a pig which weighed 74lb.

Saturday
16 December   Kill'd a hog which weighd 15 score & 11lb.

							£	s	d
Let to Andrew Valentine, part of Holland House's garden							1	11	5½
	a	r	p		£	s	d		
Higher Feild	1	2	8	at 75s	5	16	3		
Dicconson's	2	0	26	at 45s	4	17	3½	10 13 6½	
He is to clear the above & pay for it								12	5	0
I have also let										
him Holland's										
Nooks	3	0	0	at 45s	which I clear			6	15	0
[Total]								19	0	0

Saturday
23 December   Kill a hog which weigh'd 13 score & 3lb.

Kill'd a cow which weigh'd 424lb, hide 60lb, tallow 20lb, suit 16lb, 520lb.

1781

Monday
8 January   I promis'd to allow John Liptrot thirty tons of soaper's waste & he is to buy at his own cost twenty tons more to add to it. He wants a carthouse & well. NB He said soaper's waste was 5s 6d per ton.

1781
Saturday
20 January   Kill'd a hog which weigh'd 16 score.

Friday
26 January   The post did not arrive then 8 o'clock at night on acc^t of the snow.

Saturday
27 January   Killed a hog which weigh'd 15 score & 9½lb.

⊗^{104}*Saturday*
3 February   Bought a bay mare with a star & four white feet, 15½ hands high, rising six, this grass of John Tyrer of the Kiln House Eccleston for £12 12s 0d.

Saturday
17 March   Paid Mr James Orrell one year's interest of £300 due to the executors of the late Mr James Bastwell the 15th September last £15 0s 0d.

                 NB I gave him a bill of £23 & he is to return the ballance which is paid.

12 April   Kill'd a cow (a megg Harry) proved very ordinary beef, & weighed the quarters 764lb, hide 105lb, tallow 40lb, suet 18lb in all 927lb.

5 July   Cost of my engine for boreing.

	£	s	d
Timber £2 10s, iron work £7 16s 11d, three legs & a block £1 2s	11	8	11
Henry Bell 17s 6d, Latham & Dicksons all carpinters £1 3s 9d	2	1	3
[Total]	13	10	2

                 NB Henry Bell had his board for six days.

Saturday
12 August   The weather had been so dry, & little grass springing in the hills & no honey falls, that I turn'd all the score into the Norley, & five heifers & six young calves of my own into the fog^{105} in the Paddock, & my milch cows into the second crop of glover [*sic*] in the West Norley.

Friday
2 November   I grounded 2 bushells of small wheat & with some flour at home, I made them into 307 loaves, & gave 4s 8d in money which makes

---

104 BTE emphasises this date with twelve '⊕' symbols.
105 One definition of 'fog' given by the Oxford English Dictionary is 'The grass that springs up immediately after the hay-crop has been taken off, aftermath.'

1781

in all 363 which was given to as many poor persons, & I gave Margaret Bankes my gardener's wife a bushell of wheat.

Saturday
17 November   Receiv'd of Jane Moss for 66 cheeses weighing 16cwt 3qtr 24lb at £1 7s per cwt, £22 17s 9d.

Wednesday
21 November   Kill'd a hog which weighed 15 score & 11lb.

Sent my harpsicord to Standish, which I have lent to my daughter Standish.

Planted the following.

15 apple & [...][106] pear trees at the Yew Tree Farm in Eccleston late Anne Seddon's, & now in possession of Joseph Bankes.

1.	Great Rarmbert
2.	Royal Pearmain
3.	London Pippin
4.	Dutton's Virgin
5.	White Coolin
6.	Palm Apple
7.	Winter Virgin
8.	Nonsuch Apple
9. & 10.	Two New Biggins
11.	Kentish Filbasket
12.	Herefordshire Pearmain
13.	Ribston Pippin
14.	Minchal Crab
15.	Doctor Bernard's Baker

[Pears]

1.	Hampton Burgunday Pear
2.	Aston Town
3.	Catharine

Friday
30 November   Killed a hog which weighed sixteen score 3lb.

Friday
7 December   Killed a seg whose quarters weigh'd 802lb, suet & tallow 68lb, hide 118lb in all 988lb.

---

106 Detail not entered, presumably BTE intended to enter '3' here, being the number of varieties of pear trees listed.

1782

Friday
4 January

Killed a cow whose quarters weighd 860lb, suet & tallow 95lb, hide 93lb in all 1,048lb.

+ Sold to George Rice the 14th ulto 24 alders & 5 ashes which grew about the furthest pit in the Cow pasture for £12 12s to be paid for on or before the 25th March next. It was something more than 10d per foot. **+** Paid.

Monday
7 January

Mr Standish's receipt for painting out of doors. ⊖⊖⊖
Take 20lb of white sand well washed, 3lb of white lead, & of oil what will be sufficient, and if you think the colour too white, mix occar with it according to your liking.

Tuesday
15 January

Killed a hog which weigh'd 15 score & 1lb.

Friday
25 January

Killed a hog which weigh'd 16 score & 14lb.

NB John Barnes's estate in Sutton, call'd Tickles, he let to Mr Platt at £54 p.a. & Platt let it to Thomas Birchall at £85 and the copper comp^y[107] agreed to pay Birchal £200 in hand & take it for the remaining part of the term which was nine years. When I leased it, it was only let at £28 p.a. & the Lord's rent was £18, so there only remain'd £10 p.a. out of it which the leys & taxes were to be paid.

Monday
28 January

Ralph Higgison came this evening to live with me as gardener at £12 12s p.a.

NB Planted in the beginning of this month, the further dingle or pit in the Cow pasture with 64 Lombardy Poplars, 48 Planted Huntington Willows and 237 cuttings of Huntington Willows, in all 349.

Monday
18 February

John Woods's tenem^t in Eccleston, call'd Tyth Barn Farm, contains 13a 2r 33p & was set by Mr John Ford of Ormskirk to sundries for £36 10s p.a. & my dear son is willing that I let it to my trusty servant Peter Johnson for his life for £21 p.a. and that I may likewise settle upon my serv^t Margret Talbot £10 p.a. for her life, as likewise upon my serv^t Mary Seddon £5 p.a. for her life.

107   The Copper Company – The Parys Mine Company, see entry 2 Jan. 1783.

1782
ΘΘΘΘ   Planted last month in late Joseph Houghton's Moss Feild in the Watery Lane containing 2a 0r 30p the following: 430 oaks, 405 firs, 314 elms, 41 willows, 414 beeches, in all 1,604. NB for the above feild I was only offer'd 30s p.a. for the price it was then let for.

25 February   Planted in late Joseph Houghton's Moss Feild Watery Lane which is 0a 2r 25p and valued at 15s p.a. the price it was let for: 200 poplars, 100 sycamores, 100 ashes and 94 alders, 83 willows, in all 577 plants.

Friday
8 March   I had three young stirks[108] died this day by eating the clipings of yew, & three others were very ill, but by pouring into them oil & goose grease they recover'd.

Good Friday
29 March   I had this day 360 peace egg gatherers to whom I gave 15s.

NB In Samuel Ball's lease Nº 43 dated 25 March 1769, it is mention'd to contain one dwelling house 3 bays with a kitchen adjoining, one stable containing one bay adjoining Crouchley barn, one smithy & hovell, & one barn containing one bay, all which is now held by the late John Whitlow's heir, (except the 3 tonns & the garden) & contains the following: four small new houses adjoining the Sun Ale House, Samuel Appleton's & a stable by Croutchley's barn.

Monday
26 August   Agreed with Mr Nicholas Sewell for the house & grounds where Henry Edwards lives for £200, he to receive this year's rent and the purchase to be paid the 2ᵈ February next.

The late Mr Thomas Lyon's tenemᵗ farm'd by James Alcock was valued by Richard Greenall as followeth

	a	r	p	at	£	s	d
House, barn, cowhouse, orchᵈ & garden	0	1	31		0	12	6
Back Side Hey	1	3	34	45s	4	8	4¾
Parlour Hey	1	0	0	45s	2	5	0
+ Well Meadow	1	3	18	30s	2	15	10½
Long Meadow	1	1	0	25s	1	11	3
Cow Hey	2	2	8	42s	5	7	1
Coalpitt Feild	3	1	24	42s	7	2	9½
Gorsey Brow	3	0	0	40s	6	0	0

108 Stirk – A young bullock or heifer, usually between one and two years old.

1782

	a	r	p	at	£	s	d
Charcoal Feild	1	2	26	40s	3	6	6
+ Three Rod Land	0	3	27	15s	0	13	9¼
+ Little Carr	0	1	26	30	0	12s	4½
+ Nearer Little Feild	1	0	0	15	0	15s	0
Alder Walks	1	3	26	36	3	8s	10
Further Little Feild	0	3	34	38	1	16s	6¾
Middle Little Feild	1	1	18	40	2	14s	6
+ Carr Lane	1	3	06	30	2	13s	7½
Moss Feild	2	2	28	28	3	14s	10¾
[Total]	28	0	26		49	18	11½

Leys to be deducted, & the house, out housing, gates, pails, walls &c. to be kept in tenantly repair by the landowner - but if any money is advanced in draining, clearing or ditching to have so much for it as may be agreed upon.

NB the above feilds mark'd with a + to be cover'd with water if agreeable

	a	r	p	£	s	d
Part of Well Meadow about	0	3	0	1	2	6
Three Rod Land	0	3	27	0	13	9¼
Little Carr	0	1	26	0	12	4½
Nearer Little Feild	1	0	0	0	15	0
Carr Lane	1	3	6	2	13	7½
[Total]	4	3	19	5	17	3¼

Monday
26 August

Agreed with James Alcock for part of late Mr Lyon's tenem^t for £40 p.a. clear of all leys & taxes, for nine years BTE to allow him for the first three years 20 tons of soaper's waste annually, & Alcock to find 30 tons more annualy for the said first three years. BTE to do all necesary ditching & Alcock afterwards to keep all the ditches and hedges & gates in good repair, & to keep the ground clear of all gorse, alders & all other rubish, not to plow more then three acres in any one year without leave in writing, nor to stuble, or burn any part, to attend the court. BTE to have liberty of geting coal or cannel[109] or any other mineral or sand paying trespass & of planting any waste part of the ground or cops. Pay days 29th September & 2^d February & term for nine years. BTE to have free liberty of hunting, coursing, shooting, fishing &c. not fulfilling the covenants the articles to be void.

---

109 Cannel – fine-textured soft, black coal that burns with a bright flame.

1782
Wednesday
18 September   Peter Johnson agreed with Mathew Plumbley that he should hold the estate his late father held containing 4a 2r 4p for £10 p.a. clear of all leys & taxes.

Saturday
12 October   Miss Porter of Bath's receipt to make lavender water.

To a pint & a half of rectified spirits of wine, put a quarter of an ounce of chemical oil of lavender drops & upon a large lump of sugar. Put the sugar into the spirits for some hours. When taken out, stop it up very close, and it improves by keeping.

Mr Standish's hozier is Mr Marsh in The Strand near Temple Bar, London.

Wednesday
23 October   Settled with Mr William Shaw in the following manner.

	£	s	d
For the ballance of	224	6	6
Allowed him for his great improvements	120	0	0
His share of 7 acres of wheat computed at	60	0	0
For 22 thousand of bricks I had of him at 8s per	8	16	0
The ballance he is to pay me	35	10	6
[Total]	224	6	6

NB if the wheat is valued at above £12 per acre he is to have the surplus.

23 October   Agreed with Adam Crompton to let him the grounds lately held by Mr William Shaw of Prescot, containing 40a 3r 24p for fourteen years for £105 p.a. To plow no stuble nor push nor burn, but may plow 10 acres annually, & I am to allow him £5 yearly for manure, he also adding £5 more yearly to it. Pay days 29th September & 2d Febuary. The last year of his term to have no more wheat growing then [...]110 & to leave his dung on the premises.

Saturday
26 October   Let to Henry Edwards the house & land where Thomas Houghton formerly lived at £8 8s clear of all leys & taxes.

Tuesday
29 October   Killed a cow whose quarters weigh'd 590lb, tallow 57lb, suet 30lb and the hide 97lb in all 774lb.

---

110 Detail not entered by BTE.

1782
Saturday
2 November   Gave this day 320 loaves & money to 39 more, in all 359 poor persons.

Thursday
14 November   Mr John Chorley paid this day for the bark of the trees fallen by my son £100 & for some scrubs that I fell £1 15s all making £101 15s, which I paid to Peter Johnson for my son's use.

Saturday
16 November   Kill'd a hog which weighed 15 score & 2lb.

Saturday
23 November   Kill'd a hog which weighed seventeen score & 2lb.

Wednesday
27 November   Sold Jane Moss 109 cheeses weighing 1 ton 2cwt 0q 25lb at 35s per cwt, £38 17s 3½d[111]. I milked fourteen, & sometime fifteen, cows. NB I kept thirty-eight cheeses for my own use.

Friday
20 December   Kill'd a hog which weigh'd fifteen score.

Friday
27 December   Kill'd a cow, whose quarters weigh'd 856lb, tallow 69lb, suit 39lb & hide 102lb in all 1,066lb.

1783

Thursday
2 January   Killd a bull whose quarters weigh'd 738lb, hide 118lb fat, 25lb in all 881lb which I distributed amongst the poor of this township according to the numbers they were in each family, & those that had no beef, & whose families consisted of only two or three, I gave them 2s per family, & those that were only one I gave them 1s. The hide made 24s 6d, the fat 5s 8½d, £1 10s 2½d.

NB The Paris Mine Co.[112] paid Mr Thomas Tetlaw & Thomas Makin for the remainder of the term in late James Williamson's tenement for the goodwill thereof the sum of £100 and pays £28 p.a. rent, and for the goodwill of late Mr Daniel Lawton's £50 and pays £16 p.a. rent, and to Mr Thomas West for the remainder of the lease of late Johnathan Tyrer's for the good will thereof £42 and pays £9 p.a. to Martha Tyrer & her heirs.

111 £38 17s 3½d has been crossed out and the £ sign over-written probably with pd, but this is not entirely clear.
112 The Parys Mine Co – Paris Mine Company, mined copper ore on Parys Mountain, Anglesey, and set up a smelting works at Ravenhead, St Helens. See J.R. Harris, *The Copper King: a Biography of Thomas Williams of Llanidan* (Liverpool U.P., 1964).

1783
Friday
17 January   Kill'd a hog which weigh'd 18 score & 16lb.

Saturday
8 February   Deliver'd to Mr John Chorley of Prescot to negotiate for me two
                 bills drawn by James Morton of Liverpool, on Samuel Bevington
                 of London, the one drawn 26th December last at two months due
                 1st March for £20 0s 0d, the other 9th January at 75 days after date
                 due 28 March £20 14s 6d. NB Mr Chorley return'd me the above
                 two bills the same day advising me to negotiate them.

                 A clause to be inserted in a lease.
                 To quit the premises on Candlemass day after six months notice
                 in writing &c. and in case the said NN refuse so to do, then it
                 shall & may be lawful to & for the said BTE to enter into & take
                 possession of the said premises in such manner as he shall think
                 proper without being lyable as a trespasser for so doing.

Saturday
8 March   Yesterday's post did not come in than about 8 o'clock this
                 morning, on accot of the deep snow.

Tuesday
22 April   This year wheat sold per bushell of 70lb weight from 9s 6d to
                 10s, barley per Winchester bushell at 6s, 6s 6d & some at 7s. Seed
                 oats 4s 6d, oat meal 42s per load & malt from 46s to 52s per load
                 & our country cheese at 35s per hundred of 120lb & potatoes at
                 3s per bushell to 3s 6d or 4s.

Friday
16 May   Mr Wyndham of Worksup Manour told me that one Mr
                 Drinkwater builded a mill nine sash windows in front, which
                 frontes the sea, has only three pair of French stones in it & employs
                 only three millers, and that it grinds in twelve hours sixty quar-
                 ters, or four hundred & eighty bushells of wheat, that vessels of
                 three hundred tons can anchor at the Mill door. It is scituated at
                 a place call'd Sisenhurst about five miles from Chichester Sussex,
                 and when the tide comes in, it grinds with a horizontal wheel.[113]
                 Drinkwater broke by living too well, and treating with French
                 wines, so that it is now let to one Coots who pays £10 rent per
                 week for it and does all repairs.

Wednesday
28 May   My bay mare foaled a filly with a white roach.

---

113 BTE is referring to Sidlesham Mill, built in 1755 on the site of an earlier mill. Eccleston's
     description of the mill and its ownership were accurate, but the location details were not. K.M.
     Newbury, 'Sidlesham Mill,' *West Sussex History* no. 20, pp. 5–10.

1783
Saturday
6 September

The last season prov'd very unfavourable, all kinds of grain and potatoes both scarce & dear. Wheat sold at 10s per bushell of 70lb, barley 6s 6d to 7s per bushell, oat meal 40s & 42s per load, potatoes 3s & 3s 6d per bushell. That the poor were much distress'd, but a subscription was open'd and you will see hereafter what each one contributed to the support of them. Now this year the crops of corn & potatoes have been remarkably good, & all that was housed ten days ago were in fine order, but since the weather broke, & has continued so & this day was very remarkable for a very wet forenoon & afterwards a most violent tempest of wind which continued then 9 at night & it blew down some twenty rods of the Norley troughs next to the Paddock & some of my trees. Hay grass was very thin throughout the county.

Mr Trapps of Nidd, Yorkshire. An excelent receipt for the jaundice or a belious complaint.

Take of groundsel, dandelion, chickweed & celandine of each one handful, bruised, & put into three pints of water, & boiled down to a quart. Take of this decoction one tea cupfull morning & evening with one teaspoonfull of brandy in each dose.

An account of what was subscribed in 1782 towards the relief of the poor in Eccleston and the subscriber's names vizt.

	£	s	d
BTE	21	0	0
Mrs Eccleston of Cowley Hill	6	6	0
Miss Bold of Bold who farmes the Great Tyths	3	3	0
Lord Derby per Mr Wareing his steward	2	2	0
Mrs Williamson who owns Scholes	2	2	0
Richard Greenall who rents the mills	2	2	0
Margret Liptrot a rack tenant	0	10	6
Peter Moss owner of different tenements	1	11	6
Jane Moss his sis[r] a shopkeeper	1	1	0
Robert Myers sen[r] formerly a blacksmith	1	1	0
William Brighouse owner of a small tenement	0	10	6
Mrs Allison a widow & rents the late James Greenough's	0	10	6
Mr John Davenport of Sennacres	0	5	0
Henry Lyon owner of a small tenement	0	2	6
Mr Weldon, of Scholes, Presb[r]	0	10	6
John Plumb, owner of a small tenement	0	5	0
George Rice, land of inheritance	2	2	0
William Sadler, both lands and tenements	2	2	0
Thomas Making Esq., lands	1	1	0

1783

	£	s	d
John Woods, tanner, lands	0	10	6
Peter Johnson, steward, tenements	1	1	0
Paris Mine C°. or the copper works	2	2	0
Rachel Dagnall, comb maker	0	10	6
Mr John Chorley of Prescot, a small tenement	1	1	0
Mr Hunt of Liverpool, the Anchor, a large tenement	0	10	6
Mr Thomas West tenant to George Rice	1	1	0
Mr Atherton tenant at late Thomas Holding's	0	1	6
Mrs Jane Helme housekeeper at Scholes	0	1	0

Thursday
11 September   Agreed with Robert Bankes of the Yew Tree House for the Moss Meadow lately holden by the late Doc^r Leafe, deceased, for £6 p.a. to allow him £3 for ridding & ditching the same & liberty to plow it for two years to bring it into condition. Also the two feilds that Joseph Hewitt holds for £10 p.a. & after two years to have liberty to plow one acre annually, but never to plow the Great Moss Meadow.

The tempest of wind on Saturday afternoon the 6th ins^t brought with it a great quantity of sea spray which fell on the west side of the hedges & trees, & kill'd the leaves & made them appear as after a very hard frost in winter, the alders & thorns seem'd to have suffer'd the most.

Monday
29 September   I never remember'd so early a harvest, all kinds of grain being generaly got in, the begining of housing was very fine weather, then we had rain for some ten days which was succeeded by very fine, warm, sunshine which put the summer works into fine order & promises a very fine wheat seeding.

Cost of my little vault & iron door

	£	s	d
1,400 bricks 11s 3d, 2½ bushells of lime 1s 8d	0	12	11
Brick setter, carpinter & laboures	1	1	2
2 common locks 7s, a brass padlock 9s, painting 1s 11d	0	17	11
An iron door £3 15s, a set of pigeon holes £1 18s	5	13	0
[Total]	8	5	0

The late Mr Falconer, missioner of the West Indies, receipt for the rhuematism.

Ung. altheq ⅓ and diaplasma make a plaister of it and put it on the place effected and let it remain on & gives ease.

1783

Cost of my gates & pillars at the bottom of the Avenue

	£	s	d
Stone for the pillars £2 11s, working up the stone £7 19s	10	10	0
Wood for the gates & posts £2 15s, working up wood £7 9s 8d	10	4	8
Iron work £2 3s, painting £1 10s 2d, four magpies 4s	1	14	2
2 flower de luces 5s 3d[114], 2 locks & 6 keys 10s	0	15	0
[Total][115]	23	3	10

Monday
3 November   Ground 3 bushells of wheat & barley & made it into 314 loaves & gave in money 7s 11½d to 505 poor people this day.

Wednesday
5 November   This is the first year that the township has not had a bonefire as this day.

Thursday
20 November

	£	s	d
Elizabeth Unsworth my dairy maid through negligence spoild me 40 cheeses which were sold for £15 4s 7d, commision 15s, clear	14	9	7
53 more good weigh'd 9cwt 3q 3lb & sold at 35s per cwt	17	2	1½
[Total]	31	11	8½

I milked 14 cows & kept 35 cheeses for the family use.

Friday
5 December   Killed a hog which weighed sixteen score or 320lb.

Friday
12 December   Killed a hog which weigh'd seventeen score & 5lb, 345lb.

Tuesday
16 December   Poor Mrs Constantia Terningham died the 19th November last at three o'clock in the evening, being Wednesday, of a lethargy at the Prince Esterhazy in Germany, & buried at Esterhazy.[116] R.I.P.

Friday
26 December   Kill'd a cow which weigh'd 760lb, tallow 38lb, suit 15lb and the hide 116lb, in all 929lb.

114 0d crossed out and 3d inserted.
115 BTE's arithmetic is apparently in error in several places in this table.
116 Esterhazy is in eastern Austria.

1784

Tuesday
6 January   I had this Christmas 49 carrol singers.

Friday
10 January   Agreed this day with Thomas Birchall the father & Henry & William Birchall his sons for part of the late Mr Lyon's tenements in Eccleston for the term of eleven years to pay £46 p.a. clear of all leys & taxes. BTE to allow them £6 the first year for dung & they to find the same quantity the five first years. To plow seven acres the first five years & five acres the last six years. Not to stubble or burn nor plow more then the quantity specified under the penalty of £5 for every statue acre. They may be loose at the end of five years & to be allow'd 2 acres of wheat at the end of the term, but to be in part of the 5 acres allowed the last six years. BTE to have liberty to sow clover on any of the plowed feilds in the last year, of the 5 or 11 years; to leave all the dung on the premises at the end of the term. To consume all the produce, or for every load of hay sold to find two good loads of dung, & for a load of straw one good load of dung. To keep the hedges, ditches & windows in good repair. To attend the court as often as calld upon & to keep a dog & a cock if requir'd.

Friday
16 January   Kill'd a hog which weigh'd sixteen score & 6lb or 326lb.

Friday
24 January   Kill'd a hog which weigh'd fifteen score & 10lb, or 310lb.

Friday
6 February   Kill'd a hog which weigh'd fourteen score & 15lb, or 295lb.

Saturday
10 April   Kill'd a cow which weighd 710lb, hide 90lb, suit 39lb, tallow 37lb, in all 876lb.

                I had this day 421 persons for peace eggs.

Friday
16 April   Sign'd a contract this day along with my son, in order to secure to Miss Eleanor Clifton, his intended wife, a jointure of £500 p.a. clear after his death, & £100 p.a. pin money during his life. The security being on Eccleston demesne & mills, the late Lancaster's, Mr Lyon's & John Wilcox's farmer.

Low Monday
19 April   My son was this day married to Miss Eleanor Clifton of Lytham.

1784
Friday
4 June

My bay mare that was cover'd by Bandy, foaled this day a colt with a bald face.

Monday
7 June

Told my man James Wilson I would pay for his two children's schooling which is 3d per week for both of them.

Tuesday
6 July

I advanced to my son £125 from the coalworks lately held by John Mackay Esq.

I have not seen this year one martin at Eccleston & there are but few swallows, blackbirds or thrushes, which I suppose the late hard frosty winter destroy'd.

Wednesday
7 July

Receivd from the coalworks, late John Mackay's Esq., two bills dated 1st ins^t at 2 mo for £125 which is for the money advanced to my son the 6th ins^t.

Wednesday
11 August

Lent to my son T.E. fifty guineas paid 16 February 1785.[117]

Tuesday
7 September

Mr Meynell set off for London at quarter past seven o'clock this morning.

Thursday
30 September

Mr N Sewall came to live with me.

Friday
1 October

This evening about eleven o'clock, the barn, cow house, stable & counting house at German's belonging to Richard Greenall were all consumed by fire. The barn was intirely full of wheat, four horses in the stable worth from £80 to £100, in the counting house, his dairy of cheeses, £70 worth of malt, several dry planks & cordage for the mills & cotton manufactory, all his horse's geers & utensells for farming, & five to six hundred empty corn sacks, besides several other articles were all burn'd & consum'd to ashes.

Saturday
23 October

Fish'd the Engine Pond of warm water & put into the following pits the carps taken out of it, they were about two years of age

8 brace	Little Damn
8	Great Damn
6	Lower Damn

117 £52 10s 0d has been crossed out.

1784

6 brace	Richard Greenall's Pit
8	Avenue Pit
36	

There was only one skeleton alive of the large carps that I stored it with, the rest were either stolen or got out when the Damn head broke which hapned twice.

Tuesday
2 November

Gave soul loaves to 355 persons & 5s 6d in a halfpenny to each poor person, is 132 persons so the poor that came this day for charity were 487 persons.

Wednesday
17 November

Receiv'd of Jane Moss for 62 cheeses weigh'd 12cwt 2qtr 2lb, 5 of them one with another weighed better than 120lb, at 38s per cwt, £23 15s 7½d.

Sunday
21 November

It had frozen so hard for these two or three nights past, that numbers were scating this day on the Great Damn.

Saturday
27 November

Kill'd a hog which was lame & only weigh'd eleven score.

10 December

Kill'd a hog which weighed sixteen score & 6lb.

Friday
17 December

Killed a hog which weigh'd eighteen score & 3lb.

Wednesday
22 December

Killed a cow which weighed, the quarters 756lb, suet 83lb, tallow 38lb, & hide 96lb, in all 973lb.

1785

Friday
14 January

Killed a hog which weigh'd eighteen score & 9lb.

Lately leas'd by Mr Barton of Penworthen for three lives the following estates & the following rents reserved vizt. Broad Oak in Parr, and old house & outhousing in bad condition containing about 44 acres, three of which are occupied by timber & let at £100 p.a. the taxes to be deducted thereout the fine £560 & to pay £60 p.a.

Burtonhead in Sutton, a new brick house & outhousing containing about [...][118] acres & let at £40 p.a. and clears about £30. The

---

118 Quantity not entered by BTE.

1785

fine £220 and to pay £25 pa. This was purchased by Philip Alfleck Esq.

Friday
21 January   Killed a hog which weighed fourteen score.

Friday
28 January   Killed a hog which weighed fourteen score & 2lb.

Monday
7 February

	£	s	d
Let to Henry Wilcock the late Thomas Wilcox's tenement all but a garden and one dwelling & the folly clear of all taxes for	21	0	0
Let to John Watkinson the garden dwelling & folly for	3	3	0
& after the first year he is to be advanced more	0	10	6

Eccleston
17 May   I agree that mess[rs] John Rowe & John Tarleton, executors of the late Mr John Pyke of Everton, may sell by auction or otherwise the tenement he held of me in Eccleston for the term of the lease, reserving the Lord's rent & boons to myself, and they paying to me for this licence £18 18s on the day of such sale or bargain. BTE

Monday
23 May   Mr John Pyke's tenement that he held under me was sold this day at the Old Legs of Man in Prescot for £220. There were two lives in being, both women, one of 61 years the other 24. It was let at £24 & clear'd about £18. Miss Pyke the life bought it.

Thursday
26 May   My mare foaled this morning a colt foal.

Monday
13 June   Sent her & her foal to Scarisbrick to be cover'd by my son's horse.

Friday
1 July   Sent the following to run upon Martin Mere. 1 filly two years old, 1 colt one year old, 3 calves one year old, 2 calves two years old.

Thursday
21 July   Receiv'd of Mess[rs] John Rowe & John Tarleton for the lience granted them to sell the late Mr John Pyke's estate £18 18s 0d.

I allow'd Richard Greenall in account for rebuilding the barn, stables & cow house that were consumed by fire £106 11s 10½d.

1785

The cost of my new house (called Valencia), stable, cow house, barn, hog stie & necessary house vizt.

	£	s	d	£	s	d
To laying 364¾ yards brick & half at 5d	7	12	0			
To 178 yards brick length, 3½d	2	11	11			
To eight chimney drafts or smoaks						
at 6s	2	8	0			
To eleven arches, 1s	0	11	0			
To slating roof 3 rods 144 feet, 10s 6d	1	15	3½			
To pointing roof 133¼ yards, 1¼d	0	13	10½			
To geting & laying 91¼ yards of						
flags, 1s	4	11	3			
To geting & laying hearth 4 stones in						
the chambers	0	4	0			
To laying 16 yards large flags, 7d	0	9	4			
To cieling tops 94¼, 2½d	0	19	7½			
To plaistering 445 yards, 1½d	2	15	7½			
To plaistering 46 yards the above is all						
for the house, 1d	0	3	10	24	15	9
To laying 467½ yards brick & half in						
the barn, 5d	9	14	9½			
To laying 53½ yards brick length, 3½d	0	15	7			
To four arches	0	4	0			
To slating 5 rods & 208 feet, 10s 6d	2	17	11½			
To pointing 227¼ yards, 1½d	1	8	4½	15	0	8½
To laying 334½ yards brick & half,						
stable &c., 5d	6	19	4½			
To laying 56½ yards brick length, 3½d	0	16	6			
To eleven arches	0	11	0			
To slating 4 rods 293 feet, 10s 6d	2	9	8	10	16	6½
To laying 43¼ yards brick length work						
in the necessary house & hogstie, 3½d	0	12	7			
To dressing & laying 17 yards stone in						
the necessary house & hogstie, 1s 2d	0	19	10			
To slating roof 166 feet, 10s 6d	0	4	4	1	16	9
[Sub total]				52	9	9
To measuring at 3d per £ is, £0 13s my half				0	6	6
Paid William Forber a bill of day						
wages for Valencia				4	4	9
Paid William Forber a bill for day wages				0	11	8
William Forber's work came to				57	12	8
To 137¾ yards in the house roofs at 2d	1	2	11½			
20 yards & 2 feet wall plating & eave						
poling, 2d	0	3	5			

1785

	£	s	d	£	s	d
106½ yards cieling joice, 2d	0	17	9			
106½ yards joice under boarded floors, 2½d	1	2	2			
92¼ yards of flooring, 3½d	1	6	11			
19 yards stiling over kitchen, 2d	0	3	2			
14 stair steps, 2s 6d each	1	15	0			
8 yards pannel work about stairs, 1s 8d	0	13	4			
2 yards rail at top of stairs, 1s 8d	0	3	4			
3¼ yards in 1 pannel door, work & half, 1s 8d	0	5s	5			
3½ yards architrave & caseing round door, 1s 8d	0	5	10			
11 door cases 1s	0	11	0			
26¼ door cases in 11 cross barr doors, 1s 2d	1	10	7½			
Hanging 13 doors & 5 casements, 4d	0	6	0			
32 sash squares with caseings, 6d	0	16	0			
25 lights, 6d	0	12	6			
Making 2 borrowed light frames, 6d	0	1	0			
8 window boards at front & back 3¾ yards, 1s	0	3	9			
Fixing 32 window rods	0	1	6			
16 nogs in buttery, 2d	0	2	8			
4 bolts in the house, 4d	0	1	4			
Triming 4 hearth stones, 6d	0	2	0			
Lintells & attending bricklayers at the house	0	10	6	12	18	2
48 yards in 2 pair of principles in the barn, 1s	2	8	0			
232½ yards in the roof, 2d	1	18	9			
Pieceing 6 pan^s & first piece 7 joints, 10d	0	5	10			
51¼ yards in 4 barn doors, 1s	2	11	3			
4¾ yards in 2 flakes, 1s 4d	0	6	4			
11¾ yards boarding barn door tops, 6d	0	5	10½			
31 yards wall plating & eave poling, 2d	0	5	2			
1¼ yards in pitch hole door, 1s	0	1	3			
Making 2 large door heads of oak, 1s	0	2	0			
Making 1 large oak lintle over cart house	0	1	0			
Making 2 oak grainery summers, 1s	0	2	0			

1785

	£	s	d	£	s	d
Making 2 grainery posts, 10d	0	1	8			
52½ yards in 2 grainery floors at 6d	1	6	3			
8¾ yards in two bings, 1s 4d	0	11	8			
1 door case for grainery	0	1	0			
2¼ yards for ditto, 1s	0	2	3			
Hanging 5 doors 4s & grainery ditto, 6d	0	4	6			
1 two light window case & slide	0	1	8			
1 window board	0	0	2			
Making an oak frame & steps into the grainery	0	7	6			
2 cross bars for the barn doors	0	1	4			
To lintells & attending bricklayers at the barn	0	7	6	11	12	11½
27 yards in 2 pair of principles in stable & cow house	1	7	0			
203¼ yards in the roof at 2d	1	13	10½			
32½ yards of wall plating & eave poling, 2d	0	5	5			
Pieceing first piece	0	0	10			
17 yards bosting in stable, 1s	0	17	0			
4 stable posts of oak at 1s	0	4	0			
18 stable pegs, 2d	0	3	0			
50¾ yards in 2 ranges 2 racks cowhouse, 1s	2	10	9			
21½ yards large bosting in cowhouse, 1s	1	1	6			
7¾ yards little bosting in cowhouse, 1s	0	7	9			
½ yards milk bench cowhouse	0	0	6			
Six large posts in cowhouse, 1s	0	6	0			
Nine lesser in cowhouse, 6d	0	4	6			
Sixteen bosting stakes, 4d	0	5	4			
10¾ yards in 4 doors, 1s	0	10	9			
2½ yards in 3 dung holes, 1s	0	2	6			
4¼ yards in 4 wicket holes, 1s	0	4	3			
Hanging the above doors at 8d & calf ditto 4	0	7	0			
142¼ yards flooring stable & cow house, 5d	2	19	5½			
27 yards in stable cratch manger & back, 1s	1	7	0			
Lintells & attending bricklayers at cow house	0	7	6	15	5	11

1785

	£	s	d	£	s	d
Squaring 1ˢᵗ peice littlehouse & hogstie	0	0	8			
13 yard in roof of littlehouse & hogstie at 2d	0	2	2			
4¾ yards henhouse floor, 5d	0	1	11½			
Littlehouse door case	0	1	0			
Henhouse door frame	0	1	0			
2 yards in little house door at 1s	0	2	0			
0½ yards in hen house	0	0	6			
¾ yards in seal board	0	0	9			
1 yard in swine coat door	0	1	0			
2 stumps in swine coat door	0	1	0			
Hanging 3 doors & a latch & carrier	0	1	0			
My half of measuring £40 10s 1d, 3d per £	0	5	0	0	18	0½
John Dickson carpinter's bill of job work				1	13	1
Patrick the smith's bill for the house	0	19	2			
Patrick the smith's bill for stable & cow house	1	12	5			
Patrick the smith's bill for the barn	3	14	4			
Patrick the smith's bill for the grainery	0	3	3			
Patrick the smith's bill for necessary, hog & hen house & calf cribb	0	5	4	6	14	6
Paid Robert Myers, smith, as per his bill for a ditto				1	16	10½
Paid John Dickson going twice to Liverpool to buy timber				0	3	4
Paid Henry Hatton per bill for bolts, hinges &c. &c.				0	18	11¾
Paid sundry sawers				18	12	9
Paid 20 tons boler stones £5 & paveing £1 13s 9d				6	13	9
Paid for 1207½ feet Riga dale at 14¾d	74	4	2½			
Paid for 206 feet Danzick, 12¾d	10	18	10½			
Paid carting [timber] from Liverpool, 1¼d	7	7	3	92	10	4
Paid for 372 feet of oak & ash, 3½d				20	18	6
Paid for 178,000 bricks at 10s				89	0	0
Paid for 4 kilns my lime or 560 bushells, 6d	14	0	0			
Paid for 115 bushels Liverpool lime at 7d, £3 7s 1d, carriage £1 0s 0d	4	7	1	18	7	1
Paid wheeling bricks to the bricklayers				1	16	8

1785

	£	s	d	£	s	d
Paid 1cwt old nails 20s new nails per bill £4 15s				5	15	0
Paid 50 bushells of hair at 1s 6d, per & tar 5s				4	0	0
Paid oak laths & sap ditto & valu'd per John Dickson				5	0	0
Paid 60 loads of sand at 1s 2d per load				3	10	0
Paid George Hatton for glazeing, plumbing & painting as per bill				9	4	9
Paid 42 yards 2 feet ridgeing stones, 13½d, £2 8s 0d, rearing thrice £2				4	8	0
Paid 14 rods slate £29 8s, carting slate at 15s per £10 10s				39	18	0
Paid sundry laboures &c. &c. &c.	5	10	7¾			
Cost of Valencia				435	0	0

20 October   I believe few persons remember a drier or hoter summer then the last, the pastures were very thin of grass, parched up, and the meadows in as bad condition that I had not more than half the quantity of hay I used to have other years, but we had more grass in our pastures now then we had in summer. Apples universally missed, I had only eight in all.

Wednesday
2 November   I ground four bushels of corn, half wheat & half barley, and made 511 soul loaves of it, & distributed to the poor 413. There were 74 poor people less than last year.

Monday
21 November   Halsal School rent day.

    This day at eleven o'clock my daughʳ Eccleston was safely deliver'd of a son & heir christned Thomas.

Friday
2 December   Killed a hog which weighed 17 score & 2lb.

Friday
9 December   Killed a hog which weighed 18 score & 9lb.

Tuesday
20 December   Sold all my dairy of cheeses to Jane Moss & Mary Dwerryhouse and some few odd hundreds to neighbours, the whole together weighing 1 ton 1cwt 2qtr 18lb at 38s per cwt came to £41 0s 10½d. Paid. I kept 32 cheese which might weigh about 5cwt 2qtr 0lb.

1786

Tuesday
4 January   Killed a hog which weighed 13 score & 14lb.

Saturday
7 January   I had only twenty carrol singers this Christmas.

Friday
13 January   Killed a hog which weighed 15 score & 5lb.

Friday
20 January   Killed a hog which weighed 14 score & 1lb.

A certain cure for the falling sickness, particularly if the person be under seventeen years of age. It cured me when I was a student at Douai. It was given by an Irish soldier belonging to the Irish Brigade.

If the patient perceives the fit before he falls he must be let blood under the tongue, & then take the juice of a small handful of the herb call'd St. John's wort in a pint of strong drink, ale or beer for three nights successively going to bed. In case the patient beats himself, or shews any violent symptoms, he must be let blood in the cephalick vein in the arm & tongue, & then take a vomit of tartar emetick, after which the draught must be made as followeth. Take three pints of strong beer, the juice of three handfuls of the herb St. John's wort, one ounce of alum burnt and powder'd, as much of album grecum powder'd as can be laid on a halfpenny at thrice, work all these together, give him a pint three nights as above. If the fits happen at certain periods viz. at the full moon, change or equinox, let him take the remedy the three nights before the said periods. N.B The herb St John's wort is called hipericum or hepericon of which there are two sorts, one of which has smooth leaves, the other rough. The former is far the better.

Monday
6 February   Bored in the sough that was making in the Paddock to drain the Great Pond, thro' the finestone marl. It was 5 yards & 1 foot thick & bottoms on red rock, it will be found thicker in the pond.

Planted in the Larger Moss Feild late Joseph Houghton's in Watery Lane 920 young oaks. They were from acrons [*sic*] procured from Warwickshire & 380 in the other Long feild that belonged to late Joseph Houghton.

Tuesday
28 March   Let the Paddock pit intirely dry, the sough does the whole except

1786

about two hours laveing occassion'd by the slutch as is got into it. I only found 21 brace of fine, well-fed carp, 1 small brace mongrells mixt with tench, some 8 middle-sized pike, 24 eels & some few small perch & roach. N.B I heard this day that trouts will not live in a pond above 5 or 6 years.

Thursday
5 April

	£	s	d
From the 2ᵈ May 1785 I paid 4 books Poor ley at 9d per £	57	15	0
& this day I paid a 5ᵗʰ book Poor ley, all for the demesne at 6d	9	12	6
& for lands that I have purchased & the tenements out of lease valued in the rate books at £452 four books at 9d per	67	16	4
& this day a 5ᵗʰ book was paid at 6d	11	6	0
Paid for the demesne & the above lands poor lay for 12 months	146	9	6
My Sutton estates are valued at £58 10s & if rated for the poor as above would come to	10	4	9
The township of Eccleston must have paid to the poor this year	444	6	6

Good Friday
14 April

I had this day 422 poor people for peace eggs.

	£	s	d
N.B I paid 5 books of 9d & one of 6d to the poor for the demesne	81	16	3
& for lands I purchased & tenements out of lease	96	1	0
[Total]	177	17	3
The whole of the township paid this year to the poor	539	10	9
One book at 6d per £ on the whole townshp comes to	63	9	6
And of course one of 9d per £ comes to	95	4	3
And there still remain'd a debt of	165	0	0

Thursday
11 May

Planted 191 firs about the Holland's Pits.

Monday
29 May

The following trees were sold to Mr Hughes of the copper works, & valued by John Dickson, according to his judgement what they would be worth in twenty years vizt. 16 that grows in Williamson's estate with 5 cyphers in Alder Lane, 14 & 5 cyphers

1786

in Foord's 5 in all, 35 trees & 10 cyphers for which I debit said Mr Hughes as per the valuation £17 5s 1d.[119]

Thursday
1 June

I have observed for these two last years very great plenty of dandy lion & them years proved hot & dry, and this year there is great plenty of it & it promises to be both hot & dry.

Tuesday
24 October

I paid Mr Michael Hughes this day £10 which I had been owing to him at the time he gave me a bill for £50 & his rent only came to £40.

Finished all my wheat seeding in the New Meadow as also geting up all my potatoes.

Thursday
2 November

Distributed 355 loaves to 355 poor persons and gave 4s 4d in half-pennies to 104 poor persons in all 459.

Saturday
18 November

Killed a hog which weighed 19 score & 1lb.

Thursday
30 November

Agreed with [...][120] Smith for the Yew Tree & Tunstall's in Sutton exclusive of the cottage for [...][121] years for £53 p.a. clear. I am to allow him twenty tons of soaper's waste for the three first years & he is to pay for twenty tons more & cart the whole & set it upon the estate.

Saturday
2 December

Kill'd a hog that weighed 20 score & 2lb.

Monday
5 December

Sold my dairy of cheeses as followth to

	Cheeses	Cwt	qtr	lb		£	s	d
Mary Dweryhouse	54	11	1	2	at 40s	22	10	8
Jane Moss	48	10	2	11	at 40s	21	3	8
Sundries	17	4	0	20	at 40s	8	6	8
[Total] cheeses	119	26	0	3		52	1	0
I kept at 6s per cwt	28	4	2	0				
& cheeses for my use	7	1	2	15				
[Total] cheeses	154	32	0	18				

119 Michael Hughes (1752 –1825) of Sherdley, an important figure in the history of the Parys Mine Company and its Lancashire companies; Harris, *The Copper King*; John Rowlands, *Copper Mountain* (Llangefni: Anglesey Antiquarian Society, 1981).
120 Forename not entered by BTE.
121 Term not entered by BTE.

1786

NB I milked 16 cows & in August a heifer calved which made the number seventeen.

22 December   Killed a hog which weighed 24 score & 3lb.

1787

6 January   I had only forty-three carrol singers this Christmas.

Paid from the 12th August 1785 to the 5th instant in jointures

	£	s	d
Interest land & all other taxes as per book	740	1	11
From Vose when broken up as per book	29	15	8
From Liptrot £7 6s 9¼d, in potatoes £6 4s 4d as per book	13	11	1¼
Paid for a quantity of cows hair as per book	3	10	0
Paid for barrilla[122] as per book	62	6	5
Sundries from Richard Greenall as per book	76	9	2
In house keeping, servants & labourers wages &c. &c. &c.	839	11	0
[Total]	1,765	5	3¼

Monday
15 January   Mrs Williamson, owner of Scholes, thought herself agrived in the assesment of the township of Eccleston. The proper officer (Richard Greenall) waited upon her & proposed a town's meeting, that if they thought she was overrated they would do her justice to her own satisfaction, but nothing could please her, but that she would apply to the Quarter Sessions held this day at Wigan before the mayor Mr Hodson & Messrs Thomas Seel, Falconer, William Fleetwood of Liverpool, Mr Lyon of Warrington, the Rever^d Mr Whitehead & [...][123] & they all unanimously aggreed that a town's meeting should be call'd & to settle the thing amongst ourselves. Accordingly we had a meeting on Wednesday the 24th ins^t at the Eccleston Arms & all present to the amount of about thirty aggreed that it should be left to the decision of Mr James Wareing, Steward to the Right Honourable Edward of Derby, & accordingly all sign'd a paper to that effect.

---

122   Barrilla – an impure alkali made from burning a plant grown extensively in Spain. Used to make glass, soap and soda.
123   Name not entered by BTE.

1787
Thursday
8 February   My daugh^r Standish's receipt for a cold.

Elixir Paragoine twenty drops in a glass of water to be taken going to bed.

Daugh^r Standish's receipt for the rheumatism.
Volatile essence of guiacum twenty drops upon a lump of sugar & then dissolved in water.

Monday
12 March   Begun to sow oats in the Burying Hill.

Friday
17 March   Finished sowing the above hill 10a 2r with 95 bushells of oats & 2½ bushells of barley.

N.B I sow'd half a bushell of each for a trial with Brongniart's powder & followd exactly his directions.

	£	s	d		£	s	d
A year's land tax of this township comes to	76	16	8½	I pay	14	3	0
Window tax	59	2	10	I pay	10	17	0
House tax	10	0	10½	I pay	0	18	9
Horse tax	7	0	0	I pay	2	10	0
Cart tax	13	10	0	I pay	0	4	0
Carriage tax				I pay	7	0	0
Servants tax				I pay	7	10	0
[Total]	166	10	5	I pay	43	2	9

Good Friday
6 April   Killed a hog which weighed 13 score & 17lb.

I gave to 457 poor children that came beging for peace eggs.

Saturday
14 April   Killed a hog which weighed 13 score less 3lb.

Friday
27 April   The following estates belonging to Scholes were this day sold at the Legs of Man, Mr Taylor's in Prescot, to the following persons

	£	s	d
Meads House in Eccleston to Mr Ashcroft, grocer in Prescot containing 22 acres for the widow Mrs Williamson	1,260	0	0
Timber thereon for	90	0	0
New House in Eccleston to Mr James Wareing, steward to Lord Derby, purchased for myself cont^s 4 acres	555	0	0
Timber thereon for	40	12	0

1787

	£	s	d
Ritherope in Rainhill to Mr Bispham of Prescot, mercer, cont^s 22a 2r 26p for the widow Mrs Williamson	1,110	0	0
Timber thereon for	70	10	0
Sparrow Lane Meadow in Prescot cont^s 1a 1r 10p to Mr Richard Hill	195	0	0
Cross Acre in Prescot cont^s 1 acre to Mr John Houghton also of Prescot	140	0	0

Saturday
5 May

	£	s	d
Richard Vivian & his helpmate were 25 days geting soughing stones on the hill the one at 1s 6d the other 1s 4d per diem which came to	3	10	10

The ley for cattle at Atherton from the 12th May to 6th October is as followeth

	£	s	d
An aged or 3 year's old horse	3	0	0
A two years old horse	2	10	0
A one years old horse	2	0	0
A milch cow	2	0	0
A feeding cow	1	18	0
A two years old cow	1	5	0
A one year old cow	0	19	0

Corpus Christi
Thursday
7 June

I was siezed on Thursday Morning (in bed) 24th May, with a violent swiming in my head if I offerd to rise. If I lay quiet I was easy & could sleep, but durst not venture to get up before 12 o'clock. Formby, the apothecary, order a blister between my shoulders & Doc^r Green ordered me to loose eight ounces of blood & to take a dish of ginger tea with a teaspoonfull of æther in it morning & night which I continued for ten days & now take the æther in pure water as it was left to my option. Yesterday & this day I find myself without any swiming tho' I did not the preceeding days.

Tuesday
19 June

Sowed one acre & a half in Fairfield with 4lb of Norfolk turnep seed, the preceding night we had a good quantity of rain tho' the ground was not in fine condition for want of earlyer rains.

Wednesday
20 June

Turn'd 17 milch cows into the West Norley that was sown with rape seed.

1787
Friday
22 June   Sow'd 20lb of Norfolk turnip seed amongst all my wheat sown in the New Meadow.

Friday
29 June   Killed a pig which weighd seven score & 5lb, 145lb.

Friday
13 July   My dear sis^r Palmes died this evening betwixt 5 & 6 o'clock. R.I.P.

Friday
2 November   Ground 4 bush^s of small wheat which was made only into 265 loaves & gave in halfpence 8s 2d to 196 poor persons, 461 poor people.

Saturday
10 November   The New Meadow as I sow'd with wheat contains 6a 1r 38p of plow land produced as followeth vizt.

	£	s	d
5 loads of wheat of 70lb sow'd in the West Norley at 26s per	6	10	0
50 loads sold to Richard Greenall at 26s	65	0	0
45 loads sold to Richard Greenall at 27s	60	15	0
11 loads kept for house use at 27s	14	17	0
4 loads mixed with cone wheat at 27s	5	8	0
50 loads light valued at	7	10	0
[Total]	160	0	0
191 threave of straw at 1s 6d per	14	6	6
Reaping £3 12s 0d Threshing £9 6s 0d }	12	18	0
[Labour costs deducted from £14 6s 6d]	1	8	6

Makes £24 12s 3½d per acre

Killd a hog which weigh'd 16 score & 3lb.

Friday
14 December   Kill'd a black hog which weigh'd 15 score & 15lb.

1788

Friday
4 January   Killed a hog which weighd 17 score & 15lb.

Saturday
5 January   I had only 40 carrol singers this year & 9 more from Prescot Church.

                  Put into the Paddock pitt 110 brace of small carp, & into the

1788

Resovoir two months ago 44 brace & sent to Mr Hughes of Sutton Lodge 30 brace, they were all taken out of the Wall pond.

Friday
11 January   Killed a hog which weighed 17 score & 2lb.

Friday
18 January   Killed a hog which weighed 15 score & 2lb.

Thursday
21 February   Put into the Resovoir out of the Horse Pool 56 brace small carp, & into the Paddock pitt all very small 30 brace small carp.

Monday
3 March   N.B my white faced Suffolk went dry the 17th January last & the red one this day.

Saturday
15 March   My daughter Eccleston was delivered this morning at half an hour past twelve o'clock of a girl christianed Anne.
                 N.B. the annversary day of my barn being blown down 31 years ago.

Monday
17 March   My white faced Suffolk calved a bull this morning.

Friday
21 March   I had this day 324 persons for peace eggs.

Thursday
3 April   Bottled off Mr Chadwick's hogshead of red port of 35 gallons which filled 21 dozn & nine quart bottles of different sizes.

Tuesday
17 June   Doctr Bromley of Liverpool's receipt for a dropsy.
                 Take of dryed fox gloves (the leaves & flowers) one ounce, cimmer in 3 pints of water to a quart, give a tablespoonfull to the patient every afternoon.

Tuesday
15 July   Begun drinking of the hogshead of Mr Frank Chadwick red port.

31 October   Mr N. Sewall left me today to live at Scholes.

3 November   I ground 4 bushells of wheat & barley & made there from 553 loaves & distributed 506 so there remained 47 loaves.

Friday
7 November   Killed a pig which weigh'd 8 score & 14lb.

Wednesday
12 November   My old aquaintance Mrs Constantia Smith died this evening about nine o'clock at John Townley's Esq. at Corney House, Chiswick.

1788
Thursday
13 November   Mr Peter Westby died this evening at Scholes about half past eight o'clock. S.J.

Friday
14 November   Lent to Mr Moorcroft, apprentice to Doc[r] Lyon the 1st & 2[d] volumes of Don Quixote.

Friday
5 December   Kill'd a hog which weighed 17 score & 14lb.

Friday
12 December   Killed a hog which weighed 16 score 15lb.

1789

7 January   I had only 39 carrol singers this last year.

16 January   Killed a hog which weighed 15 score & 4lb.

Friday
23 January   Killed a hog which weighed 14 score & 14lb.

An account of the cost for repairing the new house as followeth vizt.

	£	s	d
250 bushells of lime at 7d, & carting 2d per bushells	9	7	6
25 Leigh lime & carting	1	3	8
41 loads of sand £3 1s 6d, & 30 bush[s] of hair £2 5s 0d	5	6	6
Laths £3 3s 10d & 2 rods slate & carting £5 14s 0d	8	17	10
34 yards of flags £1 19s 8d & carting 7s 6d	2	7	2
Glazeing £3 7s 0d, & nails £3 11s 6d	6	18	6
Blacksmith £4 19s 1d, cants[+] & more nails £3 19s 7d ([+]rails)[124]	8	18	8
Bricksetters £40 15s 2½d, labourer's bill £6 16s 1d	47	11	3½
Carpinter's bill	20	17	1½
Oak, dale, iron, sawing & new gates as per bill	6	1	8
[Total]	117	9	11

1788

[125]To sundry stuf used for the new house

	£	s	d
To 10 foot of oak for the barn door chickes at 14d per	0	11	8

124 BTE appears to be clarifying the meaning of the word cants.
125 This entry is on a loose sheet of paper inserted at this date.

1789

				£	s	d
To 60 foot of dale for barn door & floors at 15d per				3	15	0
To sawing				0	12	0
To 2 new gates 1 at 11s the other 7s				0	18	0
To iron work				0	5	0
[Total]				6	1	8

	Ton	Cwt	qtr	lb		£	s	d
Received for	1	3	0	14	of last year's make of cheese at 35s	40	9	1
Received for	0	2	2	16	of last year's make of cheese at 32s 6d	4	5	7
	1	5	3	0		44	14	8
	0	0	3	16	cheese for my use at 35s	1	10	11
27 cheeses	0	3	3	16	for family use at 32s 6d	6	6	2½
[Total]	1	10	2	2		7	17	1½

Saturday
4 April

Planted 63 grains of American wild oats in 3 pots of good earth 21 grains in each pot. One was placed in the hot bed, an other under a south wall & the 3ᵈ under a south wall which I kept filled with water, about one inch above the earth.

Friday
10 April

Gave to 468 in lieu of peace eggs 19s 6d, a half penny each, 468 poor.

Monday
13 April

The two cluster potatoes of my son's weighed 2lb & 13oz.

Tuesday
21 April

Set the above clusterd potatoes cut into 30 sets about 1 yard asunder in the Paddock Garden.

Friday
15 May

⊕ My bay mare as was covered by North Star foaled this morning, a bay foal with a star in his forehead & two white feet behind.

Appendix

To make lavender water.
To a pint and a half of rectifyed spirits of wine put a quarter of an ounce of chemical oil of lavender dropt upon a large lump of sugar. Put the sugar into the spirits for some hours. When taken out stop it up very close, and it improves by keeping.[126]

---

126 This entry is on a loose, undated sheet inserted in the first volume.

INDEX OF PERSONAL NAMES

Note: family relationships cited in this index are to Basil Thomas Eccleston.

INDEX OF PLACES

INDEX OF SUBJECTS